HOW TO MAKE ALL THE "MEAT" YOU EAT OUT OF WHEAT

Books by Nina and Michael Shandler:

THE MARRIAGE AND FAMILY BOOK
YOGA FOR PREGNANCY AND BIRTH
WAYS OF BEING TOGETHER

How to Make All the "Meat" You Eat Out of Wheat

INTERNATIONAL GLUTEN WHEAT "MEAT" COOKBOOK

by

Nina and Michael Shandler

RAWSON, WADE PUBLISHERS, INC.
New York

Library of Congress Cataloging in Publication Data

Shandler, Nina.
  How to make all the "meat" you eat from
wheat.

  Bibliography: p.
  Includes index.
  1. Cookery (Wheat)   2. Cookery (Gluten)
3. Cookery, International.   I. Shandler, Michael,
joint author.   II. Title.
TX809.W45S48   641.6′311   79-67641
ISBN 0-89256-126-2
ISBN 0-89256-131-9 pbk.

Published simultaneously in Canada by McClelland and Stewart, Ltd.
Manufactured in the United States of America
Composition by American–Stratford Graphic Services, Inc.
  Brattleboro, Vermont
Printed and bound by R. R. Donnelley & Sons,
  Crawfordsville, Indiana
Designed by Jacques Chazaud

First Edition

To our daughter

MANJU

who loves wheat "meats"

ACKNOWLEDGMENTS

We are grateful to the oral tradition that has passed gluten making from one person to another. Our special thanks goes to Jayanti Peterson, who first served us gluten steaks. And we are indebted to our daughter, Manju, and Nina's parents, who dutifully endured tasting all of the experiments that preceded the successful development of these wheat "meats." Lastly, we thank Frank Wade, who patiently and painstakingly photographed the cover picture.

AUTHORS' NOTE

Whenever the first person singular is used
in the text, it refers to Nina.

CONTENTS

ACKNOWLEDGMENTS *vii*

AUTHORS' NOTE *ix*

PART I

Introducing Wheat "Meat"

CHAPTER ONE

The Cost of the Meat-Centered Diet 3

 How Meat Consumption Affects Ecology,

  Economy and Health *4*

 Food Economy *4*

 Fuel Conservation *5*

 Water Reserves and Pollution *6*

 Heart Disease, Cancer and Meat Eating *7*

 Premature Aging *8*

 Chemical Residues in Meat *9*

 Medical Costs *10*

CHAPTER TWO

Introducing Wheat "Meat": a Low-Cost, Homemade

 Alternative to Meat *11*

 Wheat "Meat" Protein *12*

 "Meat" without Cholesterol *13*

 A Food for the Calorie Conscious *13*

 The Low Cost of Wheat "Meats" *14*

 Enjoying Wheat "Meats" *14*

CHAPTER THREE

How to Make "Meat" from Wheat 16

Preparing Raw Gluten 17
Seven Varieties of Wheat "Meat" 18
Cutlets: A Veal Substitute 18
Steak: A Mock Beef Steak 19
Ground Gluten: A Hamburger Taste-Alike 20
Spiced Links: An Alternative to Sausage 21
Roast with a Beef Flavor 22
Using the Reserved Starch, Bran and Germ 23
Seawheat: A Clam Alternative 23
Poultry Pieces: Chicken-Flavored Wheat "Meat" 24
Gluten-Free Crackers 24
Cold, Crunchy Cereal 26

PART II

Hundreds of International Ways to Serve Wheat "Meat"

CHAPTER FOUR

All-American Wheat "Meat" Recipes 29

All-American Soups 30
All-American Cutlet Main Dishes 38
All-American Steak Main Dishes 40
All-American Ground Gluten Main Dishes 46
All-American Spiced Link Main Dishes 53
All-American Roast Main Dishes 55
All-American Main Dishes with Poultry Pieces 59
All-American Seawheat Main Dishes 62
All-American Breakfast Dishes with Spiced Links 63
All-American Barbecued Cutlet Recipes 71
All-American Charcoaled Steak 73
All-American Ground Gluten Barbecue Dishes 77

CHAPTER FIVE

Mexican Wheat "Meat" Food 79

Mexican Cutlet Dishes 80
Mexican Steak Dishes 83
Mexican Ground Gluten Dishes 85
Mexican Spiced Link Dishes 93

CHAPTER SIX

Latin American Ways to Serve Wheat "Meat"   95
  Latin American Steak Recipes   96
  Latin American Ground Gluten Dishes   101
  Latin American Poultry Dishes   104

CHAPTER SEVEN

British Wheat "Meat" Dishes   108
  British Cutlet Dishes   109
  British Roast Dishes   111
  British Poultry Recipes   114
  British Spiced Link and Mixed Wheat "Meat"
    Recipes   116

CHAPTER EIGHT

French Wheat "Meat" Cuisine   120
  French Cutlet Recipes   121
  French Steak Recipes   127
  French Spiced Link and Mixed Wheat
    "Meat" Dishes   129

CHAPTER NINE

Spanish Cooking with Wheat "Meat"   131
  Spanish Cutlet Recipes   132
  Spanish Steak Recipes   134
  Spanish Roast Recipes   137
  Spanish Poultry Recipes   138
  Spanish Mixed Wheat "Meat" Dishes   140

CHAPTER TEN

Italian Wheat "Meat" Recipes   142
  Italian Cutlet Recipes   143
  Italian Steak Dishes   145
  Italian Ground Gluten Recipes   146
  Italian Spiced Link Recipes   151
  Italian Mixed Wheat "Meat" Dishes   154

CHAPTER ELEVEN

Austrian Wheat "Meat" Cooking   159
  Austrian Cutlet Recipes   160
  Austrian Steak Recipes   167
  Austrian Mixed Wheat "Meat" and
    Ground Gluten Recipes   168

CHAPTER TWELVE
Greek Wheat "Meat" Recipes   173
  Greek Cutlet Recipes   174
  Greek Ground Gluten Recipes   178
  Greek Poultry Recipes   182

CHAPTER THIRTEEN
African Cooking with Wheat "Meat"   186
  African Cutlet Recipes   187
  African Steak Recipes   190
  African Ground Gluten Dishes   192

CHAPTER FOURTEEN
Indian Cooking with Wheat "Meat"   195
  Indian Cutlet Recipes   196
  Indian Ground Gluten Dishes   201
  Indian Poultry Recipes   205

CHAPTER FIFTEEN
Chinese Wheat "Meat" Food   207
  Chinese Cutlet Dishes   208
  Chinese Steak Recipes   217

CHAPTER SIXTEEN
Japanese Wheat "Meat" Cooking   221
  Japanese Cutlet Recipes   222
  Japanese Poultry Dishes   226
  Japanese Seawheat Recipes   229

  BIBLIOGRAPHY   232
  INDEX   233

PART I

Introducing Wheat "Meat"

CHAPTER ONE

The Cost of the Meat-Centered Diet

If you wonder, "How can someone get 'meat' from flour unless he's a magician?" we'll let you in on a secret! Very few people are aware that ordinary wheat flour can be transformed into a high-protein substance called gluten, simply by adding a little water and kneading it in a specific way that we will describe.

This high-protein gluten, or wheat "meat" as we call it, can be easily seasoned and cooked to taste remarkably like a large variety of meats—at a fraction of the price of the real thing. Nutritionally, two thirds of a cup of raw gluten will supply 56 grams of protein, slightly over the recommended daily allowance for a 167-pound man. This portion can be served for the princely price of about twenty cents, without a drop of cholesterol *and with a third fewer calories than beef.*

In these times of rampant inflation and skyrocketing meat prices, eating grain-based meats and other protein-rich alternatives to meat is motivated mainly by the need to cut costs at the cash register. However, reducing the consumption of meat may be beneficial both to personal health and to the environment.

How Meat Consumption
Affects Ecology, Economy and Health

It is axiomatic that agricultural land is the source of food. In the United States, we use five acres to feed each person, while in more vegetarian-oriented countries, it takes as little as a quarter acre for each individual. This is due largely to our dependence on animals for food. Cattle particularly consume large amounts of vegetation that otherwise could be eaten directly by humans. Their need for enormous quantities of food begins with grazing, and excessive grazing can have devastating effects on the environment.

The ruination of depleted land through the grazing of cattle can be seen in Africa, where the Sahara Desert is creeping southward at the rate of fifty miles per year, bringing untold and little publicized famine, misery and death to millions of Africans. The same phenomenon is occurring to some degree in the United States.

While we have not reached the stage of famine caused by defoliation, there is no unused grazing land in this nation. In fact, at this moment 42 percent of the total land in this country is used for grazing livestock, while only 17 percent is used for growing crops, large portions of which are fed directly to livestock. Consumer demand for increasing quantities of meat makes the temptation to overgraze for greater "production" and higher profit ever-present. If, as too often is the case, immediate profit becomes a greater motivator than long-term ecological considerations, our abundant land resources could be rendered unusable.

Food Economy

If there is doubt that livestock can contribute so substantially to the kind of ruination we have described, a look at the voracious appetites of these innocent beasts will allay all skepticism.

Beef cattle eat grass and processed feed doctored with antibiotics and other drugs to make them grow fast and fat until

nearly the age of slaughter; then they are incarcerated in feedlots where they are fed to their hearts' content and far beyond.
During this final four-month period, a steer does not move
from an enclosed cubicle and is fattened from approximately
500 pounds to a hefty weight of 1,200 pounds and then slaughtered. During this crash weight-gain diet, a single animal will
be fed well over a ton of grain while at the feedlot, plus
legumes, protein supplements and some miracle drugs to
stupefy and sterilize him. If the appetite of one animal is mul-
tiplied by the millions of cattle it takes to supply the butcher
shops and restaurants of this country, the result is that U.S.
livestock consume 97 percent of the nation's legumes, 90 percent of its grain and 80 percent of its fish while they only supply 20 percent of the country's food. In her book, *Diet for a
Small Planet*, Frances Lappe estimates that the grain lost in
feeding our livestock could put a bowl of grain on the table
of every person in the world every day of the year.

Fuel Conservation

If land and food, however incorrectly, seem like resources
we can afford to waste, fuel is a well-publicized commodity
everyone wants to preserve. As a matter of fact, the food producers and distributors in the United States use as much oil
and gasoline as all of us use to drive our cars. Of course, this is
entirely justifiable: we do have to eat. But if we're trading fuel
for food, it should be as fair and economical a trade as possible
in this era of OPEC.

In this regard, grain growers drive a totally fair bargain.
The machinery used for plowing, planting and harvesting their
crops uses less than one calorie of fossil fuel energy to produce
one calorie of food energy. Meat producers, on the other hand,
make out like bandits. They not only need to produce food for
livestock to consume, but need to transport large quantities of
feed from storehouses to ranches and feedlots. They must transport cattle from ranches to feedlots and to slaughterhouses.
The overall result is that producing meat takes one hundred
calories of petroleum-based energy to provide one calorie of
food energy. Or, as Jean Mayer, President of Tufts University,

and Mary Rawitscher explain, if the 220 million people who populate this country were to substitute one pound of bread for one pound of meat just once a month, the energy saved would be equivalent to 121 million barrels of oil. If grain-based "meats" were substituted entirely for beef, 1.2 billion barrels of oil would not need to be imported from the Middle East. This would constitute a 40-percent reduction in the amount of oil imported from OPEC.

The diminishing world-wide reserves of fossil fuel could well be used more wisely in ways essential to our well-being rather than to raise a billion head of cattle that are slaughtered primarily for the luxury of their taste, and for the profit of a few.

Water Reserves and Pollution

Our questionable use of resources does not stop here. Water, like land and fossil fuel, is a commodity needed in huge volumes to produce food. To be specific, in the United States it takes 2,400 gallons of water a day to feed just one person.

Crops need to be irrigated or watered, and the majority of these food crops are eaten by livestock. This same livestock needs to drink water as well. Again, a disproportionately large quantity of a precious resource is consumed by meat producers. A beef producer needs eighty times more water than a producer of tubers or bananas. With water shortages occurring in the West and Southwest, we might well query if we can afford to give so much of it to the animals.

To add insult to injury, not only do our cattle, chickens and pigs consume a tremendous amount of water, they pollute it as well. More than half the water pollution in the United States comes from feedlots, broiler installations and hog facilities. All our sewage and industrial waste combined do not equal the water pollution caused by livestock. When and if feedlots are required to install the same pollution controls that other industries are now required by law to use, the price of beef will skyrocket an estimated additional one dollar per pound. Tack that onto inflation and someday only the very rich will be able to afford the price of hamburger.

Heart Disease, Cancer and Meat Eating

However, the most convincing evidence that heavy meat consumption is best reduced or eliminated comes not with reference to conservation—frightening as the facts about land, oil and water are—or even in relation to cost—as astronomical as it promises to become—but in consideration for personal health. Heart disease and cancer are the two largest destroyers of human life in our society, and both of these diseases have been linked to meat eating.

Fully half of the people who die in this country suffer from cardiovascular diseases. Today's beef contains three to six times as much fat, most of it saturated, as it did in the 1950's. The "beautifully" marbled effect in present-day grocery store beef is the result of modern methods of cattle raising, which cause animals at the age of slaughter to be 30 percent fat. Beef consumption, thus, can be accurately described as a risk factor in developing arteriosclerosis.

The fact that vegetarians suffer fewer heart attacks than meat eaters has not been brought to the public view with any great enthusiasm. Likewise, the recent findings from Harvard that a vegetarian diet contributes substantially to a reduction in high blood pressure has gone almost without attention. Once these facts become known, the conclusion that cutting down on meat consumption can be beneficial to the health of the heart is unavoidable.

Cancer, that great perpetrator of physical suffering, and ultimately death, to millions of Americans, has been linked to meat eating as well. At the laboratories of Cornell University, to cite only one scientific study, Dr. Willard Visek, formerly of Cornell University, found ammonia, which is produced in high concentrations when meat is metabolized, to be dangerously carcinogenic. If laboratory tests seem questionable proof of the connection between human meat consumption and cancer, the studies of Seventh-Day Adventists may provide more acceptable evidence.

The dietary habits of Seventh-Day Adventists vary. Some are vegetarian while others consume an average American quantity of meat. Comparing these two types of Seventh-Day Adventists is especially valuable since both groups have virtually identical racial and ethnic backgrounds and lifestyles. The results of comparison show without any doubt that those Seventh-Day Adventists who are vegetarian suffer far less cancer than those who eat meat.

Beyond the information associating butcher shop meats with cancer there is continually mounting specific, substantial and frightening information linking cancer with processed meats containing the additive sodium nitrite. Sodium nitrite, a coloring and preservative agent, is found in virtually every hot dog, sandwich meat, sausage, smoked meat and smoked fish eaten in this country. It is one of three ingredients necessary to form nitrosamines. The others are a mildly acid solution, which is often the condition in the human stomach, and amines, which are found in many foods, nonprescription drugs, drinks and cigarette smoke. The list of amine-containing substances that enter the body includes beer, wine, fish, cereals, oral contraceptives, tranquilizers, muscle relaxants, decongestants, diuretics and antihistamines. It is obvious that quite accidentally and unknowingly the stomach can be the perfect test tube for the formation of nitrosamines, which are acknowledged by the F.D.A. to be "one of the most formidable and versatile groups of carcinogens yet discovered." They are such potent cancer producers that they have produced the disease in every animal tested after just one low dose. The innocent All-American habit of having a hot dog and a can of beer at the baseball park becomes a questionable practice when this knowledge is considered.

Premature Aging

Old age is a debility that everyone would prefer to postpone as long as possible. In his best selling book, *How to Get Well*, nutritionist Dr. Paovo Avola reports the findings of two European doctors on aging. Dr. P. H. Schwartz of Frankfurt University, West Germany, and Dr. Ralph Bircher of Zurich, have recently reported that aging is stimulated by amyloid, which is a by-product of protein metabolism. When excessive protein is consumed, amyloid is deposited in all the connective tissue, causing tissue and organ degeneration. This explains why the Masai, an African tribe who eat far larger quantities of flesh food than we Americans, become aged in their twenties. They, along with other heavy meat eaters—Eskimos, Greenlanders, Laplanders and Russian Kirghiz tribes—look forward to a life expectancy of thirty to forty years. Cultures known for their longevity—Hunzas, Bulgarians, Russian Caucasians, Yucatán Indians and East Indian Todas—eat little meat and can boast an average life expectancy of ninety to one hundred years. Among industrialized countries, we occupy twenty-first place in life expectancy.

Chemical Residues in Meat

Meat is also suspect on the issue of chemical residues. Although the effects of chemical residues from pesticides, fertilizers and most important from feedlot procedures are not entirely understood, it may be found that they, like many chemical additives, are more injurious to our health than is now admitted. There is thirteen times as much chemical residue in meat as in its taste-alike, gluten wheat "meat."

This extraordinary concentration of chemicals in meat can be understood by recalling the tremendous quantity of chemically saturated food an animal consumes. These chemicals do not pass through his system but remain in the meat even after the animal is slaughtered. In addition to the pesticides and fertilizers in the grain and legumes the animal ingests, steers are fed large doses of antibiotics to prevent disease and increase rapid weight gain. The problem with routine use of antibiotics is that bacteria become resistant to the drugs. This has caused the F.D.A. to warn that there has been a marked increase of resistant bacteria in animals for slaughter. Since meat from diseased animals can produce food poisoning in humans, at least one noted microbiologist has warned of possible epidemics of salmonellosis.

To make a steer content with confinement, feedlot procedures include the use of high doses of tranquilizers, as well as hormones, some ingested and some injected as pellets into the ears. DES, one of the most popular hormones, is always injected into the ears because in 1973 it was banned from cattle feed. Why was it banned? Because it is a proven carcinogen. However, although not ingested, the drug may still reside in meat and no one knows in what quantities.

Perhaps the most infamous of chemicals is DDT. It is so prevalent in meat products that it has endangered the breast milk of human mothers. According to the F.D.A., the concentration of DDT in the milk of meat-eating mothers is so high that their milk is classified as unsafe for consumption by infants. Vegetarian mothers' milk, on the other hand, remains a safe food for nurturing babies, containing less than one third as much the DDT.

Medical Costs

Medical costs are a direct reflection of America's lack of good health. Between 1960 and 1976, the total cost of medical care in the United States rose from $27 billion to $137 billion. This increase of $110 billion over a brief sixteen-year period, while owing in part to inflation, is due largely to the care required for increasing numbers of people suffering from arteriosclerosis, cancer and diabetes. There is growing evidence that those suffering from these diseases are more apt to be meat eaters, so it should be no surprise that as our health costs have increased over the last twenty years, our meat consumption also has rapidly increased. In 1950, the average American ate 60 pounds of beef a year. By 1978, that consumption more than doubled to 122 pounds.

CHAPTER TWO

Introducing Wheat "Meat": a Low-Cost, Homemade Alternative to Meat

Despite the overwhelming evidence of the adverse effects of meat consumption on health and natural resources, as well as its devastating effect on the family food budget, it can be said, to use a somewhat shopworn phrase, that meat is as American as apple pie. The American palate craves its texture and taste, which is why most people eat it.

Our diet has been meat-centered for generations and most of us, it would seem, are hooked for life. Even those of us who have become vegetarian sometimes experience involuntary salivation at the smell of steak cooking. Often there is a nagging voice of nostalgia saying, "Soybeans, lentils, grains, eggs and dairy products are all wonderful sources of protein, but they simply don't make it at a barbecue!"

Homemade gluten "meats," properly prepared, have meat's tasty goodness and texture, yet qualify as excellent vegetarian foods. They can be made to resemble a variety of meats and can be served at any meal from breakfast to a dinner banquet. Although a lover of rare sirloin never will be fooled by a wheat "meat" steak, cut it up and put it in Stroganoff and she or he never will notice the difference.

When my husband and I, who had been vegetarians for ten years, discovered gluten, it was like reopening a treasure chest that had been lost in childhood. We were served gluten steaks while visiting friends. As soon as we tasted this chewy food, a craving, locked up for years, surfaced and our minds went wild fantasizing everything we would make from gluten: sausages, fried clams, wienerschnitzel.

Although we made a diligent search, few gluten recipes were forthcoming in any cookbooks. We decided to set to work to fulfill our suppressed desires. The results, which we began to call wheat "meat," were delicious; so delicious in fact that even our meat-loving parents, who visited us at the height of our experimentation, had to admit, with more than a little enthusiasm, that we had indeed been able to create the taste and texture of meat without chemicals, cost or cholesterol.

Wheat "Meat" Protein

During our experimentation, we were involved in research for a book on nutrition for children. Hours each day were spent mulling over nutrition charts and studying the vitamin, mineral and protein content of various foods. On one such day we spied gluten flour on a nutrition table. Our curiosity was immediately aroused. When we looked closely at the protein content figures, we found the information impressive. So impressive that we checked with another source to make certain the information was accurate. The statistic was correct: one cup of gluten flour contains 85 grams of protein. That figure may not seem extraordinary unless you know that one half pound of steak contains 72 grams of protein. As our fingers ran down the protein column of the nutrition chart, it soon became clear that *no single food contains as much total protein as gluten.*

Our research has taught us that protein is a complex matter and that quality as well as quantity must be considered. The highest quality protein contains, in proper proportions, eight amino acids essential to human growth and maintenance and is therefore called "complete protein." Only three classes of foods are so-called complete proteins: eggs, milk products and flesh foods. Gluten is weak in one amino acid: lysine. However, this weakness is easily offset by preparing wheat "meat" dishes with eggs, beans, bean flours, nutritional yeast, wheat germ, milk or other dairy products high in lysine. Spiced Links and Ground Gluten are substitutes for sausage and hamburger which, when made with the addition of lysine-rich foods according to our instructions, need no further complementation. Other wheat "meats" can be served or prepared with any foods high in lysine and the quality of the protein becomes as usable to the body as that in flesh foods. Simply drinking a glass of milk with a serving of wheat "meat" will provide abundant quantities of complete protein.

"Meat" without Cholesterol

Minimizing the intake of saturated fat is advisable for everyone who would like to reduce the possibility of arteriosclerosis. The almost total elimination of cholesterol-containing foods is advantageous to anyone with a history of heart problems or a tendency toward high blood pressure. Our recipes for basic wheat "meats"—cutlets, steaks, ground gluten, spiced links, "poultry" pieces, roasts—and seawheat are entirely free of cholesterol. Therefore, people with even the most severe heart difficulties can enjoy them without fear. For these same individuals, the large amount of saturated fat in beef, sausages and pork makes them high-risk foods.

Most people do not need to maintain a totally cholesterol-free diet. As most of us know, eggs and dairy products contain cholesterol. Because we believe that the positive nutritional value of these foods outweighs their negative aspects, we use them in our All-American and International dishes along with wheat "meats." Since the wheat "meats" are cholesterol-free, these can be used by those on restricted diets. There is little doubt that the person who has been restricted to two or three eggs a week will thoroughly enjoy the opportunity to have three or four "sausages" with those eggs, a treat that may have been denied for many years.

A Food for the Calorie Conscious

For those who have to count calories, wheat "meats" are an efficient way to eat protein while cutting calorie intake. By eating three ounces of hamburger, 21 grams of protein are obtained. One third cup of prepared raw gluten will give the same amount of protein. The wheat "meat" substitute has approximately one third fewer calories. A similar comparison with steak shows beef steak to have approximately 42 percent more calories than gluten steak. Sausage has nearly twice the calories of its gluten counterpart. Consequently, people who are concerned about weight gain or reduction can enjoy more satisfying meals with the addition of wheat "meats" to their diets.

The Low Cost of Wheat "Meats"

Of course, inflation makes any actual cost statistic today obsolete by tomorrow. However, it safely can be assumed that meat prices will rise more rapidly than whole wheat flour prices. Today hamburger will cost more than three times as much as gluten for equal amounts of protein. Steak will cost four to six times as much, and veal, with its exorbitant price, will be a full ten times the cost of equivalent wheat "meat" cutlets, which are a very good likeness of veal. Even a partial introduction of gluten into a meat-loving household will save the cost of this book in one trip to the supermarket. At present prices, eighteen "sausages" will cost seventy-five cents, four large breaded "veal cutlets" sixty-five cents, a "roast" fifty-five cents and three cups of "fried clams" seventy cents. For between twelve and fourteen cents a serving, you can eat a delicious, nutritious main dish. By making "meats" from gluten, the standard of eating does not need to suffer, even though the cost of living is accelerating so rapidly as to threaten our standard of living in other areas.

Enjoying Wheat "Meats"

The results of our nutritional curiosity, cooking experimentation and cost consciousness are the unique recipes for a variety of wheat "meats" that come directly from our kitchen to yours. Wheat "meats" are simple to prepare, natural, low-calorie and delicious foods that are free of the cholesterol, chemical residues and additives that plague meat. Because they are extremely inexpensive and versatile, they can be used in hundreds of dishes previously denied the vegetarian, the health conscious and now, because of the high cost of meat, the cook who loves the taste of meat but can't afford it as often.

We hope you enjoy the preparation, the taste, the good health and the savings that go hand in hand with using the wheat "meat" recipes in this cookbook as a regular part of a varied and balanced diet.

CHAPTER THREE

How to Make "Meat" from Wheat

The preparation of gluten wheat "meats" at home is a simple process that requires little time. All wheat "meats" are made from raw gluten, which can be extracted from whole wheat flour in approximately forty minutes. Once the sinuous, tasteless, protein-rich raw gluten is isolated, several methods can be used to create taste-alikes for veal cutlets, steak, hamburger, roast, chicken, clams and sausages. These wheat "meats" take from ten minutes to several hours to flavor and cook.

Any wheat "meat" can be made in large quantities and stored for later use. They remain fresh in the refrigerator for several days or can be frozen for an indefinite period of time with no loss of flavor or texture.

Making wheat "meats"—cutlets, steaks, ground gluten, spiced links, roast—and seawheat, requires a few natural foods that may not be available at the supermarket but can readily be found at natural or Oriental food stores. Tamari soy sauce, soy flour, miso (fermented soybean paste), nutritional yeast and liquid barley malt are the special ingredients needed to flavor gluten. In addition, common spices and herbs are used. Gathering these basics can be done before beginning to make "meats" from wheat.

A meat grinder or food processor is necessary for making ground gluten and spiced links, but no other kitchen appliances are required.

PREPARING RAW GLUTEN

Yield: About 2 Cups
Preparation Time: 40 minutes

2½ cups to 3 cups water   1 quart cold water (for soaking)
  7 cups whole wheat flour   3 quarts cold water (for rinsing)

Stir water into flour. Mix well. Form a stiff dough. Using your hands, press dough into a rough ball.

Pour 1 quart of cold water over the dough and allow to stand covered with water for at least 20 minutes but no longer than 4 hours.

After soaking the dough, knead it in water gently. The starch, bran and germ of the flour will separate from the gluten protein, causing the water to become milky. Continue kneading, being careful to keep the dough intact. When water becomes thick with starch, bran and germ, pour this solution into a 1-gallon container. Be careful not to discard any solid portions of dough. If your dough is not adhering to itself, it will be helpful to strain the solution off through a metal colander and return solid pieces of dough to the bowl.

Add another quart of water to the bowl containing the dough and again knead until the water has become thick and creamy. By now the dough will adhere to itself and you will be able to see the formation of sinuous strings of gluten in your dough. Again, pour the thick creamy solution into the same gallon container, using a colander to strain if necessary. Place solid dough back in the bowl, cover with water and repeat this process until the rinsing water is completely clear. It is essential that the water be clear because any starch remaining in the gluten will cause the wheat "meat" to be doughy rather than chewy. The entire kneading and rinsing process will require 10 to 15 minutes and about a gallon of rinsing water.

The dough that remains is an elastic, sinuous substance. This raw gluten is the concentrated protein of wheat, which is basic to making wheat "meat." About two cups of raw gluten should be obtained from rinsing seven cups of whole wheat flour. If you are left with substantially less than two cups, it is likely that the flour you are using is too coarsely ground. However, this is unusual since nearly all commercial whole wheat bread flours are perfectly ground to produce a maximum yield of good quality gluten. Whole wheat pastry flour is an exception. It is milled from a strain of wheat with a low gluten content and your yield will be minimal.

The raw gluten can be flavored and cooked immediately into a variety of wheat "meats." If, however, you do not wish to use the gluten immediately, it should be covered with water and stored in the refrigerator. Gluten that is allowed to stand without being soaked in liquid becomes tough and rubberlike.

The starch, bran, germ and water solution that has been reserved from rinsing contains much of the valuable vitamin and mineral content of whole wheat. It is a nutrition-packed solution that should not be discarded. Rather, set it aside while preparing your wheat "meat" and later it can be used to make delicious Scandinavian-style hard bread. The simple recipe for making these crackers follows the next seven basic wheat "meat" recipes.

Seven Varieties of Wheat "Meat"

Seven kinds of wheat "meat" can be made from raw gluten. These wheat "meats" resemble veal cutlets, steak, hamburger, sausage, roast, chicken and clams. The next seven recipes will show you how to make these wheat "meats": cutlets, steak, ground gluten, spiced links, roast, poultry pieces and seawheat. Later, in the second part of this cookbook, under All-American and International Wheat "Meat" Recipes, hundreds of ways to use these delicious meat taste-alikes will be given.

CUTLETS: A VEAL SUBSTITUTE

Makes 4 to 6 cutlets
Preparation Time: 10 minutes
Cooking Time: 3–7 minutes

2 cups raw gluten	1 tablespoon tamari soy sauce
3 cups water	1 teaspoon lemon juice
½ teaspoon garlic powder	¼ teaspoon black pepper
1 tablespoon nutritional yeast	1 teaspoon cumin, ground
1 tablespoon oil	1 teaspoon coriander, ground

Break gluten into 4 to 6 pieces. Pound with a meat mallet to desired thickness: ¾ inch for thicker cutlets, ¼ inch for thinner cutlets. When cooked, the cutlets will increase in size and thickness.

Pour water into a saucepan. Add garlic powder, nutritional yeast, oil, soy sauce, lemon juice, black pepper, cumin and coriander. Bring water and flavorings to a gentle boil. Drop cutlets into this gently boiling broth. (If liquid is boiling rapidly, the texture of the cutlets will become spongy rather than veallike.)

The cutlets will sink to the bottom of the pan when they are dropped in. Allow them to cook, uncovered, only until they float to the surface of the liquid; for thin cutlets approximately 3 minutes, for thick cutlets 5 to 7 minutes. Remove cutlets with a slotted spoon and drain on paper towels. In this form, these cutlets resemble raw veal. They can be dusted with cumin powder and fried in oil on both sides or prepared and used according to any of the cutlet recipes in the All-American or International recipe sections of this book.

The liquid used to flavor cutlets makes an excellent broth for use in soups and gravies. It can be saved in the refrigerator for a week or longer to be used as needed.

STEAK: A MOCK BEEF STEAK

Makes 4 to 6 steaks
Preparation Time: 10 minutes
Cooking Time: 50 minutes

2 cups raw gluten	1 teaspoon cumin, ground
3 cups water	1 teaspoon coriander, ground
¼ cup tamari soy sauce	½ teaspoon garlic powder or 1
½ teaspoon black pepper	clove garlic, minced
1 tablespoon oil	

Divide raw gluten into 4 to 6 pieces. Pound with a meat mallet into steak-size pieces. Combine all remaining ingredients in a pot. Add gluten steaks. Place pot on medium heat for 50 minutes. Cook, uncovered, without boiling. Long, slow cooking allows the seasonings to penetrate the raw gluten, creating a dense beeflike texture. If boiled steaks take on a spongy texture, they have been boiled too rapidly for too long a period of time.

Steaks can be served immediately, but a more beeflike appearance will be obtained if they are fried in oil on both sides before serving. There are a multitude of recipes using wheat "meat" steak in the All-American and International chapters of this cookbook.

The liquid used to flavor wheat "meat" steaks makes an excellent broth for use in dark gravies, stew and soups. It can be stored in the refrigerator for a week or longer and used as needed.

GROUND GLUTEN: A HAMBURGER TASTE-ALIKE

Yield: 3 cups
Preparation Time: 15 minutes
Cooking Time: 15 minutes

3 cups water
2 tablespoons burdock root, ground (obtainable at health food stores, optional)
2 cups raw gluten

1 tablespoon oil
2 teaspoons miso
½ teaspoon garlic powder
1 teaspoon cumin, ground
1 teaspoon coriander, ground

1 tablespoon nutritional yeast

In a saucepan, combine water with ground burdock root, if available. Place saucepan on high heat and bring to a gentle boil. Reduce heat to medium and continue to boil water gently. Tear gluten into small teaspoon-sized pieces and drop into water. Allow to cook for 15 minutes while water continues to boil gently. Remove gluten pieces with a slotted spoon and drain on paper towels.

Grind gluten pieces in a food processor or meat grinder until it resembles the texture of coarsely ground steak. In a bowl, mix oil, miso, garlic powder, cumin, coriander and nutritional yeast. Add ground gluten and mix well.

Ground gluten can be eaten directly or sautéed in oil for a few minutes. It is a loose "meat" that will not hold its shape without a binding material. Soy flour or chickpea flour are recommended for binding the loose ground gluten since these bean flours provide a complementary protein. For recipes for hamburgers and meatballs, refer to the All-American and International sections of this cookbook.

SPICED LINKS: AN ALTERNATIVE TO SAUSAGE

Makes 18 Spiced Links
Precooking: 15 minutes
Preparation Time: 30 minutes
Cooking Time: 15 minutes

2 cups raw gluten
1 tablespoon burdock root, ground (obtainable at health food stores, optional)
3 cups water
4 teaspoons miso
1½ teaspoons garlic powder
1½ teaspoons ginger, powdered
1½ teaspoons black pepper

½ teaspoon sage
½ teaspoon rosemary
½ teaspoon thyme
½ teaspoon tarragon
½ teaspoon basil
½ teaspoon dry mustard
2 tablespoons nutritional yeast
1 cup soy flour

⅓ cup water mixed with 2 teaspoons oil

PRECOOKING

Tear raw gluten into small teaspoon-size pieces. Set aside. Combine water with burdock, if available, in a saucepan. Add gluten pieces. Bring to a gentle boil. Allow to boil for 15 minutes. Remove gluten pieces with a slotted spoon. Drain on paper towels.

PREPARATION

Mince gluten pieces in a food processor or meat grinder to the consistency of coarsely ground steak. Set aside. In a bowl, combine miso, garlic powder, ginger, black pepper, sage, rosemary, thyme, tarragon, basil and dry mustard. Mix well. Add ground gluten pieces. Mix until thoroughly combined with seasonings. Stir in nutritional yeast and soy flour. Mix to make a stiff dough that can be easily shaped. If dough is sticky, add additional flour. With moistened hands, shape into 18 cylinders resembling sausages.

COOKING

Pour water and oil mixture into a frying pan with a cover. Place on medium-high heat and bring to a gentle boil. Place links in pan, cover and continue to cook in gently boiling water for 15 minutes. Check periodically to ensure that water does not entirely evaporate. Add 3 tablespoons additional water if necessary.

Spiced links can be served immediately or fried in oil for a more sausagelike feel and appearance. In addition, there are many breakfast, lunch and dinner serving suggestions for spiced links in the All-American and International sections of this cookbook.

ROAST WITH A BEEF FLAVOR

Serves 4 to 6
Preparation Time: 5 minutes
Cooking Time: 10 hours in an oven,
16 hours in a slow cooker

2 cups raw gluten	3 tablespoons tamari soy
1½ cups water	sauce
¾ teaspoon garlic powder	2 teaspoons cumin, ground
½ teaspoon black pepper	1 teaspoon coriander, ground
½ teaspoon onion powder	

Shape gluten into a ball. Place it in a covered baking dish or a slow cooker (crock pot). Measure water into a mixing bowl. Stir in all remaining ingredients. Pour water mixture over gluten. Bake, covered, in a 250-degree oven for 10 hours or overnight. Or cook in a slow cooker, set on low, for 16 hours. The long, slow cooking time permits the seasonings to penetrate the "roast" and gives a texture that enables the "roast" to be sliced very thin. Wheat "meat" roast makes an excellent sandwich meat as well as a tasty pot roast. There are numerous recipes using roast in the All-American and International recipe sections of this cookbook.

SEAWHEAT: A CLAM ALTERNATIVE

Makes 3 cups seawheat
Preparation Time: 10 minutes
Cooking Time: 3 minutes

½ cup firmly packed seaweed,
(dulse, kombu or wakame,
obtainable at Oriental food
stores, optional)
3 cups water

1 tablespoon liquid barley malt
½ teaspoon salt
1 tablespoon oil
2 tablespoons fresh lemon juice
2 cups raw gluten

Tear seaweed, if available, into 1-inch pieces. Place in a saucepan. Add water. Stir in malt, salt, oil and lemon juice. Break gluten into small clam-size pieces and set aside.

Bring water mixture to a gentle boil. Drop the gluten pieces into boiling broth. The gluten will sink. As soon as they rise to the top of the liquid, remove them with a slotted spoon and drain on paper towels. The seawheat will be cooked in about 3 minutes and will have the chewy texture of clams. If they have a spongy texture, the water has boiled too rapidly or the gluten has been cooked too long.

Seawheat can be eaten immediately, dipped in sauce, or it can be breaded and deep-fried to resemble fried clams. In addition, there are numerous recipes using seawheat in the All-American and International sections of this cookbook.

POULTRY PIECES: CHICKEN-FLAVORED WHEAT "MEAT"

Makes 8 pieces
Preparation Time: 10 minutes
Cooking Time: 45 minutes

2 cups raw gluten
3 cups water
1 tablespoon nutritional yeast
½ teaspoon salt
½ teaspoon celery seed
¼ teaspoon sage
¼ teaspoon thyme

½ teaspoon cumin, ground
½ teaspoon coriander, ground
¼ teaspoon garlic powder
¼ teaspoon tarragon
¼ teaspoon rosemary
½ teaspoon turmeric
2 teaspoons corn oil

Divide raw gluten into 8 pieces. Using a meat mallet, pound

these pieces into the shape of boneless chicken breasts. In a saucepan, combine water with all remaining ingredients to form a poultry-flavored broth. Add raw gluten pieces to broth.

Cook gluten in broth over medium heat for 45 minutes without boiling. Slow cooking allows the poultry flavoring to penetrate the gluten. If the broth is allowed to boil, the texture of the poultry pieces will become spongy, but if cooked slowly, it will resemble chicken breasts.

Poultry pieces are best when dipped in batter or flour and then fried in oil. However, they can be diced or chopped immediately for use in soups or salads. Many recipes for poultry pieces can be found in the All-American and International recipe sections of this cookbook.

The poultry broth used in flavoring poultry pieces is an excellent base for soups and gravies. It can be stored in the refrigerator for a week or longer and used as needed.

Using the Reserved Starch, Bran and Germ

The creamy solution you washed away and saved while making raw gluten contains the vitamin- and mineral-rich starch, bran and germ of whole wheat. This solution should not be wasted but used to make gluten-free crackers or crunchy cereal. By making either crackers or cereal, the nutritional value of whole wheat is not lost and another money-saving, wholesome food is added to your diet.

Both crackers and cereal are simple to make. They require no kneading or rolling, but your friends will be astonished that they're not a new, delicious Scandinavian import or a recent addition to the Post line of cold cereals. Not only will you enjoy assuring them that you made them yourself, you will also appreciate the bonus to your food budget.

GLUTEN-FREE CRACKERS
Makes 3 cookie sheets of crackers
Preparation Time: 2 to 3 hours standing for liquid and solids
to separate, plus 1 hour for yeasted mixture to rise
Baking Time: 2 hours

Reserved solution from one   2 tablespoons liquid barley
    recipe of raw gluten   malt
¼ cup lukewarm water   1 tablespoon baking yeast

Allow reserved mixture of water, starch, bran and germ to stand at room temperature for 2 to 3 hours or in the refrigerator overnight. The starch, bran and germ will form a thick sediment at the bottom of the container. This sediment will be used to make crackers.

Pour off the liquid at the top of the container and store in the refrigerator for use in soups, gravies and sauces. This liquid contains the water-soluble vitamins in whole wheat, notably B vitamins, and will add a nutritional boost to any recipe calling for water. Often, our recipes in the All-American and International sections of this cookbook will call for using either this liquid, which we call wheat water, or water, interchangeably.

Stir the residue at the bottom of the container and pour it into a bowl. In a separate bowl, combine warm water with malt. Stir until malt completely dissolves. Malt is superior to simple sugar in its ability to activate baking yeast. Sprinkle yeast over the water and malt solution. Allow to stand for 5 minutes until dissolved. Stir into the starch, bran and germ mixture. Cover with a warm damp towel and let stand in a warm place for 30 minutes, then stir with a spoon. Pour equal portions onto 3 well-oiled cookie sheets. Allow to stand in a warm place for 30 minutes longer.

Set oven at 300 degrees. Place cookie sheets in warmed oven and bake for 2 hours until crackers are fully dried out and crisp. These crackers, which are very much like Scandinavian hard bread, only fresh, warm and homemade, can be broken into serving-size pieces.

VARIATION 1

For a thicker cracker, pour the yeasted batter onto 1 or 2 well-oiled cookie sheets rather than 3. This heavier version will require 2 to 3 hours baking, depending on the thickness of the crackers.

For variety, try adding a tablespoon of caraway seeds, a tablespoon of fennel seeds, a teaspoon of garlic powder or a tablespoon of minced onion to the cracker batter before allowing it to rise.

COLD, CRUNCHY CEREAL

Makes 1 quart
Preparation Time: same as cracker preparation
Baking Time: same as cracker baking time

The ingredients and procedure for making breakfast cereal from the reserved starch, bran and germ are the same as for making gluten-free crackers, the previous recipe. After crackers are made, crumble them between your fingers or chop them in a food processor until they reach desired consistency. This cereal is similar to Grape Nuts. It can be stored in a covered jar and eaten for breakfast with milk and fruit.

VARIATION 1

For a sweeter cereal with added calcium and iron, add 3 tablespoons of blackstrap molasses to the batter before allowing it to rise.

VARIATION 2

For a cinnamon and raisin cereal, add 1 teaspoon cinnamon to batter before allowing it to rise. After cereal has been crumbled or chopped, add 1 cup of raisins.

PART II

Hundreds of International Ways to Serve Wheat "Meat"

CHAPTER FOUR

All-American Wheat "Meat" Recipes

All-American recipes provide the most straightforward way to introduce wheat "meats" into the diet without changing your usual menus or having to run to a specialty food store for exotic ingredients. Nutritional yeast, soybean flour, or chickpea flour, miso and tamari soy sauce are already on your kitchen shelves if you've prepared wheat "meats."

By slipping wheat "meats" into soups, gravies, pot pies, pancakes and hamburger buns, you can save dollars and accustom your family to this new taste adventure.

ALL-AMERICAN SOUPS

CREAM OF TOMATO WITH CUTLET CHUNKS

Serves 4 to 6
Preparation Time: 15 minutes
Cooking Time: 20 minutes
Elementary

3 tablespoons oil	½ teaspoon tarragon
1½ cutlets, cut in 1-inch cubes	1 teaspoon basil
2 onions, chopped	1 teaspoon salt
4 cups vegetable broth	1 cup dried milk powder
5 unpeeled tomatoes, chopped	

Heat oil in a frying pan over medium heat. Add cutlet chunks and fry until lightly browned. Add onions and sauté until transparent. Set aside.

Mix broth with herbs, salt, milk powder and tomatoes. Purée in an electric blender or food processor until smooth. Pour into a pot and cook over medium heat without bringing to a boil. Add onions and cutlet chunks. Serve when cutlets are fully heated.

TOMATO AND STEAK SOUP

Serves 4 to 6
Preparation Time: 15 minutes
Cooking Time: 20 minutes
Elementary

2 tablespoons olive oil	2 green peppers, chopped
1 cup steak, sliced ⅛ inch thick and 1 inch square	2 tablespoons parsley, chopped
	5 unpeeled tomatoes, chopped
2 onions chopped	1 tablespoon tomato paste
4 cups vegetable broth	

Heat oil in a heavy-bottomed pot large enough to hold entire soup. Add steak and sauté for 2 minutes. Add onions and cook until transparent. Add green peppers and parsley. Cook for 3 minutes. Stir in chopped tomatoes and cook for 3 more minutes. Stir in tomato paste. Pour in broth and continue to cook until well heated.

CREAM OF CUTLET SOUP

Serves 4 to 6
Preparation Time: 10 minutes
Cooking Time: 15 minutes
Elementary

2 tablespoons oil	1 cup light cream
1½ cups cutlet cut in ½-inch cubes	3 tablespoons whole wheat pastry flour
1 cup chopped chives or scallions	½ teaspoon salt
3 cups milk	½ teaspoon black pepper
	1 tablespoon butter

Heat oil in a heavy-bottomed pan over medium heat. Add cutlet cubes and sauté until lightly browned. Add chives or scallions and sauté for an additional minute. Add milk. Stir cream slowly into flour so it does not lump. Add to soup. Season with salt and pepper. Dot with butter. Cook over medium heat, stirring occasionally, until soup has thickened and there is no taste of raw flour.

SPLIT PEA SOUP WITH SPICED LINKS

Serves 6 to 8
Preparation Time: 4 hours soaking time plus 10 minutes
Cooking Time: 1 hour
Elementary

2 cups split green or yellow peas	1 teaspoon salt
7 cups water or wheat water	½ teaspoon black pepper
2 carrots, diced	2 bay leaves
2 celery stalks, diced	½ teaspoon thyme
1 garlic clove, minced	3 tablespoons oil
2 onions, chopped	6 spiced links, sliced

Soak dried peas in water for four hours. Transfer peas and water to a pot and bring to a boil. Continue to boil for 5 minutes. Reduce heat to medium. When boiling subsides, add vegetables, salt, pepper and herbs. Continue to cook for 45 minutes until peas are creamy. Heat oil in a frying pan over medium heat. Brown sliced links in hot oil. Pour soup into serving bowls and top with spiced links.

CREAM OF SPLIT PEA AND SPICED LINK SOUP

Serves 4 to 6
Preparation Time: 4 hours soaking time plus 10 minutes
Cooking Time: 1 hour
Elementary

1 cup split green or yellow peas	1 tablespoon fresh or 1 teaspoon dried mint
4 cups water or wheat water	1 teaspoon salt
1 tablespoon nutritional yeast	1 cup sour cream mixed with
1 onion, finely chopped	½ cup water
2 garlic cloves, minced	2 tablespoons butter
8 spiced links, sliced	

Soak peas in water for 4 hours in a pot large enough to hold the entire soup. Bring to a boil. Allow to boil for 5 minutes. Reduce heat to medium. Stir in nutritional yeast, onion, garlic, mint and salt. Cook for 45 minutes until peas are soft. Purée in an electric blender or food processor until smooth. Stir in sour cream and water mixture. If a hot soup is desired, return to stove until thoroughly heated before serving. If a cold soup is preferred, place in the refrigerator to cool. In a heavy frying pan, melt butter over medium heat. Sauté spiced link slices until lightly browned. Add to soup and serve.

LENTIL SOUP WITH SPICED LINKS

Serves 4 to 6
Preparation Time: 4 hours soaking time plus 10 minutes
Cooking Time: 1 hour
Elementary

1 cup lentils	1 teaspoon salt
4 cups water or wheat water	½ teaspoon black pepper
3 tablespoons oil	2 bay leaves
2 onions, chopped	1 tablespoon whole wheat pas-
2 carrots, chopped	try flour mixed with 2 table-
1 potato, diced	spoons water
1 teaspoon cumin, ground	2 teaspoons lemon juice
1 teaspoon thyme	2 tablespoons olive oil

10 spiced links, sliced

Cover lentils with water and soak for at least 4 hours. Heat oil in a heavy-bottomed pan large enough to hold entire soup. Add onions and cook until transparent. Add carrots and potato. Sauté until lightly browned. Add lentils and water. Stir in cumin, thyme, salt, pepper and bay leaves. Cover and cook over medium heat for 30 minutes. Stir flour and water mixture into soup. Cook for 20 minutes longer. Stir in lemon juice. In a heavy frying pan, heat oil over medium heat. Brown link slices in hot oil. Stir into soup and serve.

BLACK-EYED PEA SOUP WITH SPICED LINKS

Serves 4 to 6
Preparation Time: 6 hours soaking time plus 15 minutes
Cooking Time: 3 hours
Elementary

1 cup dried black-eyed peas	2 bay leaves
5 cups water or wheat water	½ teaspoon salt
1 tablespoon oil	½ teaspoon black pepper
3 onions, chopped	4 spiced links, crumbled
2 garlic cloves, minced	2 tablespoons butter

6 spiced links, sliced

Soak peas in water for 6 hours or overnight. Place peas and water in a pot large enough to hold entire soup. Bring to a boil. Continue to boil 5 minutes and reduce heat to medium.

In a heavy frying pan heat oil over medium heat. Add onions and sauté until transparent. Add garlic and cook until onions are lightly browned. Add onions and garlic to cooking peas. Stir in bay leaves, salt, pepper and crumbled links. Cook until peas are soft, about 2 hours and 30 minutes.

In a heavy frying pan, melt butter over medium heat. Add sliced links. Sauté until lightly browned. Stir into pea soup before serving.

MINESTRONE

Serves 4 to 6
Preparation Time: 20 minutes
Cooking Time: 30 minutes
Elementary

¾ cup fresh or precooked kidney beans
6 cups water
3 tablespoons oil
2 onions, chopped
1 leek, chopped
2 carrots, chopped
1 cup celery, chopped
½ cup fresh or frozen corn kernels

½ cup fresh or frozen peas
2 tablespoons olive oil
10 spiced links, sliced
1 tablespoon tomato paste
2 unpeeled tomatoes, chopped
1 tablespoon parsley, chopped
1 teaspoon sage
1 garlic clove, minced
1 teaspoon salt
½ cup Parmesan cheese, grated

In a pot large enough to hold entire soup, combine kidney beans and water. Cook over medium heat.

In a heavy frying pan, heat oil over medium heat. Add onions and sauté until transparent. Add leek and carrots. Sauté for 3 minutes. Stir in celery, corn and peas. Sauté for 1 minute. If vegetables begin to brown, add 1 tablespoon water.

Drop sautéed vegetables into cooking beans. Return frying pan to heat. Add olive oil. Sauté spiced links. Add links to cooking soup. Stir in tomato paste, tomatoes, parsley, sage, garlic and salt. Cook until vegetables are tender. Stir in cheese before serving.

RICE AND SPICED LINK CHOWDER

Serves 4 to 6
Preparation Time: 15 minutes
Cooking Time: 1½ hours
Elementary

2 cups water or wheat water	3 cups milk
½ cup brown rice	2 tablespoons butter
2 tablespoons corn oil	6 spiced links, sliced
3 onions, chopped	2 eggs, beaten
2 potatoes, chopped	½ teaspoon salt

½ teaspoon black pepper

In a covered pot large enough to hold entire soup, bring water to a boil. Add rice, cover and reduce heat to low. Allow to cook for 40 minutes.

In a heavy frying pan, heat corn oil over medium heat. Add onions and sauté until transparent. Stir in potatoes and cook for 10 minutes. If potatoes begin to burn, add 1 tablespoon water. Add onions and potatoes to cooking rice. Cook for 15 minutes until potatoes are soft. Add milk and increase heat to medium. Cook, covered, without boiling for another 15 minutes.

Return frying pan to burner and melt butter. Brown sliced spiced links. Add links to soup. Stir in eggs. Cook for 5 minutes. Season with salt and pepper before serving.

POULTRY NOODLE SOUP

Serves 4 to 6
Preparation Time: 15 minutes
Cooking Time: 20 minutes
Elementary

2 tablespoons corn oil	2 celery stalks, finely chopped
1½ cups poultry pieces, cut in ¼-inch cubes	4 cups poultry broth (p. 24)
1 cup scallions or leeks, finely chopped	1 cup whole grain flat noodles or broken whole grain spaghetti
2 tablespoons parsley, finely chopped	

In a heavy frying pan, heat oil. Add small cubes of poultry and sauté until lightly browned. Add scallions or leeks and sauté until tender. Add remaining vegetables and cook until deepened in color. Remove from heat and set aside.

In a pot large enough to hold entire soup, bring broth to a boil. Add whole grain pasta. Boil gently for 10 minutes. Stir in vegetables and cook for 3 minutes. Serve before vegetables have wilted.

SEAWHEAT AND MUSHROOM BISQUE

Serves 4 to 6
Preparation Time: 10 minutes
Cooking Time: 15 minutes
Elementary

4 tablespoons butter	1 tablespoon liquid barley
1 cup mushrooms, sliced	malt
4 tablespoons whole wheat	1 cup seawheat, diced
pastry flour	1½ cups light cream
2½ cups water or wheat water	1 tablespoon tomato paste

½ teaspoon salt

In a heavy frying pan, melt butter over medium heat. Add mushrooms and sauté until they have decreased in size and darkened in color. Stir in flour until thoroughly mixed with frying pan juices. Stir in water and malt. Cook, stirring occasionally, for 10 minutes until liquid has thickened. Add seawheat. Remove from heat and stir in cream. Return to burner and reduce heat to low. Cook until hot. Stir in tomato paste until thoroughly mixed. Add salt before serving.

MANHATTAN CHOWDER

Serves 4 to 6
Preparation Time: 20 minutes
Cooking Time: 30 minutes
Elementary

2 tablespoons oil
1 onion, chopped
1 potato, diced
2 celery stalks, diced
2 green peppers, diced
3 unpeeled tomatoes, chopped
2 carrots, diced

4 cups vegetable broth
3 tablespoons tomato paste
1 teaspoon dried parsley
¼ teaspoon garlic powder
½ teaspoon black pepper
½ teaspoon salt
1 cup seawheat, diced

2 teaspoons arrowroot starch dissolved in 1 tablespoon water

In a heavy frying pan, heat oil over medium heat. Sauté onions until transparent. Add remaining vegetables and sauté for 3 minutes. Set aside.

In a pot large enough to hold entire soup, mix broth with tomato paste. Stir in dried parsley, garlic powder, black pepper and salt. Add sautéed vegetables. Place on medium heat and cook for 20 minutes until potatoes are tender. Add seawheat. Stir in starch and water mixture. Continue cooking, stirring constantly, until soup has thickened slightly. Serve.

NEW ENGLAND CHOWDER

Serves 4 to 6
Preparation Time: 20 minutes
Cooking Time: 45 minutes
Elementary

1 tablespoon oil
3 potatoes, diced
2 onions, chopped
1 garlic clove, minced

2 cups seawheat, diced
4 cups milk
1 teaspoon salt
½ teaspoon black pepper

1 tablespoon arrowroot starch mixed with 1 tablespoon water

In a heavy frying pan, heat oil over medium heat. Add potatoes and sauté for 5 minutes. If potatoes begin to stick to frying pan, add 1 tablespoon water. Add onions and garlic. Sauté until onions are transparent. Set aside.

In a pot large enough to hold entire soup, combine seawheat, milk, salt and pepper. Add potatoes, onion and garlic. Cook over medium heat without boiling for 20 minutes until potatoes are soft. Stir starch and water mixture into soup. Continue to cook, stirring constantly, until soup thickens, then serve.

ALL-AMERICAN CUTLET MAIN DISHES

CUTLETS WITH CHEESE

Serves 4
Preparation Time: 10 minutes
Cooking Time: 15 minutes
Intermediate

4 slices Cheddar or Swiss
  cheese
4 cutlets, pounded thin
¼ cup soy or chickpea flour
⅛ teaspoon salt
⅛ teaspoon black pepper
½ teaspoon cumin

2 eggs, lightly beaten
1 tablespoon milk
1 cup whole grain soft breadcrumbs
½ cup oil
8 lemon slices
4 sprigs parsley

Place a slice of cheese over one half of each thinly pounded cutlet. Fold cutlets over cheese and secure with a toothpick.

Arrange 3 soup-size bowls close to your cooking surface. In the first, mix soy or chickpea flour with salt, pepper and cumin. In the second, beat eggs with milk. In the third, place bread-crumbs.

Coat both sides of each cheese-stuffed cutlet with seasoned flour. Next dip each cutlet in egg mixture and thoroughly moisten. Lastly, dredge in breadcrumbs.

Heat oil in a heavy frying pan until water dances when sprinkled into it. Place cutlets in hot oil and fry until golden brown on both sides. Drain on paper towels. Serve garnished with lemon slices and parsley.

STUFFED CUTLETS

Serves 4
Preparation Time: 20 minutes
Cooking Time: 25 minutes
Intermediate

½ cup mozzarella cheese,
grated
½ cup feta cheese, crumbled
1 onion, finely chopped
1 garlic clove, minced
1 egg, lightly beaten
½ cup ripe olives, chopped
¾ cup whole wheat bread-
crumbs

¼ teaspoon oregano
¼ teaspoon black pepper
4 cutlets, pounded thin
4 tablespoons butter
3 tablespoons oil
¼ cup whole wheat pastry flour
½ cup vegetable broth
1 cup yogurt or sour cream
¼ cup fresh parsley, chopped

Combine grated mozzarella cheese, feta cheese, onion, garlic, egg, olives, breadcrumbs, oregano and black pepper to make stuffing.

Place stuffing in the center of each cutlet. Fold cutlet over the stuffing and secure with a toothpick.

Heat oil and butter in a heavy frying pan until water sizzles when sprinkled onto the hot fats. Dredge each stuffed cutlet in flour. Fry on both sides until golden brown. Remove from pan and set aside, covered with foil.

Add broth to frying pan. Stir in sour cream or yogurt. Add chopped parsley. Cook for 3 minutes. Pour sauce over stuffed cutlets before serving.

CHOPS WITH HERBS

Serves 4
Preparation Time: 20 minutes
Cooking Time: 15 minutes
Elementary

4 tablespoons butter
1 teaspoon tarragon
½ teaspoon onion powder
½ teaspoon garlic powder

pinch of black pepper
1 teaspoon cumin, ground
pinch salt
4 cutlets, 1 inch thick
1 lemon, cut in wedges

In a saucepan, melt butter with tarragon, onion powder, garlic powder, black pepper, cumin and salt. Brush cutlets with warm herb butter. Allow to stand for 15 minutes. Heat a heavy frying pan over medium heat. Place cutlets in hot pan, pouring in any herb butter that has collected while cutlets have been waiting. Brown on both sides and serve with lemon wedges.

LEMON CUTLET LOAF

Serves 4 to 6
Preparation Time: 15 minutes
Baking Time: 1 hour
Elementary

4 cutlets	1 cup soy flour
4 tablespoons butter, melted	1 teaspoon salt
2 onions, grated	½ teaspoon black pepper
1 teaspoon lemon peel, grated	1 lemon, thinly sliced
3 eggs, lightly beaten	3 tablespoons whole grain
½ cup sour cream	breadcrumbs

Grind cutlets in a meat grinder or food processor to the consistency of coarsely ground steak. Combine ground cutlets with 2 tablespoons of the melted butter, onion, lemon peel, eggs, sour cream, soy flour, salt and pepper. Pour into a well-oiled loaf pan. Top with sliced lemon and sprinkle with breadcrumbs. Drizzle the remaining 2 tablespoons of melted butter over the loaf. Bake at 350 degrees for 1 hour until lightly browned.

ALL-AMERICAN STEAK MAIN DISHES

CHUNKY STEW

Serves 4 to 6
Preparation Time: 25 minutes
Cooking Time: 40 minutes
Elementary

4 tablespoons oil
4 onions, chopped
3 carrots, cut into 1-inch chunks
2 potatoes, cut into 1-inch chunks
4 cups vegetable broth
½ teaspoon garlic powder

¼ teaspoon black pepper
1 teaspoon mustard seeds
¼ cup fresh parsley, chopped
2 cups steak, cut into 1-inch cubes
3 stalks celery, diced
3 green peppers, diced
4 tomatoes, cut in wedges

1 tablespoon arrowroot starch mixed with 1 tablespoon water

In a heavy-bottomed pot large enough to hold entire stew, heat oil over medium heat. Add onions and sauté until transparent. Stir in carrots and potatoes. Sauté for 5 minutes. If vegetables begin to brown, add 1 tablespoon water. Add broth, garlic powder, black pepper, mustard seeds and parsley. Cover and cook without boiling for 20 minutes until carrots and potatoes are tender.

Stir in steak cubes, celery, green peppers and tomatoes. Cook for 10 minutes without boiling. Add arrowroot starch and water mixture. Cook, stirring constantly, until sauce thickens.

STEAK WITH MUSHROOMS

Serves 4
Preparation Time: 10 minutes
Cooking Time: 15 minutes
Elementary

2 tablespoons oil
¼ teaspoon salt
¼ teaspoon black pepper

4 steaks
2 tablespoons butter
2 cups mushrooms, sliced

In a heavy frying pan, heat oil over medium heat. Add salt and pepper. Brown steaks on both sides in seasoned oil. Add butter and melt. Add mushrooms and reduce heat to low. If steaks and mushrooms begin to stick to the pan, add 1 tablespoon water. Cover and cook for 10 minutes until mushrooms have darkened in color and decreased in size. Arrange steaks on a platter and spoon a generous serving of mushrooms on each.

STEAK AND GRAVY

Serves 4
Preparation Time: 10 minutes
Cooking Time: 15 minutes
Elementary

1 tablespoon oil	3 tablespoons soy flour
4 steaks	¼ teaspoon black pepper
2 onions, chopped	1 teaspoon cumin, ground
1½ cups water or wheat water	1 teaspoon coriander, ground
1 tablespoon tamari soy sauce	

In a heavy frying pan, heat oil over medium heat. Brown steaks in oil on both sides. Add onions and sauté until transparent. If steaks or onions begin to stick to the pan, add 1 tablespoon water. Remove steaks from pan and set aside, covered with foil.

In a bowl, mix water with flour, pepper, cumin, coriander and soy sauce until flour is dissolved. Pour flour mixture into frying pan. Increase heat to medium-high and bring to a gentle boil, stirring constantly. When gravy thickens, serve in a gravy boat along with browned steaks.

BREADED FRIED STEAK

Serves 4
Preparation Time: 15 minutes
Cooking Time: 20 minutes
Elementary

⅓ cup soy or chickpea flour	⅔ cup soft whole grain bread-
1 egg	crumbs
1 tablespoon milk	½ cup oil
4 sprigs parsley	

Arrange three soup-size bowls in a line near your cooking surface. In the first, place flour. In the second, beat egg and milk together. In the third, place breadcrumbs. Thoroughly coat each steak, first with flour, next with egg mixture and lastly with breadcrumbs.

In a heavy frying pan, heat oil until water sizzles when sprinkled onto it. Add breaded steaks and sauté on both sides until lightly browned and crisp. Serve garnished with parsley.

SWISS STEAK

Serves 4
Preparation Time: 10 minutes
Cooking Time: 15 minutes
Elementary

⅓ cup soy flour
⅛ teaspoon salt
¼ teaspoon black pepper
1 teaspoon cumin, ground
4 steaks
4 tablespoons oil

1 garlic clove, minced
2 onions, chopped
⅔ cup vegetable broth
1 tablespoon arrowroot starch
mixed with 1 tablespoon
water

Mix flour with salt, pepper and cumin. Thoroughly coat steaks with seasoned flour. In a heavy frying pan, heat oil over medium heat. Brown steaks on both sides in hot oil. Remove from pan, place on a platter and cover with foil.

Add garlic and onions to frying pan. Sauté until onions are transparent. Stir in broth. Cook until broth begins to bubble around the edges of the pan. Add starch and water mix. Continue cooking, stirring constantly, until broth thickens. Pour gravy over steaks and serve.

STEAK WITH ONIONS AND PEPPERS

Serves 4
Preparation Time: 10 minutes
Cooking Time: 15 minutes
Elementary

2 tablespoons oil
1 teaspoon cumin
¼ teaspoon salt
¼ teaspoon black pepper
½ teaspoon garlic powder

4 steaks
2 onions, sliced in rings
1 tablespoon water
1 green pepper, sliced
1 red pepper, sliced

Heat oil in a heavy frying pan over medium heat. Stir in cumin, salt, black pepper and garlic powder. Brown steaks in seasoned oil on both sides. Remove from pan and cover with foil.

Add onion rings and cook until transparent. Add water, green and red peppers. Sauté until their color deepens and they are still crisp. Serve steaks topped with peppers and onions.

POT PIES

Serves 4
Preparation Time: 45 minutes
Cooking Time: 40 minutes
Intermediate

DOUGH INGREDIENTS

⅓ cup lukewarm water
1 egg, lightly beaten
1 tablespoon vinegar

1 tablespoon butter, melted
1½ cups whole wheat pastry
flour
¼ teaspoon salt

FILLING INGREDIENTS

2 potatoes, diced
2 carrots, diced
2 cups water
3 tablespoons butter
1½ cups steak, cut in 1-inch
cubes
2 tablespoons whole wheat
pastry flour
1 onion, finely chopped
1 celery stalk, finely chopped

¼ cup fresh or frozen corn
kernels
¼ cup fresh or frozen peas
1 tablespoon nutritional yeast
½ teaspoon black pepper
2 teaspoons tamari soy sauce
1 teaspoon liquid barley malt
1 teaspoon cumin, ground
1 teaspoon coriander, ground
¼ teaspoon salt
pinch of cayenne (optional)

DOUGH

To make dough, combine water, egg, vinegar and melted butter. In a separate bowl, mix flour and salt. Pour flour and salt into liquid mixture. Stir ingredients for 5 minutes. Turn dough onto a well-floured board and knead. If dough begins to stick to board, add flour. Cover and allow to sit for 30 minutes while preparing filling.

FILLING

To make filling, cook potatoes and carrots in water until tender. While these vegetables are cooking, melt butter in a heavy frying pan over medium heat. Add steak to hot butter and brown. Stir in flour. Gradually add carrots and potatoes along with the water they have been cooked in. Stir in remaining ingredients. Cook, stirring occasionally, until gravy thickens. Remove from heat and set aside.

ASSEMBLING

To assemble individual pot pies, divide dough into 8 small balls. Roll out each ball of pastry on a floured board into circles approximately 5 inches in diameter. Line 4 individual pie plates with pastry. Spoon filling into each. Roll out top crusts, cover pies, slash to let steam escape and pinch edges.

Bake at 350 degrees for 40 minutes until top crust is lightly browned.

STROGANOFF

Serves 4
Preparation Time: 10 minutes
Cooking Time: 20 minutes
Elementary

3 cups water
½ pound flat spinach noodles
4 tablespoons butter
4 steaks, sliced ⅛ inch thick
   and cut in 1-inch squares
1 onion, grated
1 cup mushrooms, sliced

½ teaspoon salt
¼ teaspoon black pepper
pinch of nutmeg
½ teaspoon basil
1 cup sour cream mixed
   with ¼ cup water

Bring water to a boil. Cook noodles in boiling water for 10 minutes until tender.

While noodles cook, heat 2 tablespoons of butter in a heavy frying pan. Sauté steak pieces on both sides until lightly browned. Add onion and sauté until transparent. Add remaining 2 tablespoons butter. When melted, stir in mushrooms and cook until color darkens. Stir in salt, pepper, nutmeg and basil. Add sour cream and water mixture. Cook until hot.

Drain noodles. Pour onto a serving platter and top with steak and sour cream mixture before serving.

ALL-AMERICAN GROUND GLUTEN MAIN DISHES

HEARTY GRAVY AND MASHED POTATOES

Serves 4 to 6
Preparation Time: 10 minutes
Cooking Time: 40 minutes
Elementary

POTATO INGREDIENTS

5 potatoes, chopped	3 tablespoons milk
2 cups water	½ teaspoon salt
	2 tablespoons butter

GRAVY INGREDIENTS

½ cup cooked lentils	2 tablespoons oil
2 tablespoons chickpea flour	2 onions, chopped
1 teaspoon tamari soy sauce	1 garlic clove, minced
½ teaspoon black pepper	1 green pepper, chopped
2½ cups vegetable broth	1½ cups ground gluten

POTATOES

To make mashed potatoes, boil potatoes in water for 15 minutes until soft. Drain and discard water. Add milk, salt and butter. Mash with a potato masher, electric mixer or food processor. Turn potatoes into a covered baking dish and keep warm in a 200-degree oven while making gravy.

GRAVY

To make gravy, combine cooked lentils, flour, soy sauce, black pepper and broth in an electric blender or food processor. Purée until smooth and set aside.

In a heavy frying pan, heat oil over medium heat. Add onions and sauté until transparent. Stir in garlic and cook until onions have browned. Mix in green peppers and cook until darkened in color and still crisp. Add ground gluten and puréed lentil mixture to sautéed vegetables. Continue to cook until thoroughly heated.

Remove potatoes from oven and serve with hot, hearty gravy.

BROWN LOAF

Serves 4 to 6
Preparation Time: 15 minutes
Baking Time: 1 hour
Elementary

3 cups ground gluten	1 onion, finely chopped
3 tablespoons fresh parsley, chopped	1 teaspoon black pepper
	1 cup whole grain bread-
2 teaspoons cumin, ground	crumbs
2 eggs, lightly beaten	½ teaspoon salt

Spread gluten on a cookie sheet. Bake at 300 degrees for 10 minutes. Remove from oven and combine with all remaining ingredients. Mix well. Pour into a well-oiled loaf pan. Bake at 350 degrees for 50 minutes until loaf is firm. Remove loaf from pan to a serving plate and slice. Serve hot as a main dish or cold as a sandwich "meat."

BROWN LOAF WITH CREAM

Serves 4 to 6
Preparation Time: 15 minutes
Baking Time: 1 hour
Elementary

3 cups ground gluten
1 onion, finely chopped
1 teaspoon savory
1 garlic clove, finely chopped
1 teaspoon cumin, ground

1 egg, lightly beaten
1 cup whole grain breadcrumbs
2 tablespoons butter, melted
1 tablespoon whole wheat pastry flour

¾ cup cream

Spread ground gluten on a cookie sheet. Bake at 300 degrees for 10 minutes. Combine onion, savory, garlic, cumin, egg and breadcrumbs. Remove gluten from oven and stir into breadcrumb mixture. With moistened hands, mold a rounded oval loaf on an oiled oblong baking dish.

Bake at 350 degrees for 50 minutes, brushing with melted butter occasionally. Sprinkle loaf with flour and pour cream over it. Bake for 5 additional minutes before serving.

STUFFED CABBAGE

Serves 4 to 6
Preparation Time: 20 minutes
Cooking Time: 20 minutes
Intermediate

4 cups water
8 large cabbage leaves
4 cups ground gluten
2 onions, finely chopped
2 tablespoons fresh parsley, chopped
½ teaspoon thyme

1 garlic clove, minced
2 tablespoons cider vinegar
3 tablespoons liquid barley malt
½ cup sour cream mixed with ¼ cup water

Bring water to a boil. Place cabbage leaves in boiling water for 2 minutes until wilted. Drain. Set aside.

To make stuffing, combine ground gluten with onions, parsley, thyme, garlic, vinegar and malt. Mix well. Place equal portions of filling on each cabbage leaf and roll into a cylinder. Secure each roll with a toothpick.

Arrange in a shallow baking dish. Pour sour cream mixture over the rolls. Bake at 350 degrees for 20 minutes until tender.

TOMATO SAUCE VARIATION

Pour ⅔ cup tomato or vegetable juice over the assembled rolls rather than sour cream and water mixture.

MASHED POTATOES 'N' HASH PIE

Serves 4 to 6
Preparation Time: 10 minutes
Precooking Time: 20 minutes
Baking Time: 25 minutes
Elementary

MASHED POTATO INGREDIENTS

5 potatoes, diced
2 cups water
3 tablespoons milk

½ teaspoon salt
¼ teaspoon black pepper
2 tablespoons butter

HASH INGREDIENTS

1 tablespoon oil
1 tablespoon butter
2 onions, chopped
2 cups ground gluten

1 unpeeled tomato, chopped
½ teaspoon salt
½ teaspoon black pepper
1 tablespoon melted butter

POTATOES

To make mashed potatoes, boil potatoes in water for 15 minutes until soft. Drain. Add milk, salt, pepper and butter. Mash with a potato masher, electric mixer or food processor. Set aside.

HASH

To make hash, heat oil and butter in a heavy frying pan. Add onions and sauté until transparent. Stir in ground gluten and cook until lightly crusted. Add tomato and cook for 3 minutes. Season with salt and pepper.

To assemble pie, line the bottom of a shallow, oiled baking dish with half of the mashed potatoes. Cover with hash. Top pie with remaining mashed potatoes, spread decoratively over the hash. Brush with melted butter and bake at 400 degrees for 25 minutes until top is crusted and lightly browned.

SLOPPY JOES ON WHOLE WHEAT BURGER BUNS

Serves 4 to 6
Preparation Time: 2 hours for Whole Wheat Burger Buns
10 minutes for Sloppy Joe Topping
Baking Time: 20 minutes for Whole Wheat Burger Buns
Cooking Time: 15 minutes for Sloppy Joe Topping
Intermediate

INGREDIENTS FOR WHOLE WHEAT BURGER BUNS

3 tablespoons oil
¼ cup liquid barley malt
½ teaspoon salt

1 cup milk, scalded
1 tablespoon baking yeast
3¼ cups whole wheat flour

2 tablespoons butter, melted

SLOPPY JOE INGREDIENTS

3 tablespoons butter
2 onions, finely chopped
3 cups ground gluten
½ cup celery, finely diced
¼ cup green pepper, finely diced

½ cup tomato paste mixed with
1¼ cups water or wheat water
½ teaspoon garlic powder
1 teaspoon tamari soy sauce
pinch of cayenne

8 sprigs parsley

BURGER BUNS

To make buns, begin by mixing oil, malt and salt in a large bread bowl. Add scalded milk and stir until malt is dissolved. When milk cools to lukewarm, sprinkle yeast over the mixture. Allow to sit for 5 minutes until yeast begins to foam. With a wire whisk or electric mixer beat in ¾ cup flour. Continue beating for 3 minutes. Allow to stand in a warm place for 10 minutes. Gradually mix in remaining flour. Turn onto a well-floured board and knead for 5 minutes. Place kneaded dough in a well-oiled bowl, cover with a warm, damp towel and let rise for 1 hour. Punch down. Form into 8 to 12 burger buns. Place buns on an oiled cookie sheet. Allow to rise, covered with a dry towel, for another 30 minutes. Brush melted butter on buns and bake at 350 degrees for 20 minutes until lightly browned.

SLOPPY JOE TOPPING

To make Sloppy Joe topping, heat butter in a heavy frying pan over medium heat. Add onions and sauté until transparent.

Stir in ground gluten and cook until lightly browned. Add celery and green pepper. Sauté for 3 minutes until green pepper has deepened in color and is still crisp. Stir in tomato paste mixture, garlic powder, tamari soy sauce and cayenne.

Remove buns from oven, cut them in half and top with Sloppy Joe mixture. Garnish with parsley before serving.

WHEAT "MEAT" BALL SUBMARINES

Serves 4 to 6
Preparation Time: 2 hours for Whole Wheat Submarine Bread
20 minutes for Wheat "Meat" Balls and Sauce
Baking Time: 20 minutes for Submarine Bread
Cooking Time: 30 minutes for Wheat "Meat" Balls and Sauce
Intermediate

SUBMARINE BREAD INGREDIENTS

3 tablespoons oil	1 teaspoon garlic powder
3 tablespoons liquid barley malt	1 cup milk, scalded
	1 tablespoon baking yeast
½ teaspoon salt	3¼ cups whole wheat flour

2 tablespoons melted butter

WHEAT "MEAT" BALL INGREDIENTS

3 cups ground gluten	½ teaspoon black pepper
1 onion, grated	1 tablespoon nutritional yeast
1 cup soy flour	1 tablespoon miso

TOMATO SAUCE INGREDIENTS

¾ cup tomato paste	½ teaspoon onion powder
2¼ cups water or wheat water	1 teaspoon garlic powder
2 tablespoons olive oil	½ teaspoon allspice, ground

1 teaspoon tamari soy sauce

SUBMARINE BREAD

To make submarine bread, mix oil, malt, salt and garlic powder in a large bread bowl. Add scalded milk and stir until malt is dissolved. Allow milk mixture to cool to lukewarm. Sprinkle yeast over cooled milk mixture. With a wire whisk or electric mixer, beat ¾ cup flour into the milk mixture. Continue to beat for 3 minutes. Gradually add remaining flour. Turn dough onto a well-floured board and knead for 10 minutes. Place kneaded dough in a well-oiled bowl, cover with a warm, damp towel and allow to rise for 1 hour. Punch down and shape into 8 to 12 oval submarine loaves. Place sandwich loaves on an oiled baking sheet. Cover with a dry towel and allow to rise for 30 minutes longer. Brush loaves with melted butter. Bake at 350 degrees for 20 minutes.

WHEAT "MEAT" BALLS

To make wheat "meat" balls, combine ground gluten, onion, flour, black pepper, nutritional yeast and miso. With moistened hands form into 24 balls. Set aside.

SAUCE

To make sauce, combine tomato paste, water, olive oil, onion powder, garlic powder, allspice and soy sauce in a saucepan. Heat sauce to a gentle boil. Reduce heat to medium. When boiling subsides, add wheat "meat" balls. Continue to cook for 25 minutes until wheat "meat" balls are firm and have no taste of raw flour.

To serve, cut submarine loaves in half and top with wheat "meat" balls and sauce.

BURGERS

Serves 4
Preparation Time: 15 minutes
Cooking Time: 25 minutes
Elementary

2 cups ground gluten	1 tablespoon nutritional yeast
1 teaspoon miso	2 teaspoons cumin, ground
⅔ cup soy flour	1 tablespoon oil
½ teaspoon black pepper	½ cup water

Combine all ingredients except oil and water. Mixture should be stiff enough to shape easily. If necessary, add more soy flour. With moistened hands, shape into burger patties.

Heat oil and water in a covered frying pan to a gentle boil. Add burger patties and cover. Cook in gently boiling water for 15 minutes until burgers are firm.

In a well-oiled frying pan, brown burger patties on both sides before serving. Burgers can be served with gravy or on a bun. There is a recipe for whole wheat burger buns in the recipe for Sloppy Joes on Whole Wheat Burger Buns (page 50).

CHEESEBURGER VARIATION

After burgers have been browned on one side in an oiled frying pan, turn and top with slices of cheese. Continue to cook until cheese melts.

ALL-AMERICAN SPICED LINK MAIN DISHES

SPICED LINKS WITH GREEN PEPPERS

Serves 4 to 6
Preparation Time: 10 minutes
Cooking Time: 10 minutes
Elementary

¼ cup olive oil
12 to 16 spiced links
5 green peppers, sliced
4 garlic cloves, minced
1 tablespoon vinegar

pinch oregano
pinch black pepper
2 tablespoons fresh parsley, chopped

In a heavy frying pan, heat oil until water sizzles when sprinkled onto it. Add links and brown on all sides. Push to one side. Add green peppers and garlic. Cook until peppers begin to brown. Add remaining ingredients and cook for 2 minutes. Arrange spiced links on a serving plate, topped with peppers and parsley mixture.

SPICED LINKS WITH SAUERKRAUT

Serves 4 to 6
Preparation Time: 10 minutes
Cooking Time: 45 minutes
Elementary

8 medium-sized whole potatoes	½ teaspoon black pepper
1 quart water	1 tablespoon raisins in 2 cups water or wheat water
2½ cups sauerkraut	12 to 16 spiced links
1 large potato, grated	3 tablespoons olive oil

Boil potatoes in water until easily pierced with a fork. Drain and set aside. In a saucepan, combine sauerkraut, raisin and water mixture, black pepper and grated potato. Cover and cook over medium heat for 20 minutes.

While sauerkraut mixture cooks, prepare spiced links. In a heavy frying pan, heat oil over medium heat. Brown links in hot oil.

To serve, pour cooked sauerkraut mixture into the center of a platter, top with spiced links and surround with boiled potatoes. Serve with mustard and horseradish if desired.

SPICED WHEAT "MEAT" IN CRUST

Serves 4 to 6
Preparation Time: 2½ hours
Baking Time: 30 minutes
Intermediate

1 tablespoon oil	½ teaspoon oregano
1 tablespoon liquid barley malt	½ teaspoon dried parsley
pinch salt	½ teaspoon garlic powder
⅔ cup milk, scalded	4 cups spiced link mixture (before forming into link shapes)
2 teaspoons baking yeast	
2 cups whole wheat flour	1 cup water
2 tablespoons butter, melted	

To make crust, mix oil, malt, salt and scalded milk in a large bread bowl. Allow to cool to lukewarm and sprinkle yeast over milk mixture. Let stand for 5 minutes until yeast begins to foam. In a separate bowl, combine flour, oregano, parsley and garlic powder. With a wire whisk or electric mixer, beat ½ cup of seasoned flour into milk mixture. Continue to beat for 3 minutes. Using a wooden spoon, gradually mix in remaining flour. Turn dough onto a well-floured board and knead for 10 minutes. Place kneaded dough in a well-oiled bowl, cover with a damp, warm towel and allow to rise for 1 hour.

While dough rises, form spiced link mixture into one roll with moistened hands. In a covered pot large enough to hold spiced link roll, bring water to a gentle boil. Place spiced link roll on a rack and set in pot above boiling water. Cover pot and allow roll to steam for 30 minutes until firm. Remove from pot and set aside to cool.

When dough has risen for 1 hour, place on a floured board and roll out into a piece of dough large enough to wrap around the entire outside of the spiced roll. Wrap roll in dough, allowing seams to overlap slightly and closing seams with moistened fingers.

Place on a well-oiled baking dish and allow to stand in a warm place, covered with a dry towel, for an additional 30 minutes. Uncover and brush with melted butter. Bake at 350 degrees for 30 minutes until lightly browned. Serve immediately for a hot main dish or allow to cool and serve with horseradish and mustard.

ALL-AMERICAN ROAST MAIN DISHES

OLD-FASHIONED HASH

Serves 4 to 6
Preparation Time: 25 minutes
Cooking Time: 20 minutes
Elementary

2 tablespoons oil	½ teaspoon thyme
2 tablespoons butter	½ teaspoon salt
2 onions, finely chopped	½ teaspoon black pepper
2 cups boiled potatoes, finely chopped	½ cup cream
2½ cups roast, finely diced	8 eggs
	1½ cups water

In a frying pan, heat butter and oil over medium heat. Add onions and sauté until transparent. Stir in potatoes and sauté until lightly crusted. Add roast and sauté until lightly browned. Stir in thyme, salt, pepper and cream. Cook until cream evaporates and a crust is left at the bottom of the pan. Scrape crust loose with a spatula and place in a 200-degree oven to warm while poaching eggs.

To poach eggs, pour water into a frying pan. Bring water to a gentle boil. Break one egg at a time into a ladle and gently slip into water. Be careful that the yolks stay intact. Add four eggs in this manner. Reduce heat so that water is just below the boiling point. As the eggs cook, carefully pour 1 tablespoon of the hot water they are cooking in over each egg. Remove eggs with a slotted spoon in 3 minutes when whites have become opaque. Set aside without breaking yolks. Poach the second batch of four eggs in the same manner.

Remove hash from oven and spoon onto individual serving plates. Top each serving with two poached eggs.

POT ROAST

Serves 4 to 6
Preparation Time: 15 minutes
Cooking Time: 4 hours in a Crock-Pot (slow cooker),
2 hours in an oven
Elementary

1 roast	1 green pepper, finely chopped
5 small onions, peeled	1 cup boiling vegetable broth
5 carrots, cut in 2-inch chunks	1 tablespoon arrowroot starch mixed with 1 tablespoon water
5 small potatoes	
1 stalk celery, chopped	

Cook roast as directed on page 22 in a crock pot or oven. When 4 hours remain of the cooking time in a Crock-Pot or 2 hours remain of baking time in an oven, add whole onions, carrots, small potatoes, celery, green pepper and 1 cup of boiling broth. When total cooking time for roast has elapsed, remove roast and place on a serving platter. Surround with onions, carrots and potatoes. Place broth with celery and green peppers in a saucepan and bring to a gentle boil. Stir in starch and water mixture and continue to stir until broth thickens, about 2 minutes. Pour ⅔ cup of gravy over the roast and vegetables and serve remainder in a gravy boat.

CREAM SAUCE VARIATION

Add 1 cup of sour cream or yogurt to the thickened gravy just before serving.

HOT SLICED ROAST SANDWICHES

Serves 4
Preparation Time: 10 minutes
Cooking Time: 10 minutes
Elementary

2 teaspoons butter	1 tablespoon oil
4 slices whole wheat bread	2 onions, sliced in rings
½ roast, in thin slices	2 cups vegetable broth
1 tablespoon arrowroot starch mixed with 1 tablespoon water	

Butter bread and cover with generous portions of roast slices. Place on an oiled baking sheet and bake at 300 degrees for 10 minutes while preparing gravy.

To make gravy, heat oil in heavy frying pan over medium heat. Add onions and sauté until browned. Pour in broth. Bring to a gentle boil. Stir in starch and water mixture. Continue stirring until broth thickens into a transparent gravy, about 2 minutes.

Remove sandwiches from oven and place on individual plates. Pour gravy over sandwiches and serve.

BOILED ROAST

Serves 6 to 8
Preparation Time: 10 minutes
Cooking Time: 2 hours in a Crock-Pot,
1 hour in an oven
Elementary

1 roast
1 cup water or wheat water
3 onions, sliced in rings
4 carrots, diced

2 parsnips, diced
2 green peppers, diced
3 celery stalks, diced
1 bay leaf

Two hours before a roast has completed its normal cooking time in a Crock-Pot or 1 hour before cooking time is completed in an oven, add water, vegetables and bay leaf. When normal cooking time has elapsed, serve roast surrounded by vegetables.

ROAST IN A POT

Serves 6 to 8
Preparation Time: 15 minutes
Cooking Time: 4 hours in a Crock-Pot,
2 hours in an oven
Elementary

1 roast
1 cup boiling vegetable broth
4 onions, sliced
4 carrots, in 1-inch chunks

3 potatoes, in 1-inch chunks
2 bay leaves
3 tablespoons soy flour mixed
with 3 tablespoons water

Four hours before a roast has completed its normal cooking time in a Crock-Pot or 2 hours before cooking time is completed in an oven, add boiling broth, vegetables and bay leaves. When total cooking time has elapsed, place roast on a platter surrounded by vegetables.

Pour broth into a saucepan and bring to a gentle boil. Add flour and water mixture. Stir constantly until gravy thickens. Serve gravy in a gravy boat as an accompaniment to roast.

ALL-AMERICAN
MAIN DISHES WITH POULTRY PIECES

POULTRY SALAD

Serves 4 to 6
Preparation Time: 15 minutes
No cooking
Elementary

2½ cups poultry pieces, diced	2 tablespoons olive oil
2 cups water	¼ cup mayonnaise
1 onion, finely chopped	1 teaspoon lemon juice
1 garlic clove, finely chopped	½ teaspoon salt
½ teaspoon dill weed	¼ teaspoon black pepper

8 to 10 slices whole grain bread or 4 to 6 whole lettuce leaves

Place poultry pieces and water in an electric blender or food processor. Chop fine. Drain in a wire strainer, pressing down to remove all excess water. Combine chopped poultry with onions, garlic, dill weed, olive oil, mayonnaise, lemon juice, salt and pepper. Serve spread on bread or spooned onto lettuce leaves.

CREAMED POULTRY ON TOAST

Serves 4 to 6
Preparation Time: 15 minutes
Cooking Time: 20 minutes
Elementary

4 tablespoons butter	½ teaspoon salt
4 tablespoons chickpea flour	¼ teaspoon pepper
1¾ cups milk	2 tablespoons oil
¼ cup cream	2½ cups poultry pieces, in
pinch nutmeg	1-inch cubes

4 to 6 slices of whole grain bread

In a saucepan, melt butter over medium heat. Stir in flour until completely combined. Gradually add milk and cream, stirring constantly to prevent lumps from forming. Season with nutmeg, salt and pepper. When sauce has thickened, reduce heat to simmer and cover.

In a heavy frying pan, heat oil over medium heat. Add poultry cubes and sauté until lightly browned. Add browned cubes to white sauce and continue to simmer. Toast bread. Place toast on individual serving plates, top with creamed poultry and serve.

SPICY FRIED POULTRY

Serves 4 to 6
Marinating Time: 1 hour
Preparation Time: 5 minutes
Cooking Time: 15 minutes
Intermediate

2 cups milk	8 to 10 poultry pieces
½ teaspoon garlic powder	½ cup whole wheat pastry flour
¼ teaspoon salt	¼ cup butter
½ teaspoon turmeric	¼ cup oil
pinch powdered ginger	3 tablespoons soy flour or
pinch cayenne	chickpea flour

2 tablespoons fresh parsley, chopped

Combine milk, garlic powder, salt, turmeric, ginger and cayenne. Place poultry pieces in a shallow dish. Pour milk mixture over them and allow to marinate for 1 hour. Remove pieces from milk and reserve milk mixture.

Dredge pieces in whole wheat pastry flour. Heat butter and oil in a frying pan over medium heat. Fry both sides of poultry pieces in hot fats until lightly browned and crisp. Remove from pan and drain on paper towels.

Pour all but 3 tablespoons of melted butter and oil out of the frying pan and return pan to burner. Stir in soy or chickpea flour. Gradually add reserved milk mixture, stirring constantly, until milk thickens to a white sauce. Place poultry pieces on a platter, pour white sauce over them and garnish with parsley.

SOUTHERN FRIED POULTRY PIECES

Serves 4 to 6
Preparation Time: 10 minutes
Cooking Time: 15 minutes
Elementary

½ cup whole wheat pastry flour
pinch cumin
pinch black pepper
¼ teaspoon paprika
8 to 10 poultry pieces
½ cup oil

2 tablespoons soy flour or
chickpea flour
1 cup milk
1 teaspoon butter
½ teaspoon salt
½ teaspoon black pepper

2 tablespoons parsley, chopped

Mix whole wheat pastry flour with cumin, pepper and paprika. Dredge poultry pieces in seasoned flour. Heat oil in a heavy frying pan until water sizzles when sprinkled onto it.

Fry floured poultry pieces in hot oil on both sides until golden brown. Remove from oil and drain on paper towels.

Pour all but 2 tablespoons of oil out of the frying pan. Stir in bean flour. Gradually add milk. Add butter, salt and pepper. Cook, stirring constantly, until gravy thickens. Pour gravy into a gravy boat. Garnish poultry pieces with parsley and serve.

CREOLE FRIED POULTRY

Serves 4 to 6
Preparation Time: 15 minutes
Cooking Time: 10 minutes
Intermediate

8 to 10 poultry pieces
½ cup whole wheat pastry flour
¼ cup oil
¼ cup butter
1 garlic clove, minced
1 onion, chopped
1 teaspoon thyme

4 unpeeled tomatoes, in
wedges
½ teaspoon salt
1 teaspoon black pepper
½ cup poultry broth (p. 24)
½ teaspoon arrowroot starch
mixed with 1 teaspoon water

Thoroughly coat poultry pieces with flour. Heat oil and butter in a heavy frying pan over medium heat. Place poultry pieces in hot fats and brown lightly on both sides. Push to one side of the frying pan.

Add onion, garlic and thyme. Cook until onions are transparent. Add tomatoes and cook for 5 minutes. Season with salt and pepper. Remove poultry pieces and vegetables from pan with a slotted spoon and arrange on a serving platter.

Pour broth into pan and bring to a gentle boil while scraping loose brown bits that may have stuck to the bottom of the pan. Add starch and water mixture. Stir constantly until broth thickens, about 3 minutes. Pour sauce over poultry pieces and vegetables, garnish with parsley and serve.

ALL-AMERICAN SEAWHEAT MAIN DISHES

DEEP-FRIED SEAWHEAT
Serves 4 to 6
Preparation Time: 15 minutes
Cooking Time: 10 minutes
Elementary

2½ cups seawheat	1 cup whole grain bread-
½ cup chickpea or soy flour	crumbs
1 egg, lightly beaten with 1	1 cup oil
tablespoon milk	2 cups lettuce, shredded

⅓ cup tartar sauce

In a mixing bowl, combine seawheat and flour until seawheat is thoroughly coated. Pour egg mixture into bowl. Toss seawheat until coated with egg mixture. Add breadcrumbs and toss until seawheat has a coating of breadcrumbs.

In a heavy-bottomed pan or a deep-frying utensil, heat oil until water sizzles when sprinkled onto it. If using a pan, drop in seawheat and fry until golden brown and crisp. Remove seawheat with a slotted spoon and drain on paper towels. If using a deep-frying utensil, place breaded seawheat in wire basket and set in hot oil. When seawheat is golden brown and crisp, lift out wire basket and turn seawheat onto paper towels to drain. Place beds of lettuce on individual plates. Spoon servings of fried seawheat onto lettuce and serve with 1 tablespoon of tartar sauce on top.

SCALLOPED SEAWHEAT CASSEROLE

Serves 4 to 6
Preparation Time: 15 minutes
Cooking Time: 20 minutes
Elementary

1 cup whole grain or gluten-
free cracker crumbs
½ cup whole grain bread-
crumbs
½ cup butter, melted
½ teaspoon salt
¼ teaspoon black pepper

½ teaspoon paprika
2 cups seawheat, diced
1 onion, finely chopped
2 tablespoons fresh parsley,
chopped
½ cup light cream

Mix cracker crumbs and breadcrumbs with melted butter. Stir in salt, pepper and paprika. Set aside ⅓ cup of crumb mixture. Mix remaining crumb mixture with seawheat, onion and parsley. Pour into a well-oiled baking dish. Sprinkle reserved crumb mixture over the top. Pour cream over the casserole. Bake, uncovered, at 325 degrees for 20 minutes until golden brown and crusted.

ALL-AMERICAN
BREAKFAST DISHES WITH SPICED LINKS

FRIED LINKS

Serves 4 to 6
Preparation Time: 5 minutes
Cooking Time: 10 minutes
Elementary

2 tablespoons oil
12 to 18 spiced links
8 to 12 eggs, any style

8 to 12 pieces toasted whole
grain bread

In a heavy frying pan, heat oil over medium heat. Brown links on all sides in hot oil. Serve with eggs and toast for a typical American breakfast.

HASH BROWNS WITH SPICED LINKS

Serves 4 to 6
Preparation Time: 15 minutes
Cooking Time: 15 minutes
Elementary

2 tablespoons oil
12 to 18 spiced links

4 potatoes, grated
½ teaspoon salt
¼ teaspoon black pepper

In a heavy frying pan, heat oil over medium heat. Add spiced links and potatoes. Season with salt and pepper. Cook, allowing potatoes to stick to the frying pan, until lightly browned and then loosen and turn mixture with a spatula. Continue frying in this manner until potatoes and links are evenly crusted. This dish makes a substantial addition to a hearty breakfast.

SPICED LINK HASH WITH POACHED EGGS

Serves 4
Preparation Time: 10 minutes
Cooking Time: 15 minutes
Intermediate

2 tablespoons oil
4 potatoes, boiled and diced
2 cups spiced links, crumbled
½ teaspoon tarragon

½ teaspoon salt
¼ teaspoon black pepper
8 eggs
1 cup water
2 tablespoons fresh parsley, chopped

In a heavy frying pan, heat oil over medium heat. Add potatoes and fry until they stick to the pan and become lightly browned. Loosen with a spatula, turn and repeat procedure until potatoes are crusted on all sides. Add crumbled links and sauté until they are lightly browned. Stir in tarragon, salt and pepper. Cover and set aside while poaching eggs.

To poach eggs, pour water into a frying pan. Bring to a gentle boil. Break one egg at a time into a ladle and gently slip into water. Be careful that the yolks stay intact. Add four eggs in this manner. Reduce heat so that water is just below the boiling point. As the eggs cook, carefully pour 1 tablespoon of the hot water they are cooking in over each egg. Remove eggs with a slotted spoon in three minutes when whites have become opaque. Set aside, being careful not to break yolks. Poach a second batch of eggs in the same way.

Spoon hash onto individual plates. Top with eggs and garnish with parsley.

HOMINY GRITS AND SPICED LINKS

Serves 4 to 6
Preparation Time: 5 minutes
Cooking Time: 15 minutes
Elementary

¾ cup hominy grits	1 teaspoon vanilla extract
3 cups water	2 tablespoons liquid barley malt
¼ teaspoon salt	1 teaspoon blackstrap molasses
½ cup raisins	2 tablespoons oil
12 to 18 spiced links	

In a saucepan, combine hominy, water, salt, raisins, vanilla, malt and molasses. Cook, covered, over high heat until mixture begins to boil. Reduce heat to simmer and cook until water is fully absorbed, about 10 minutes.

In a heavy frying pan, heat oil over medium heat. Add spiced links and brown on all sides. Spoon hominy into individual bowls and top with spiced links.

SPICED LINKS WITH PINEAPPLE

Serves 4 to 6
Preparation Time: 10 minutes
Cooking Time: 10 minutes
Elementary

12 to 18 spiced links	2 tablespoons oil
4 cups unsweetened canned pineapple in chunks	2 teaspoons arrowroot starch mixed with 1 tablespoon water

In a frying pan, heat oil over medium heat. Brown links lightly on all sides. Remove and set aside.

Drain pineapple chunks and reserve liquid. Sauté pineapple until very lightly browned. Add reserved liquid to frying pan. Bring to a gentle boil. Stir in starch and water mixture. Continue stirring until sauce thickens. Return spiced links to cooking pineapple and heat for 3 minutes. This dish can be served hot or cold.

SPICED LINKS WITH DRIED FRUIT

Serves 4
Preparation Time: 30 minutes
Cooking Time: 20 minutes
Elementary

2 cups boiling water	2 tablespoons oil
1½ cups mixed dried fruit	12 to 18 spiced links
2 teaspoons arrowroot starch mixed with 1 tablespoon water	

Pour boiling water over dried fruit and allow to soak for 30 minutes.

Heat oil in a heavy frying pan over medium heat. Add links and brown on all sides. Drain fruit and reserve water. Stir fruit into frying pan with links. Cook for 3 minutes. Pour in reserved water. Bring to a very gentle boil. Stir in arrowroot starch and water mixture. Continue stirring until liquid thickens, about 2 minutes. This dish is best when served hot.

SPICED LINKS AND APPLES

Serves 4 to 6
Preparation Time: 10 minutes
Cooking Time: 20 minutes
Intermediate

½ cup raisins	2 tablespoons oil
1½ cups water	6 unpeeled apples, in thin wedges
2 teaspoons arrowroot starch mixed with 1 tablespoon water	¼ teaspoon cinnamon, ground
	12 to 18 spiced links

Combine raisins and water in a saucepan. Cook over medium-high heat and bring to a gentle boil. Allow to boil for 3 minutes. Add starch and water mixture. Cook, stirring constantly, until liquid thickens. Reduce heat to simmer and prepare apples and links.

In a heavy frying pan, heat 1 tablespoon of oil over medium heat. Add apples and sprinkle with cinnamon. Sauté until apples are soft. Push to one side. Add remaining oil. Brown links on all sides.

Spoon apples onto a serving platter. Top with spiced links and pour on raisin sauce. This dish tastes best hot.

BUCKWHEAT PANCAKES WITH SPICED BITS

Serves 4
Preparation Time: 10 minutes
Cooking Time: 15 minutes
Elementary

1½ cups buckwheat flour
¾ cup whole wheat pastry flour
⅛ teaspoon salt
1 tablespoon low-sodium baking powder

⅔ cup spiced links, crumbled
1 tablespoon liquid barley malt
1 egg
1 tablespoon safflower oil
2 cups milk

In a mixing bowl, combine all dry ingredients, including crumbled spiced links. In a separate bowl, beat together malt, egg, oil and milk. Gradually add liquid mixture to dry ingredients. Stir until combined.

Heat an oiled frying pan or griddle over medium-high heat. Drop batter by spoonfuls onto hot oiled surface. Allow to cook until bubbles cover the top of the batter, about 3 minutes. Turn and fry until lightly browned on the other side. Serve with butter and syrup.

BUTTERMILK PANCAKES WITH SPICED BITS

Serves 4
Preparation Time: 10 minutes
Cooking Time: 15 minutes
Elementary

2 cups whole wheat pastry flour	1 cup spiced links, crumbled
½ cup wheat germ	1 tablespoon liquid barley malt
1 teaspoon baking soda	2 eggs, beaten
½ teaspoon salt	2½ cups milk
2 tablespoons oil	

In a mixing bowl, combine dry ingredients and crumbled spiced links. In a separate bowl, mix malt, eggs, milk and oil. Gradually add liquid ingredients to dry ingredients and stir until combined.

Heat an oiled frying pan or griddle over medium-high heat. Drop batter by spoonfuls onto hot, oiled surface. Allow batter to cook until bubbles cover the top. Turn and fry until pancakes are brown on the other side. Serve with syrup and butter.

POPPY SEED CAKES WITH SPICED BITS

Serves 4 to 6
Preparation Time: 10 minutes
Cooking Time: 15 minutes
Intermediate

2 cups whole wheat pastry flour	1 tablespoon liquid barley malt
2 teaspoons low-sodium baking powder	2 eggs, beaten
½ teaspoon salt	2½ cups milk
⅔ cup spiced links, crumbled	2 tablespoons oil
	2 tablespoons poppy seeds

In a mixing bowl, combine flour, baking powder, salt and crumbled spiced links. In a separate bowl, combine malt, eggs, milk and oil. Pour liquid ingredients into dry ingredients and stir until combined.

Heat a lightly oiled frying pan or griddle over medium-high heat. Sprinkle 1½ teaspoons of poppy seeds in a thin layer over the hot surface. Drop batter onto poppy seed–covered frying pan or griddle and cook until bubbles cover the batter. Turn and brown on the other side. Repeat until all poppy seeds and batter are used. Serve with butter and syrup.

CHOLESTEROL-FREE PANCAKES WITH SPICED LINKS

Serves 4
Preparation Time: 10 minutes
Cooking Time: 15 minutes
Elementary

1¼ cups whole wheat pastry flour
2 teaspoons low-sodium baking powder
¼ teaspoon salt

¾ cup spiced links, crumbled
2 tablespoons liquid barley malt
2 tablespoons oil
½ cup soy milk

¾ cup water

In a mixing bowl, combine flour, baking powder, salt and crumbled spiced links. In a separate bowl, beat together malt, oil, soy milk and water. Stir liquid ingredients into dry ingredients until combined.

Heat a lightly oiled frying pan or griddle over medium-high heat. Pour batter by spoonfuls onto oiled frying pan or griddle. Allow to cook until bubbles cover the surface of each pancake. Turn and cook until lightly browned on the other side. Serve with syrup.

CHOLESTEROL-FREE BUCKWHEAT CAKES WITH SPICED BITS

Serves 4 to 6
Preparation Time: 15 minutes
Cooking Time: 15 minutes
Elementary

2 cups buckwheat flour	⅔ cup spiced links, crumbled
1 cup whole wheat pastry flour	2 cups soy milk
2 teaspoons low-sodium baking powder	2 tablespoons safflower oil
½ teaspoon salt	1 tablespoon blackstrap molasses

In a bowl, combine flours, baking powder, salt and crumbled spiced links. In a separate bowl, mix soy milk, oil and molasses. Stir liquid ingredients into dry ingredients until combined.

Heat a lightly oiled frying pan or griddle over medium-high heat. Drop batter by spoonfuls onto hot oiled surface. Cook until bubbles form on pancakes. Turn and brown on the other side. Serve with syrup.

CHOLESTEROL-FREE CORN CAKES WITH SPICED BITS

Serves 4 to 6
Preparation Time: 10 minutes
Cooking Time: 15 minutes
Elementary

2 cups whole wheat pastry flour	2 tablespoons oil
2 cups corn meal	2 tablespoons liquid barley malt
½ cup salt	2½ cups soy milk
1 tablespoon low-sodium baking powder	1 teaspoon blackstrap molasses
1 cup spiced links, crumbled	

In a bowl, combine flour, corn meal, salt, baking powder and crumbled spiced links. In a separate bowl, mix oil, malt, soy milk and molasses. Add liquid ingredients to dry ingredients and stir until combined.

Heat a lightly oiled frying pan or griddle over medium-high heat. Drop spoonfuls of batter onto hot frying pan or griddle. Turn and brown on the other side. Serve with syrup.

ALL-AMERICAN BARBECUED CUTLET RECIPES

CASTILIAN-STYLE BARBECUE

Serves 4
Preparation Time: 15 minutes
Cooking Time: 10 minutes
Elementary

½ teaspoon salt	2 garlic cloves, crushed
½ teaspoon black pepper	8 toasted almonds, finely grated
1 teaspoon cumin, ground	1 teaspoon paprika
4 cutlets, 1 inch thick	4 tablespoons olive oil

In a small bowl, mix salt, pepper and cumin. Rub mixture on both sides of cutlets. In a separate bowl, combine garlic, almonds, paprika and oil to make a paste for basting. Place cutlets 4 inches above hot coals and brown on both sides, basting occasionally with paste.

SPANISH GRILLED CUTLETS

Serves 4
Preparation Time: 5 minutes
Marinating Time: 1 hour
Cooking Time: 15 minutes

4 cutlets, 1 inch thick	1 tablespoon lemon juice
½ cup olive oil	¼ teaspoon salt
2 garlic cloves, crushed	¼ teaspoon black pepper
¼ teaspoon oregano	¼ cup water or wheat water

Prick holes in cutlets with prongs of a fork or with skewers. Combine other ingredients for a marinade. Place cutlets in a shallow dish and pour marinade over them. Allow to stand, turning occasionally, for 1 hour. Remove cutlets from marinade and grill 4 inches from hot coals for 7 minutes on each side. Brush occasionally with marinade mixture. Serve when well browned on both sides.

SKEWERED CUTLETS WITH CURRY-LEMON SAUCE

Serves 4 to 6
Preparation Time: 20 minutes
Marinating Time: 2 hours
Cooking Time: 15 minutes
Intermediate

3 tablespoons olive oil	3 cups cutlets, in 1-inch cubes
3 onions, chopped	½ teaspoon salt
1 tablespoon curry powder	¼ teaspoon black pepper
1 teaspoon coriander, ground	4 bay leaves
½ teaspoon turmeric	1 garlic clove, minced
½ cup water or wheat water	1 tablespoon whole wheat
½ cup fresh lemon juice	pastry flour mixed with 2
1 tablespoon liquid barley	tablespoons water
malt	2 onions, in quarters

In a heavy frying pan, heat oil. Add chopped onions and sauté until transparent. Stir in curry powder, coriander and turmeric. Gradually add water or wheat water and lemon juice. Stir in barley malt and allow to simmer for 15 minutes. Remove from heat and add cutlets. Stir in salt, pepper, bay leaves and garlic. Allow to marinate for 2 hours.

Remove cutlet cubes and set aside. Make curry-lemon sauce by pouring marinade into a saucepan and heating it to a gentle boil. Stir in flour and water mixture. Continue stirring until sauce thickens, about 5 minutes. Set sauce aside while grilling cutlets.

String cutlet cubes and quartered onions on skewers. Grill 4 inches from hot coals, turning occasionally, until well browned on all sides.

Before serving, remove cutlet cubes and onions from skewers onto individual plates and top with sauce.

BARBECUED CUTLETS WITH ORANGE DIP

Serves 4 to 6
Preparation Time: 15 minutes
Cooking Time: 20 minutes
Elementary

¼ cup water or wheat water	1 teaspoon sour cream or
¼ cup fresh orange juice	yogurt
1 tablespoon fresh lemon juice	3 cups cutlets, in 1-inch cubes
2 tablespoons tamari soy sauce	¼ cup melted butter

Heat water, orange juice, lemon juice and soy sauce in a saucepan without boiling for 5 minutes. Remove from heat and stir in sour cream or yogurt. Set aside.

To grill cutlets, thread cubes on skewers. Grill 4 inches from hot coals, turning and brushing occasionally with melted butter. When cutlet cubes are well browned, serve with individual servings of orange dip.

ALL-AMERICAN CHARCOALED STEAK

GRILLED STEAKS WITH ITALIAN SAUCE

Serves 4 to 6
Preparation Time: 10 minutes
Cooking Time: 20 minutes
Elementary

4 to 6 steaks	1 bay leaf
¼ cup butter, melted	½ teaspoon oregano
2 tablespoons oil	2 tablespoons liquid barley
1 onion, chopped	malt
1 garlic clove, minced	½ teaspoon basil
1 green pepper, chopped	½ teaspoon salt
½ cup tomato paste	⅛ teaspoon black pepper
1½ cups water or wheat water	¼ teaspoon paprika

Brush steaks with melted butter. Grill 6 inches from hot coals for 7 minutes on each side until well browned, basting occasionally with butter.

While steaks grill, prepare sauce. In a heavy frying pan, heat oil. Add onions, garlic and green pepper. Cook until onions are transparent. Add remaining ingredients and cook for 10 minutes.

To serve, place steaks on individual plates and top with sauce.

STEAK ON SKEWERS

Serves 4 to 6
Preparation Time: 15 minutes
Cooking Time: 15 minutes
Elementary

¼ cup onion, finely chopped
2 tablespoons fresh parsley, finely chopped
1 teaspoon tarragon
½ teaspoon salt

¼ teaspoon black pepper
1 garlic clove, minced
3 cups steak, in 1-inch cubes
20 mushroom caps
⅓ cup butter, melted

In a bowl, combine onion, parsley, tarragon, salt, pepper and garlic. Press steak cubes into onion mixture so that it adheres. Thread cubes and mushroom caps onto skewers. Grill 6 inches from coals, turning and brushing with melted butter occasionally. Serve when cubes are well browned.

TERIYAKI-STYLE BARBECUE

Serves 4 to 6
Preparation Time: 5 minutes
Marinating Time: 1 hour
Cooking Time: 15 minutes
Elementary

¼ cup tamari soy sauce
⅓ cup cooking sherry or sake
3 tablespoons rice syrup
1 tablespoon fresh ginger root, grated

1 garlic clove, minced
½ teaspoon lemon peel, finely grated
4 to 6 steaks
⅓ cup sesame oil

In a bowl, combine soy sauce, sherry or sake, rice syrup, ginger root, garlic and lemon peel. Place steaks in a shallow dish. Pour soy sauce marinade over steaks and allow to stand for 1 hour.

To grill, remove steaks from marinade and grill 4 inches from hot coals for 7 minutes on each side, basting occasionally with sesame oil.

Heat marinade and pour over steaks just before serving.

RANCH-STYLE STEAK

Serves 4 to 6
Preparation Time: 10 minutes
Marinating Time: 2 hours
Cooking Time: 20 minutes
Elementary

MARINADE INGREDIENTS

2 onions, finely chopped	½ teaspoon dry mustard
1 garlic clove, finely chopped	1 teaspoon tamari soy sauce
½ teaspoon salt	¼ cup olive oil
⅛ teaspoon chili powder	¼ cup cider vinegar
½ teaspoon celery seeds	4 to 6 steaks

SAUCE INGREDIENTS

¼ cup liquid barley malt	1½ cups water or wheat water
1 teaspoon blackstrap molasses	1 teaspoon fresh lemon juice
½ cup tomato paste	pinch cayenne

⅓ cup butter, melted (for basting)

In a bowl, combine all marinade ingredients. Place steaks in a shallow dish and pour marinade over them. Allow to stand for 2 hours, turning occasionally.

To make sauce, remove steaks from marinade and set aside. In a saucepan, combine marinade with sauce ingredients. Bring to a gentle boil and cook while grilling steaks.

Grill steaks 6 inches from hot coals for 7 minutes on each side, basting occasionally with melted butter. When steaks are well browned, serve with a topping of sauce.

STUFFED STEAK ROLLS

Serves 4
Preparation Time: 20 minutes
Cooking Time: 25 minutes
Intermediate

1 tablespoon oil	4 steaks, pounded thin
2 onions, chopped	4 unpeeled tomatoes, chopped
2 green peppers, chopped	¼ cup water or wheat water
¾ cup fresh or frozen corn	½ teaspoon salt
kernels	¼ teaspoon black pepper

¼ cup butter, melted

In a heavy frying pan, heat oil. Sauté onions until transparent. Add green peppers, corn kernels and cook for 3 minutes. Spoon 1 heaping tablespoon of sautéed vegetables onto the center of each thinly pounded steak. Roll steak around vegetables in jelly-roll fashion, secure with skewers. Set aside. In a saucepan, combine remaining sautéed vegetables with tomatoes, water, salt and pepper. Cook for 10 minutes without boiling while grilling steak rolls.

Grill steak rolls 4 inches from hot coals, basting occasionally with melted butter and turning every 3 minutes to brown rolls uniformly. Serve stuffed rolls topped with sauce.

OUTDOOR SHISH KEBAB

Serves 4
Preparation Time: 10 minutes
Marinating Time: 2 hours
Cooking Time: 30 minutes
Intermediate

2 onions, sliced into rings	1 cake tofu, cut into 1-inch
2 tablespoons olive oil	cubes
4 tablespoons lemon juice	8 cherry tomatoes
½ teaspoon salt	2 green peppers, in quarters
½ teaspoon black pepper	2 tablespoons heavy cream
2 cups steak, cut into 1-inch cubes	mixed with 1 tablespoon
½ cup safflower oil	melted butter

In a deep bowl, combine onion rings, olive oil, lemon juice, salt and pepper. Add steak cubes and toss. Allow to marinate at room temperature for 2 hours, tossing occasionally.

In a heavy frying pan, heat safflower oil until water sizzles when sprinkled onto it. Add tofu cubes and fry until golden brown on all sides.

Thread vegetables, marinated steak cubes, onion rings and tofu on skewers. Grill kebabs 4 inches from hot coals, basting occasionally with butter and cream mixture and turning until well browned on all sides.

ALL-AMERICAN GROUND GLUTEN BARBECUE DISHES

GRILLED BURGERS

Serves 4 to 6
Preparation Time: 30 minutes
Cooking Time: 15 minutes
Intermediate

3 cups ground gluten	⅔ cup water
½ teaspoon black pepper	⅓ cup olive oil
1 teaspoon miso	½ cup tomato paste
1 tablespoon nutritional yeast	1 cup water or wheat water
2 onions, finely chopped	¼ cup liquid barley malt
1 garlic clove, minced	1 teaspoon dry mustard
1 cup soy flour or chickpea flour	½ teaspoon salt
	½ teaspoon allspice, ground

In a bowl, combine ground gluten with black pepper, miso, nutritional yeast, onions, garlic and soy or chickpea flour. With moistened hands, form mixture into burger patties. In a covered frying pan, bring ⅔ cup water to a gentle boil. Place patties in water, cover and cook for 15 minutes until firm.

In a saucepan, combine olive oil, tomato paste, water or wheat water, malt, mustard, salt and allspice. Cook for 15 minutes until flavors are well combined.

Grill steamed burger patties 5 inches above hot coals for 5 minutes on each side, basting occasionally with sauce. When burgers are well browned, serve with generous toppings of sauce.

ITALIAN OUTDOOR BURGERS

Serves 4 to 6
Preparation Time: 20 minutes
Cooking Time: 15 minutes
Intermediate

BURGER INGREDIENTS

3 cups ground gluten
1 teaspoon cumin, ground
½ teaspoon black pepper
1 teaspoon miso
1 tablespoon nutritional yeast

½ teaspoon garlic powder
1 teaspoon oregano
1 teaspoon fresh parsley, finely chopped
1 cup soy or chickpea flour

⅔ cup water

TOPPING INGREDIENTS

2 teaspoons oil
⅓ cup mushrooms, sliced
½ cup tomato paste
⅔ cup water or wheat water
1 garlic clove, minced
¼ teaspoon marjoram

¼ teaspoon thyme
4 to 6 slices mozzarella cheese
1 onion, sliced in rings
2 tablespoons Parmesan cheese, grated

BURGERS

In a bowl, combine ground gluten, cumin, black pepper, miso, nutritional yeast, garlic powder, oregano, parsley and soy or chickpea flour. With moistened hands, form mixture into burger patties. In a covered frying pan, bring ⅔ cup water to a boil. Place patties in gently boiling water, cover and cook for 15 minutes until firm.

TOPPING

To make topping sauce, heat oil in a heavy frying pan. Sauté mushrooms in oil until decreased in size and darkened in color, about 5 minutes. Add tomato paste, water or wheat water, garlic, marjoram and thyme. Stir until well combined and cook for 15 minutes without boiling.

To grill burger patties, place burgers 5 inches from hot coals and grill for 5 minutes on one side. Turn and top each patty with a slice of mozzarella cheese, a tablespoon of sauce, a slice of onion, another tablespoon of sauce and a sprinkling of Parmesan cheese. Grill burgers until cheeses are melted. Serve accompanied by remaining sauce.

CHAPTER FIVE

Mexican Wheat "Meat" Food

Chili, tortillas, tamales, enchiladas, tostadas are Mexican names for Mexican foods that have become almost as familiar in the United States as hot dogs and potato chips. These easy-to-make dishes are inexpensive and delicious, which accounts for their growing popularity.

Basic to Mexican cooking are tortillas, chilies, chili powder and finely ground corn flour, all of which are readily available at any well-stocked supermarket. Most of the recipes in this section can be made with these few additions to your normal grocery list. All your well-known favorite Mexican dishes can be found in this chapter, along with a few unusual surprises.

MEXICAN CUTLET DISHES

CUTLETS WITH PEANUT SAUCE

Serves 4
Preparation Time: 15 minutes
Cooking Time: 45 minutes
Elementary

4 cutlets, 1 inch thick
2 cups vegetable broth
4 celery stalks, cut in 3-inch chunks
2 carrots, cut in 2-inch chunks
2 onions, quartered
¼ teaspoon black pepper

4 tomatoes, chopped
¼ cup water or wheat water
1 tablespoon soy flour
2 tablespoons peanut butter
4 cloves
3 whole black peppercorns
1 cinnamon stick
1½ teaspoons chili powder

In a casserole dish, place cutlets, broth, celery, carrots, onions and black pepper. Cover and bake at 300 degrees for 30 minutes until carrots are tender.

Purée tomatoes, water or wheat water, soy flour and peanut butter in an electric blender or food processor until smooth.

Remove casserole from oven and stir in peanut sauce, cloves, peppercorns, cinnamon stick and chili powder. Return to oven for a final 10 minutes of cooking.

CUTLETS IN PECAN SAUCE

Serves 6
Preparation Time: 20 minutes
Cooking Time: 20 minutes
Elementary

2 tablespoons oil
1 teaspoon cumin, ground
½ teaspoon garlic powder
½ teaspoon salt
¼ teaspoon thyme
¼ teaspoon oregano
1 tablespoon butter

3 cups cutlets, cut in 1-inch cubes
½ cup pecans, chopped
1 onion, chopped
3 tablespoons whole wheat pastry flour
1 cup sour cream

In a heavy frying pan, heat oil over medium heat. Stir in cumin, garlic powder, salt, thyme and oregano. Add cutlet cubes and sauté for 5 minutes until browned. Reduce heat to simmer.

In a separate frying pan, melt butter. Sauté pecans and onions until onions are transparent. Pour sautéed pecan and onions into cutlet cube mixture.

In a small bowl beat flour and sour cream together. Stir into cutlet mixture. Heat for 5 minutes, stirring occasionally, before serving.

STEW WITH FRUIT

Serves 8
Preparation Time: 20 minutes
Cooking Time: 25 minutes
Elementary

2 tablespoons oil	½ teaspoon oregano
1 teaspoon cumin, ground	¼ teaspoon cloves
3 cutlets, cut in 1-inch cubes	6 tomatoes, chopped
1 cup water or wheat water	1 onion, chopped
1 bay leaf	2 apples, cored and sliced
1 teaspoon crushed red peppers	2 pears, cored and sliced
1 tablespoon fresh parsley, chopped	2 bananas, sliced
	⅔ cup pineapple, cut in chunks
½ teaspoon thyme	¼ cup walnuts
	¼ cup pecans

In a heavy frying pan, heat oil over medium heat. Stir in cumin. Add cutlet cubes and sauté until lightly browned. Remove from heat and set aside.

Purée water or wheat water, bay leaf, red peppers, parsley, thyme, oregano, cloves, tomatoes and onion in an electric blender or food processor until smooth.

In a flameproof casserole dish, arrange a layer of cutlet cubes, a layer of apples, a layer of pears, a layer of bananas, a layer of pineapple, a layer of walnuts and a layer of pecans. Pour tomato purée over the top. Cook over medium heat without boiling for 15 minutes until apples are tender.

GREEN, WHITE AND RED TACOS

Serves 6
Preparation Time: 20 minutes
Cooking Time: 15 minutes
Elementary

GUACAMOLE INGREDIENTS

2 avocados, pitted and peeled
2 tomatoes, chopped
½ teaspoon chili powder
2 teaspoons fresh lemon juice
½ teaspoon salt

CUTLET FILLING INGREDIENTS

2 tablespoons oil
1 red onion, chopped
2 cups cutlets, diced
3 tomatoes, chopped
½ teaspoon crushed red peppers

TORTILLAS AND TOPPING

2 tablespoons oil
12 corn tortillas
1 cup sour cream

GUACAMOLE

To make guacamole, purée avocados, tomatoes, chili powder, lemon juice and salt in an electric blender or food processor until smooth. Set aside.

CUTLET FILLING

To make cutlet filling, heat 2 tablespoons oil in a heavy frying pan over medium heat. Sauté red onion until transparent. Add cutlet and sauté until lightly browned. Purée tomatoes with crushed red peppers in an electric blender or food processor and add to cutlet and onion.

TORTILLAS AND TOPPING

To prepare tortillas, heat oil in a heavy frying pan over medium heat. Dip each tortilla in hot oil for 10 seconds until limp and drain on paper towels.

To assemble, place a serving of avocado mixture, a heaping tablespoon of cutlet mixture and of sour cream on half of each tortilla. Fold tortilla over the fillings before serving.

MEXICAN STEAK DISHES

STEAK TIDBITS

Serves 4 to 6
Preparation Time: 15 minutes
No Cooking
Elementary

3 avocados, peeled, pitted and diced
1 tomato, peeled and chopped
½ teaspoon salt
1 tablespoon onion, chopped

½ teaspoon chili powder
2 teaspoons lemon juice
½ cup sour cream
½ teaspoon garlic powder
4 steaks, cut in 1-inch cubes

Purée avocados, tomato, salt, onion, chili powder, lemon juice, sour cream and garlic powder in an electric blender or food processor until smooth. Spoon into the center of a serving plate. Place toothpicks in steak cubes and arrange around the avocado mixture. Cubes are dipped in avocado dip before eating. This dish can be served as an appetizer or a main luncheon course.

STEAK-FILLED FLOUR TORTILLAS

Serves 6 to 8
Preparation Time: 15 minutes
Cooking Time: 20 minutes
Intermediate

4 to 6 steaks
2 garlic cloves, minced
1 tablespoon chili powder
1 teaspoon cider vinegar
½ teaspoon salt

1 teaspoon cumin, ground
⅛ teaspoon black pepper
12 flour tortillas
1 cup oil
2 cups lettuce, shredded

2 cups sour cream

Grate steak with a grater or food processor. Combine grated steak with garlic, chili powder, vinegar, salt, cumin and black pepper. Mix well and set aside.

In a 350-degree oven, warm tortillas in a covered baking dish for 10 minutes. Remove from oven and spoon ¼ cup steak mixture into the center of each tortilla. Fold sides over the filling to form a rectangle. Secure with toothpicks.

In a frying pan, heat oil until water sizzles when sprinkled onto it. Fry stuffed tortillas on both sides until golden brown. Place in a 300-degree oven to keep warm while frying remaining tortillas. Place on individual plates and serve with a topping of lettuce and sour cream.

STEW IN A POT

Serves 6
Preparation Time: 20 minutes
Cooking Time: 25 minutes
Elementary

1 cup water or wheat water	¼ teaspoon cumin, ground
3 potatoes, quartered	3 fresh ears of corn, cut into
1 teaspoon crushed red pepper	2-inch sections
6 tomatoes, chopped	2 zucchini, sliced
½ cup vegetable broth	3 cups steak, cut in 1-inch cubes
2 tablespoons sesame seeds	¼ cup fresh parsley, chopped
1 garlic clove, minced	1 tablespoon tamari soy sauce

Bring water or wheat water to a boil, add potatoes and cook for 15 minutes until they can be easily pierced with a fork. Remove from heat and set aside.

Purée red pepper, tomatoes, broth, sesame seeds, garlic and cumin in an electric blender or food processor. Pour purée into a flameproof casserole along with corn, zucchini, potatoes with water or wheat water, steak cubes, parsley and soy sauce. Cook, covered, over medium heat until vegetables are tender.

MEXICAN GROUND GLUTEN DISHES

MEXICAN HASH

Serves 4 to 6
Preparation Time: 15 minutes
Cooking Time: 15 minutes
Elementary

2 tablespoons oil
2 onions, chopped
1 garlic clove, minced
3 cups ground gluten
¼ cup water or wheat water
1 apple, chopped
½ cup raisins

¼ cup fresh parsley, chopped
¼ cup almonds, chopped
1 tablespoon fresh lemon
juice
1 teaspoon liquid barley malt
¼ teaspoon cinnamon
¼ teaspoon black pepper

In a frying pan over medium heat, heat oil. Add onions and garlic and sauté until transparent. Stir in ground gluten and cook for 3 minutes. Stir in the rest of ingredients and cook for 10 minutes. Serve immediately or use as a filling for tacos or green peppers.

STUFFED CHEESE

Serves 4 to 6
Preparation Time: 1 hour
Cooking Time: 25 minutes
Intermediate

CHEESE AND FILLING INGREDIENTS

1 2-pound Edam cheese
2 tablespoons olive oil
1 onion, finely chopped
2 garlic cloves, minced
1 cup ground gluten

2 tomatoes, finely chopped
¼ cup ripe olives, pitted
½ teaspoon salt
¼ teaspoon oregano
⅛ teaspoon black pepper

¼ teaspoon cinnamon

SAUCE INGREDIENTS

1 tablespoon oil	1 teaspoon miso
1 onion, finely chopped	2 peeled tomatoes, finely
1 green pepper, finely chopped	chopped
2 tablespoons soy flour	½ cup water or wheat water

12 to 16 corn tortillas (for serving)

CHEESE AND FILLING

To prepare cheese for filling, remove red wax skin. Cut a ½-inch slice from the top of the cheese. Hollow out the inside of the cheese, leaving a ¾-inch shell. Soak shell in water for 45 minutes.

While cheese is soaking, prepare filling. In a heavy frying pan, heat 1 tablespoon oil over medium heat. Sauté onions until transparent. Add garlic and ground gluten and sauté for 3 minutes. Stir in tomatoes, olives, salt, oregano, pepper and cinnamon. Cook for 3 minutes and remove from heat.

Remove cheese from water and drain on paper towels. Brush the outside of cheese with remaining tablespoon oil. Set in a round baking dish. Spoon filling into cheese shell.

Bake for 10 minutes in a 350-degree oven until the sides of the cheese begin to melt.

SAUCE

While cheese bakes, prepare sauce. In a heavy frying pan, heat oil over medium heat. Sauté onion and green pepper until lightly browned. Stir in flour, miso, tomatoes and water or wheat water.

Remove cheese from oven and pour sauce over it. To serve, spoon portions over tortillas.

TAMALES

Serves 5 to 7
Soaking Time for Cornhusks: 2 hours (optional)
Preparation Time: 45 minutes
Cooking Time: 40 minutes
Advanced

DOUGH INGREDIENTS

25 cornhusks or 25 pieces of
6" x 8" foil or parchment
3 cups corn flour

½ cup water or wheat water
1 cup butter, soft
½ teaspoon salt

FILLING INGREDIENTS

2 tablespoons oil
1 onion, chopped
2 garlic cloves, minced
3 cups ground gluten
½ cup tomato paste
½ cup raisins
2 tablespoons fresh parsley,
chopped

¼ cup almonds, chopped
2 teaspoons liquid barley
malt
½ teaspoon miso
1 teaspoon fresh lemon
juice
½ teaspoon cinnamon
½ cup soybean flour

DOUGH

To prepare cornhusks for filling, soak husks in warm water for 2 hours. Remove excess moisture by pressing between paper towels. Foil or parchment can be used in place of soaked cornhusks.

To make dough, combine flour and water or wheat water in a mixing bowl. Allow to stand for 20 minutes. In a separate bowl, beat together butter and salt. Add flour and water mixture and beat for 3 minutes until well combined. Set aside.

FILLING

To make filling, heat oil in a heavy frying pan over medium heat. Sauté onions and garlic until transparent. Stir in ground gluten. Add remaining filling ingredients, cook for 2 minutes and remove from heat.

ASSEMBLING

To assemble tamales, place 2 tablespoons of dough in the center of each cornhusk or wrapper. Using moistened fingers, spread dough over the cornhusks or wrappers to 1 inch from the ends of each. Spoon ¼ cup of filling in a row down the center of the dough. Roll the cornhusks or wrappers around the filling and tie the ends with strings or twist foil wrappers closed. Place tamales on a rack in a frying pan. Pour water into the frying pan to just below the level of the rack. Cover pan and bring water to a gentle boil. Steam for 40 minutes, checking occasionally to make sure water does not entirely evaporate. If necessary, pour more water below the tamales. When ready, tamales will easily pull away from wrappers.

EMPANADITAS (MEXICAN TURNOVERS)

Serves 4 to 6
Preparation Time: 30 minutes
Cooking Time: 20 minutes
Intermediate

DOUGH INGREDIENTS

2 cups whole wheat pastry flour
1 teaspoon low-sodium baking powder
½ teaspoon salt
2 tablespoons corn oil
½ cup cold water

FILLING INGREDIENTS

2½ cups ground gluten
1 tablespoon cider vinegar
2 tablespoons paprika
½ teaspoon salt
pinch cayenne
½ teaspoon oregano
3 garlic cloves, minced
1 teaspoon coriander, ground
1 teaspoon cumin, ground
¼ teaspoon cloves, ground
1 egg
⅓ cup soy flour
1 cup oil for deep-frying or 2 tablespoons milk for baking

DOUGH

To make dough, combine flour, baking powder and salt in a mixing bowl. Rub in oil with fingers until mixture resembles coarse oatmeal. Add water and mix well. Turn onto a floured board and knead for 5 minutes until dough is smooth. Cover with a dry towel and set aside for 30 minutes.

FILLING

Make filling while dough is resting. In a mixing bowl, combine all filling ingredients and mix well.

ASSEMBLING

To assemble turnovers, divide dough into 20 balls. Roll each ball into a circle on a floured board. Place 1 tablespoon of filling on each circle. Fold the dough over the filling to form a half circle. Moisten edges of turnover with fingers and seal with the prongs of a fork.

If you wish to deep-fry turnovers, heat oil in a heavy frying pan until water sizzles when sprinkled onto it. Fry turnovers for 3 minutes on each side until golden brown and drain on paper towels.

If you would rather bake turnovers, arrange them on an oiled baking sheet, brush with milk and bake for 15 minutes in a 425-degree oven until golden brown.

FRIED ENCHILADAS

Serves 6
Preparation Time: 15 minutes
Cooking Time: 35 minutes
Intermediate

SAUCE INGREDIENTS

2 onions, chopped
½ cup water or wheat water
3 tomatoes, finely chopped

1 jalapeño pepper, seeded and chopped
½ teaspoon salt

FILLING INGREDIENTS

2 tablespoons oil
2 onions, chopped
2 cups ground gluten

¼ cup tomato paste
¼ cup water or wheat water
½ teaspoon salt

EGG COATING

4 eggs, separated
2 tablespoons soy flour

1 tablespoon water or wheat water

ASSEMBLING INGREDIENTS

2 tablespoons olive oil
12 tortillas

1 cup oil (for deep-frying)
2 cups shredded lettuce

1½ cups Cheddar cheese, grated

SAUCE

To make sauce, combine onions and water or wheat water in a saucepan. Cook over medium heat for 5 minutes. Purée tomatoes in an electric blender or food processor until smooth. Add puréed tomatoes to onions. Stir in chopped pepper and salt. Cook, uncovered, for 10 minutes until slightly thickened and reduce heat to simmer.

FILLING

Prepare filling while sauce simmers. In a heavy frying pan over medium heat, heat oil. Sauté onions until transparent. Add ground gluten and cook for 3 minutes. Stir in tomato paste, water or wheat water and salt. Cook for 5 minutes and set aside.

EGG COATING

To prepare egg coating for enchiladas, beat whites until stiff peaks form. In a separate bowl, beat yolks with 1 tablespoon water or wheat water. Add flour and continue to beat until this mixture becomes thick and lemon-colored. Fold into egg whites.

ASSEMBLING

To assemble enchiladas for serving, heat olive oil in a heavy frying pan over medium heat. Using tongs, dip each tortilla in oil for 10 seconds until limp. Place ¼ cup of ground gluten filling on each tortilla and roll up.

In a heavy frying pan, heat frying oil until water sizzles when sprinkled onto it. Dip each rolled, stuffed tortilla in egg mixture and deep-fry until golden on both sides. Place on individual serving plate, pour sauce over stuffed tortillas and top with lettuce and cheese.

GROUND GLUTEN TACOS

Serves 6
Preparation Time: 15 minutes
Cooking Time: 15 minutes
Elementary

TACOS AND FILLING

12 taco shells	2½ cups ground gluten
1 tablespoon oil	1 teaspoon chili powder
1 onion, chopped	½ teaspoon salt
1 garlic clove, minced	1 tablespoon water

SAUCE INGREDIENTS

2 tomatoes, chopped	1 garlic clove, minced
1 teaspoon crushed red peppers	½ teaspoon salt
1 onion, chopped	1 teaspoon liquid barley malt

1 tablespoon olive oil

TOPPINGS

1 cup Cheddar cheese, grated	1 cup lettuce, shredded
	4 tomatoes, finely chopped

TACOS AND FILLING

Arrange taco shells on a cookie sheet lined with paper towels and warm in a 200-degree oven while preparing filling.

To make filling, heat oil in a heavy frying pan over medium heat. Add onion and garlic. Sauté until transparent. Stir in ground gluten and cook for 3 minutes. Stir in chili powder, salt and water. Reduce heat to simmer and prepare sauce.

SAUCE

To make sauce, purée tomatoes, crushed red peppers, onion, garlic, salt and malt in an electric blender or food processor. In a saucepan, combine purée and olive oil. Cook over medium heat for 10 minutes.

ASSEMBLING

To assemble, fill each taco with ground gluten filling, cheese, lettuce and tomatoes. Serve with sauce.

TOSTADAS

Serves 6
Preparation Time: 15 minutes
Cooking Time: 15 minutes
Elementary

2 tablespoons oil	¼ cup oil for frying
1 onion, chopped	6 tortillas
1 garlic clove, minced	1½ cups lettuce, shredded
2 cups ground gluten	2 tomatoes, chopped
½ teaspoon chili powder	1½ cups Cheddar cheese, grated

In a heavy frying pan, heat oil over medium heat. Sauté onions and garlic until transparent. Add gluten and chili powder. Cook for 5 minutes until gluten is lightly browned. Cover, remove from heat and set aside.

In a separate frying pan heat oil for frying until water sizzles when sprinkled onto it. Fry tortillas, one at a time, until golden brown and crisp. Remove from heat and drain on paper towels.

On each fried tortilla, spread a layer of gluten mixture, of lettuce and tomatoes, and top with cheese.

HOT CHILI

Serves 6 to 8
Preparation Time: 15 minutes
Cooking Time: 3 hours
Elementary

1 cup pinto beans, soaked overnight	2 jalapeño peppers, seeded and chopped
4½ cups water or wheat water	½ teaspoon chili powder
1 tablespoon oil	½ teaspoon crushed red peppers
2 onions, chopped	
1½ cups ground gluten	½ teaspoon salt
1 green pepper, diced	½ teaspoon oregano
2 garlic cloves, minced	½ cup tomato paste

Drain soaked pinto beans and place in a saucepan. Add water or wheat water and bring to a boil. Allow to boil for 5 minutes and reduce heat to medium-low. Cook, covered, for 2½ hours until soft.

In a frying pan, heat oil over medium heat. Add onions and brown. Stir in ground gluten and cook for 3 minutes. Add green pepper and garlic. Cook for another 5 minutes. If mixture begins to stick to pan, add 1 tablespoon water. Stir in jalapeño peppers, chili powder, red peppers, salt, oregano and tomato paste. Add to beans and cook for 30 minutes.

MEXICAN SPICED LINK DISHES

SPICED LINK TARTS

Serves 6 to 8
Preparation Time: 40 minutes
Cooking Time: 30 minutes
Advanced

DOUGH INGREDIENTS

1 cup whole wheat pastry flour	1 cup ice water
2 cups corn flour	1 egg, beaten
½ teaspoon salt	¼ cup butter, melted

FILLING INGREDIENTS

2 cups spiced links, crumbled	½ cup Parmesan cheese, grated
1 tomato, chopped	2 tablespoons olive oil
1 cup oil for deep frying	

TOPPING INGREDIENTS

½ cup sour cream	½ cup ripe olives, chopped

DOUGH

To make dough, combine flour, corn flour and salt in a mixing bowl. Stir in ice water and egg until well combined. Mix in melted butter. Shape into a ball and chill for 30 minutes.

FILLING

To make filling, combine spiced links, tomato and cheese. In a heavy frying pan, heat olive oil over medium heat. Add link mixture and cook for 5 minutes. Place in a warm 200-degree oven while preparing tarts.

ASSEMBLING

Divide dough into 28 balls and cover with a towel to keep them from drying out. On a well-floured board, roll each ball into a 4-inch-long oval. Pinch up the edges of each oval together to form a tart shape.

In a heavy-bottomed saucepan, heat oil for frying until water sizzles when sprinkled onto it. Fry each tart in oil for 30 seconds until golden brown. Fill each tart with spiced link filling and top with sour cream and olives.

These tarts can be served as appetizers or as a main course.

RED ENCHILADAS

Serves 4 to 6
Preparation Time: 15 minutes
Cooking Time: 35 minutes
Elementary

3 tomatoes, chopped	5 tablespoons olive oil
¼ cup water or wheat water	½ cup heavy cream
1 onion, chopped	2 cups spiced links, crumbled
2 garlic cloves, minced	8 tortillas
½ teaspoon salt	1 cup Cheddar cheese, grated
½ teaspoon crushed red peppers	¼ cup scallions, chopped

Purée tomatoes, water, onion, garlic, salt and red peppers in an electric blender or food processor until smooth. Pour into a saucepan and add 1 tablespoon olive oil. Cook over medium heat for 10 minutes until slightly thickened. Remove from heat and stir in cream.

In a frying pan, heat 2 tablespoons of olive oil. Sauté spiced links until browned. Pour ⅔ cup of tomato-cream sauce into pan with links and remove from heat and set aside.

In a separate frying pan, heat remaining 2 tablespoons of oil. With tongs, dip each tortilla in hot oil for 10 seconds until limp. Drain on paper towels.

Place equal portions of spiced link filling on each tortilla. Roll up and place in a shallow baking dish. Pour sauce over tortillas and bake at 350 degrees for 20 minutes. Sprinkle with cheese and bake for an additional 10 minutes until cheese melts. Garnish with scallions before serving.

CHAPTER SIX

Latin American Ways
to Serve Wheat "Meat"

Latin American food is surprisingly different from Mexican food. Both regions use chilies to spice their dishes, but in Latin America there is not the preponderance of tortillas. There is, rather, an ingenious combining of tastes to produce unusual and delicious dishes. Latin American cooks will combine olives, apples and pecans with steak, or spiced links with peaches and a meringue topping. The results are a pleasure to eat and make these dishes particularly useful when you want to serve something out of the ordinary.

LATIN AMERICAN STEAK RECIPES

STEAK IN TOMATO SAUCE WITH BLACK BEANS

Serves 4 to 6
Preparation Time: 20 minutes
Cooking Time: 2½ hours
Elementary

BLACK BEAN INGREDIENTS

1 cup black beans, soaked
overnight
4 cups water or wheat water
2 tablespoons olive oil

3 green peppers, chopped
1 onion, chopped
1 garlic clove, chopped
1 tablespoon coriander seeds

¼ teaspoon salt

STEAK AND SAUCE INGREDIENTS

¼ cup olive oil
2 cups steak, cut in ½-inch
cubes
2 onions, chopped

1 garlic clove, minced
4 tomatoes, chopped
½ teaspoon cumin seeds
¼ teaspoon black pepper

BLACK BEANS

Drain soaked beans. Place in a covered saucepan with water or wheat water. Bring to a boil and allow to boil 10 minutes, then reduce heat to medium-low. Cook for 2 hours.

In a heavy frying pan, heat oil over medium heat. Sauté green peppers, onion and garlic until onion is transparent. Add sautéed vegetables to beans. Stir in coriander seeds and salt. Continue to cook while preparing steak and sauce.

STEAK AND SAUCE

In a heavy frying pan, heat oil over medium heat. Sauté steak cubes until browned. Add onions and garlic and cook until onions are browned. If ingredients begin to stick to the pan, add 1 tablespoon water. Stir in tomatoes, cumin and black pepper. Simmer for 20 minutes.

Pour steak and sauce into the center of a serving platter and surround by black bean mixture.

STEAKS IN COCONUT

Serves 4 to 6
Preparation Time: 15 minutes
Cooking Time: 40 minutes
Intermediate

1 coconut, shelled and cut into
   ½-inch cubes
reserved coconut milk mixed
   with enough water to make
   2 cups

2 tomatoes, chopped
2 onions, chopped
⅛ teaspoon salt
pinch black pepper
2 tablespoons olive oil
4 to 6 steaks

Purée coconut, coconut milk and water in an electric blender or food processor until smooth. Pour mixture into a heavy frying pan and bring to a gentle boil. Reduce heat to simmer and cook for 15 minutes until coconut mixture has thickened slightly.

Purée tomatoes and onions in a blender or food processor. Add tomato-onion purée to coconut. Stir in salt and pepper. Continue to simmer while browning steaks.

In a heavy frying pan, heat oil over medium heat. Brown steaks on both sides. Add to coconut purée and simmer for a final 5 minutes before serving.

BAKED STUFFED PUMPKIN

Serves 6 to 8
Preparation Time: 30 minutes
Cooking Time: 1 hour
Intermediate

1 10-pound pumpkin
½ cup butter, softened
2 tablespoons olive oil
3 cups steak, cut in ½-inch
   cubes
3 onions, chopped
2 green peppers, chopped
1 garlic clove, minced

3 tomatoes, chopped
½ teaspoon oregano
½ teaspoon salt
¼ teaspoon black pepper
3 sweet potatoes, diced
2 medium-sized zucchini,
   sliced

Preheat oven to 375 degrees.

To prepare pumpkin for baking, wash the outside and cut a lid 7 inches in diameter around the stem. Retain lid and stem as a cover and handle. Clean pulp from the inside of the pumpkin. Rub the inside with butter. Replace lid and bake for 45 minutes, until the shell can be pierced with a fork but is not collapsed.

While pumpkin is baking, prepare stuffing. In a heavy frying pan, heat oil over medium heat. Sauté steak cubes until browned on all sides. Add onions and sauté until transparent. Add green peppers and garlic. Cook for 3 minutes. Stir in tomatoes, oregano, salt and pepper. Reduce heat to simmer. Add sweet potatoes and zucchini. Cover and cook for 20 minutes until sweet potatoes are soft.

Remove from heat and pour into pumpkin shell. Return pumpkin shell to oven and bake for 15 minutes longer. Serve on a large platter and scoop portions of stuffing and pumpkin onto individual plates.

FILLED DUMPLINGS WITH TOMATO SAUCE

Serves 4 to 6
Preparation Time: 25 minutes
Cooking Time: 30 minutes
Advanced

DOUGH INGREDIENTS

¾ cup corn flour
½ cup whole wheat flour

¼ teaspoon salt
¾ cup water or wheat water

FILLING INGREDIENTS

¼ cup olive oil
1 onion, chopped
1 garlic clove, minced
3 tomatoes, chopped

2 cups steak, cut in ¼-inch cubes
1 tablespoon fresh parsley, chopped

¼ teaspoon black pepper

SAUCE INGREDIENTS

5 tomatoes, chopped
½ cup green pepper, chopped
2 onions, chopped

1 tablespoon olive oil
pinch salt
½ cup water

DOUGH

To make dumpling dough, combine flours and salt in a mixing bowl. Add water while stirring. Knead on a floured board until smooth. Cover and allow to stand for 20 minutes while preparing filling and sauce.

FILLING

To prepare filling, heat olive oil in a heavy frying pan over medium heat. Sauté onion and garlic until transparent. Add tomatoes and reduce heat to simmer. Cook for 3 minutes and stir in steak, parsley and black pepper. Simmer for 10 minutes, remove from heat and set aside.

SAUCE

To make sauce, purée all sauce ingredients in an electric blender or food processor until smooth. Pour into a frying pan and heat over medium heat for 5 minutes. Reduce heat to simmer and continue to simmer while preparing dumplings.

ASSEMBLING

To assemble dumplings, pull 2 tablespoon-size pieces of dough from ball and flatten between palms into 3-inch-by-4-inch ovals not more than ¼-inch thick. Place 1 heaping tablespoon of filling in the center of the pressed dough. With moistened fingers fold sides of dough over the filling and press edges together firmly. Filling should be well sealed inside. Continue this process until all the dough and filling are used.

Place dumplings in the simmering sauce and cook for 7 minutes on each side until thoroughly cooked.

STEAK PIE WITH PEACHES AND MERINGUE

Serves 4 to 6
Preparation Time: 40 minutes
Cooking Time: 40 minutes
Advanced

PASTRY INGREDIENTS

4 cups whole wheat pastry flour	4 egg yolks
1 cup butter, cut into small bits	¾ cup ice water

FILLING INGREDIENTS

½ cup raisins
1 cup water or wheat water
2 tablespoons olive oil
1 onion, chopped
2 cups steak, cut in ¼-inch
   cubes
⅓ cup liquid barley malt
½ teaspoon cinnamon

½ teaspoon cloves, ground
½ teaspoon oregano
½ bay leaf
¼ teaspoon black pepper
1 tablespoon chickpea flour
6 fresh peaches, peeled, pitted
   and halved

1 egg yolk, beaten with 1 teaspoon water for brushing top pastry

MERINGUE INGREDIENTS

4 egg whites
                    1 tablespoon liquid barley malt

PASTRY

To prepare pastry, combine flour and butter in a mixing bowl. Rub together with fingers until the mixture resembles the texture of coarse oatmeal. Add egg yolks one at a time. Mix until they are absorbed. Gradually add water, stirring with a fork. Shape dough into a ball, wrap in wax paper and refrigerate for 20 minutes while preparing filling.

FILLING

In a saucepan combine raisins and water or wheat water. Cook over medium heat for 5 minutes. Set aside.

In a heavy frying pan, heat olive oil over medium-high heat. Sauté onion until transparent. Add steak cubes and cook until lightly browned. Stir in malt, cinnamon, cloves, oregano, bay leaf and black pepper. Drain raisins and coat with flour. Add coated raisins to cooking steak mixture. Stir well and cook for an additional 5 minutes. Set aside.

ASSEMBLING

Preheat oven to 375 degrees.

Remove dough from the refrigerator and divide into two equal portions. Roll each half into a rectangle 12 inches by 16 inches on a well-floured board.

Oil an 8-inch-by-12-inch baking dish. Drape one piece of pastry loosely over the dish. Gently press the pastry into the corners of the baking dish, being careful not to tear it. Pour filling into the pastry-lined dish and spread it evenly. Arrange peach halves on top of the filling. With the second pastry, cover the peaches, allowing pastry to sink ½ inch below the rim of the baking dish. Brush with egg yolk and water mixture. Bake for 30 minutes until crust is golden brown.

MERINGUE

While pie is baking, combine malt and egg whites in a mixing bowl. Beat with a rotary or electric beater until whites are stiff and glossy. Remove pie from oven and increase oven temperature to 425 degrees. Spread meringue evenly and attractively over the top pie crust. Place back in oven for 10 minutes until meringue is golden.

LATIN AMERICAN GROUND GLUTEN DISHES

CORN PIE WITH GROUND GLUTEN, RAISINS AND OLIVES

Serves 6
Preparation Time: 20 minutes
Cooking Time: 1 hour and 10 minutes
Intermediate

¼ cup raisins	1 teaspoon paprika
½ cup boiling water	½ teaspoon salt
2 tablespoons olive oil	¼ teaspoon black pepper
3 cups ground gluten	½ cup ripe olives, chopped
4 onions, chopped	2 cups fresh or frozen corn
¼ teaspoon garlic, minced	kernels
1 green pepper, chopped	1 tablespoon milk
2 teaspoons cumin, ground	1 tablespoon butter

Cover raisins with boiling water and allow to soak for 15 minutes while preparing pie.

In a frying pan, heat olive oil over medium heat. Sauté ground gluten until browned. Add onions, garlic and green pepper and cook for 5 minutes. If mixture sticks to pan, add 1 tablespoon water. Drain raisins and add. Stir in cumin, paprika, salt and black pepper. Cook for 5 minutes, stirring occasionally. Remove from heat and add olives. Turn into an oiled casserole.

Preheat oven to 350 degrees.

Purée corn and milk in an electric blender or food processor until smooth. In a frying pan, heat butter over medium heat. Pour corn purée into heated butter and reduce heat to simmer. Stir constantly while simmering for 10 minutes until it acquires the consistency of thick cereal. Remove from heat and spread evenly over ground gluten mixture.

Bake for 30 minutes at 350 degrees. Increase heat to 450 degrees and bake for 10 minutes longer until top is golden brown and crusted.

GROUND GLUTEN WITH APPLES, OLIVES AND ALMONDS

Serves 5
Preparation Time: 15 minutes
Cooking Time: 20 minutes
Elementary

3 tablespoons olive oil	½ cup raisins
2½ cups ground gluten	10 green olives, chopped
2 onions, chopped	⅛ teaspoon cinnamon
1 garlic clove, minced	⅛ teaspoon cloves, ground
3 tomatoes, chopped	½ teaspoon salt
2 peeled apples, cored and chopped	½ teaspoon black pepper
	½ cup almonds

In a heavy frying pan, heat oil over medium heat. Stir in ground gluten, onions and garlic. Cook, stirring constantly, for 5 minutes. If mixture sticks to the pan, add 1 tablespoon water. Add tomatoes, apples, raisins, olives, cinnamon, cloves, salt, black pepper and almonds. Reduce heat and simmer for 15 minutes. Serve alone as a main dish or use as a filling for green peppers or tacos.

STUFFED CHILIES WITH
WHIPPED CREAM AND NUT SAUCE

Serves 6
Preparation Time: 40 minutes
Cooking Time: 25 minutes
Advanced

CHILIES AND STUFFING INGREDIENTS

12 fresh sweet chili peppers or
    6 large green peppers
1 tablespoon olive oil
2 cups ground gluten
2 onions, chopped
1 garlic clove, minced
5 tomatoes, peeled and
    chopped

¾ cup raisins
2 tablespoons cider vinegar
1 tablespoon liquid barley
    malt
2 teaspoons cinnamon
½ teaspoon cloves, ground
½ teaspoon salt
½ cup almonds, slivered

TOPPING INGREDIENTS

2 cups heavy cream
½ cup walnuts, finely
    chopped
½ cup almonds, finely
    chopped

2 tablespoons fresh parsley,
    finely chopped
½ teaspoon cinnamon
pinch salt

CHILIES AND STUFFING

To prepare chilies for stuffing, rinse under cold water. Immerse in cool water and remove stems and seeds with a paring knife, keeping the chilies intact. If using green peppers, core and seed them. Roast chilies or green peppers by arranging them on a rack and broiling them 3 inches from heat. Broil for 5 minutes on each side until well browned. Remove from oven, remove skin and set aside.

To prepare stuffing, heat olive oil in a heavy frying pan over medium heat. Add ground gluten, onions and garlic. Cook, stirring constantly, for 5 minutes. If mixture begins to stick to the pan, add 1 tablespoon water. Stir in tomatoes, raisins, vinegar, malt, cinnamon, cloves, salt and almonds. Continue to cook, stirring occasionally, for 15 minutes.

TOPPING

While filling simmers, prepare topping. Whip cream until it

forms peaks. Fold walnuts, almonds, parsley, cinnamon and salt into the whipped cream.

ASSEMBLING

To assemble, fill roasted peppers with filling and top with cream and nut topping. Place attractively on a serving platter.

LATIN AMERICAN POULTRY DISHES

JELLIED POULTRY WITH TOMATOES

Serves 4 to 6
Preparation Time: 15 minutes
Cooking Time: 15 minutes
Time to Gel: 2 to 4 hours

3 tablespoons olive oil	1 teaspoon summer savory
3 cups poultry pieces, cut in 1-inch cubes	½ teaspoon fresh or dried mint
	½ teaspoon salt
¼ cup lemon juice	¼ teaspoon black pepper
1 Spanish onion, finely chopped	1 teaspoon nutritional yeast
1 garlic clove, minced	2 tomatoes, chopped
¼ cup parsley, chopped	2 cups tomato juice
1 teaspoon coriander seeds	2 teaspoons agar powder

In a heavy frying pan, heat oil over medium heat. Brown poultry cubes. Add lemon juice, onion, garlic, parsley, coriander seeds, savory, mint, salt, black pepper and nutritional yeast. Sauté for 3 minutes and pour into a dish or gelatin mold. Spread a layer of tomatoes over the poultry mixture.

In a saucepan, bring tomato juice to a gentle boil. Sprinkle agar powder over boiling juice. Continue to boil for 5 minutes until agar is dissolved. Skim foam from the surface of the juice. Pour over poultry and tomatoes and allow to stand for 3 minutes until juice seeps to the bottom of the bowl or mold. Allow to gel in a refrigerator for 2 hours or at room temperature for 4 hours. Remove from mold by setting bowl or mold in a pot of hot water for 2 minutes. Place a plate over the top of the bowl or mold and turn upside down. Lift off mold or bowl.

COLD PICKLED POULTRY PIECES

Serves 4 to 6
Preparation Time: 20 minutes
Cooking Time: 10 minutes
Marinating Time: 6 to 10 hours
Elementary

⅓ cup olive oil
2½ cups poultry pieces, cut in 1-inch cubes
½ cup white wine
¼ cup cider vinegar
½ cup water or wheat water
¼ teaspoon salt
2 bay leaves
2 whole cloves
¼ teaspoon thyme
2 Spanish onions, finely chopped
¼ cup chives, finely chopped
3 tablespoons parsley, chopped
2 green peppers, finely chopped

In a heavy frying pan, heat olive oil over medium heat. Brown poultry pieces. Stir in wine, vinegar, water or wheat water, salt, bay leaves, cloves, thyme. Simmer for 5 minutes. Remove from heat and add onions, chives, parsley and peppers. Pour into a bowl and allow to marinate from 6 to 10 hours or overnight before serving.

JELLIED POULTRY WITH VEGETABLES

Serves 4 to 6
Preparation Time: 20 minutes
Cooking Time: 15 minutes
Time to Gel: 2 to 4 hours
Intermediate

3 tablespoons olive oil
2½ cups poultry pieces, diced
¼ cup lemon juice
2 cups water or wheat water
1 teaspoon nutritional yeast
½ teaspoon cumin, ground
¼ teaspoon salt
2 teaspoons agar powder
¼ cup parsley, chopped
¼ cup scallions, chopped
½ cup carrot, grated
½ cup celery, finely chopped
6 large leaves of lettuce

In a heavy frying pan, heat oil over medium heat. Sauté diced poultry until lightly browned. Set aside.

In a saucepan, combine lemon juice, water or wheat water, nutritional yeast, cumin and salt. Sprinkle agar powder over liquid mixture. Bring to a gentle boil. Continue to boil for 5 minutes until agar is dissolved. Skim foam from the surface of the liquid. Reduce heat to simmer while arranging poultry and vegetables.

In a bowl or gelatin mold, spread layers of parsley, scallions, carrot and celery. Top with poultry. Pour hot agar mixture over the vegetables and poultry, being careful not to disturb the arrangement. Allow to gel in a refrigerator for 2 hours or at room temperature for 4 hours until set.

To remove from mold or bowl, place in a pot of hot water and allow to stand for 2 minutes. Place a plate over the top of the bowl or mold and turn upside down. Lift bowl or mold off of the gelled poultry dish. Surround by lettuce leaves before serving.

POULTRY IN CHILI-NUT SAUCE

Serves 4 to 6
Preparation Time: 20 minutes
Cooking Time: 15 minutes
Elementary

1 tablespoon olive oil	½ cup water or wheat water
2 onions, chopped	2 green peppers, diced
8 poultry pieces, thinly sliced	⅛ teaspoon basil
½ cup pumpkin seeds	¼ cup almonds, slivered
¼ teaspoon tarragon	½ cup walnuts, chopped
¼ teaspoon rosemary	pinch cayenne
¼ teaspoon cumin, ground	3 tablespoons cashew butter
¼ teaspoon coriander, ground	mixed with 1 cup water or
1 teaspoon nutritional yeast	wheat water

In a frying pan, heat oil over medium heat. Sauté onions until transparent. Add poultry and sauté until lightly browned. Stir in pumpkin seeds, tarragon, rosemary, cumin, coriander, nutritional yeast, water or wheat water, green peppers, basil, almonds, walnuts and cayenne. Cook for 5 minutes. Reduce heat to simmer and add combined cashew butter and water. Allow to simmer for 5 minutes before serving.

POULTRY IN TOMATO SAUCE

Serves 4 to 6
Preparation Time: 15 minutes
Cooking Time: 20 minutes
Elementary

2 tablespoons olive oil	1 garlic clove, minced
2½ cups poultry pieces, diced	½ teaspoon oregano
½ cup pecans	⅛ teaspoon cinnamon
¼ cup almonds	⅛ teaspoon cloves, ground
3 tomatoes, chopped	¼ teaspoon salt
½ cup onion, chopped	pinch cayenne

In a heavy frying pan, heat oil over medium heat. Sauté poultry until lightly browned. Add remaining ingredients and simmer for 15 minutes.

POULTRY WITH FRUIT JUICE

Serves 4 to 6
Preparation Time: 10 minutes
Cooking Time: 15 minutes
Marinating Time: 4 hours
Elementary

⅔ cup orange juice	¼ teaspoon cumin seeds
⅓ cup lemon juice	¼ teaspoon cloves, ground
¼ teaspoon garlic powder	¼ teaspoon cinnamon
¼ teaspoon oregano	⅛ teaspoon black pepper
2½ cups poultry pieces, diced	

In a saucepan, combine all ingredients and simmer for 15 minutes. Remove from heat and allow to marinate for 4 hours. Serve cold or reheat before serving.

CHAPTER SEVEN

British Wheat "Meat" Dishes

One afternoon as we sat discussing food with friends, one of our English companions began to be chided about the quality of British cooking. One man jokingly remarked, "There's only one kind of British cuisine—dull!" Although this lady was used to such indictments of her home country's eating habits, she decided on this occasion to come to its defense. "Good English food is expensive and time-consuming to prepare so you can never find it in restaurants, but home cooking is sometimes excellent."

Her protestation reminded us that we had always loved steak and kidney pie and that Yorkshire pudding was among our favorites. We decided to do some cookbook and kitchen research. Wheat "meats," it turned out, are very adaptable to good English cooking without much fuss and with, of course, very little expense.

BRITISH CUTLET DISHES

CUTLETS WITH MINT SAUCE

Serves 5
Preparation Time: 15 minutes
Cooking Time: 25 minutes
Elementary

SAUCE INGREDIENTS

½ cup water or wheat
  water
2 tablespoons rice syrup

¼ cup fresh mint leaves,
  chopped, or 2 tablespoons
  dried mint

½ teaspoon arrowroot starch mixed with 1 teaspoon water

CUTLET INGREDIENTS

3 tablespoons oil
½ teaspoon black pepper
1 teaspoon cumin, ground

⅛ teaspoon salt
1 teaspoon rosemary, crushed
5 cutlets, pounded thin

SAUCE

To make sauce, combine water or wheat water, rice syrup and mint in a saucepan. Bring to a gentle boil. Stir in starch and water mixture. Cook, stirring constantly, for 2 minutes until sauce thickens. Reduce heat to simmer.

CUTLETS

In a heavy frying pan, heat oil. Stir in pepper, cumin, salt and rosemary. Fry cutlets in seasoned oil on both sides until browned.

Place cutlets on a serving platter and pour sauce over them.

CUTLETS AND APPLE PIE

Serves 4 to 6
Preparation Time: 20 minutes
Baking Time: 1 hour and 15 minutes
Elementary

2 tablespoons oil
1½ cups cutlets, cut in 1-inch
  cubes
4 onions, chopped
½ teaspoon sage
½ teaspoon salt
⅛ teaspoon black pepper

2 tablespoons butter, softened
4 peeled apples, cored and
  sliced
½ cup water or wheat water
6 potatoes, diced
¼ cup milk
3 tablespoons butter, melted

In a frying pan over medium heat, heat oil. Sauté cutlet cubes until lightly browned. Remove from heat and set aside.

In a bowl, mix onions, sage, salt and black pepper. Coat the inside of a casserole dish with softened butter. Spread ⅓ of cutlets over the bottom of the casserole. Sprinkle ⅓ cup onion mixture over cutlets. Make a layer of apples, using half of the sliced apples. Repeat layers and top with remaining third of cutlets. Pour water over casserole and bake, covered, for 1 hour.

While casserole is baking, boil potatoes for 20 minutes until tender. Drain and pour into a bowl. Add milk and 1½ tablespoons melted butter. Whip until smooth, using a potato masher, electric mixer or food processor.

Remove casserole from oven and spread potatoes attractively over cutlet cubes. Brush with remaining 1½ tablespoons melted butter. Return casserole, uncovered, to oven. Increase temperature to 400 degrees for 10 minutes until top is lightly browned. Place under a broiler for 10 seconds to enrich color before serving.

LANCASHIRE HOT POT

Serves 6
Preparation Time: 30 minutes
Cooking Time: 20 minutes
Intermediate

3 tablespoons butter
1½ cups mushrooms, sliced
3 onions, sliced
2 tablespoons oil
1 teaspoon cumin, ground

½ teaspoon salt
¼ teaspoon black pepper
6 cutlets, pounded thin
6 potatoes, boiled and sliced
¼ cup water

In a heavy frying pan, melt butter over medium heat. Sauté mushrooms and onions until mushrooms have decreased in size and darkened in color and onions are transparent. Pour into a bowl and return frying pan to heat.

Heat oil over medium heat. Stir in salt, pepper and cumin. Fry cutlets on both sides until lightly browned. Remove from heat.

In a shallow baking dish, make a layer of potatoes, using half of the potatoes. Spread half the mushroom-onion mixture over the potatoes. Place cutlets on top of onion-mushroom mixture. Cover cutlets with remaining half of onion-mushroom mixture and top with remaining potatoes. Pour water gently down the sides of the baking dish. Cover and bake at 300 degrees for 20 minutes.

BRITISH ROAST DISHES

SPICED ROAST

Serves 6 to 8
Preparation Time: 15 minutes
Cooking Time: 30 minutes
Elementary

1 roast, thinly sliced	½ teaspoon allspice
½ cup liquid barley malt	1 teaspoon black pepper
½ cup water or wheat water	¼ teaspoon salt
¼ teaspoon cinnamon	¼ cup raisins

In a well-oiled, shallow baking dish, arrange roast slices in a single overlapping layer. In a bowl, mix malt, water or wheat water, cinnamon, allspice, black pepper, salt and raisins. Pour over roast slices. Bake at 300 degrees, uncovered, for 30 minutes.

SHEPHERD'S PIE

Serves 4 to 6
Preparation Time: 20 minutes
Baking Time: 1 hour
Elementary

FILLING INGREDIENTS

2 tablespoons oil
2 cups roast, cut in ½-inch cubes
3 tablespoons soy flour
1½ cups water or wheat water
1 cup fresh or frozen corn kernels

¼ teaspoon black pepper
1 teaspoon cumin, ground
½ teaspoon coriander, ground
1 tablespoon tamari soy sauce
1 teaspoon nutritional yeast

MASHED POTATO TOPPING INGREDIENTS

5 potatoes, chopped
2 cups water
3 tablespoons butter

5 tablespoons milk
½ teaspoon salt
1½ tablespoons melted butter

FILLING

In a heavy frying pan, heat oil over medium heat. Sauté roast cubes until lightly browned. Stir in soy flour. Gradually add water or wheat water, stirring constantly to prevent lumps from forming. Reduce heat to simmer and add corn kernels. Stir in black pepper, cumin, coriander, soy sauce and nutritional yeast. Pour into a loaf pan or baking dish.

POTATO TOPPING

To mash potatoes for topping, boil potatoes in water for 15 minutes until soft. Drain and discard water. Add butter, milk and salt. Mash with a potato masher, electric mixer or food processor until smooth.

ASSEMBLING

Spoon potatoes over corn and roast filling. Using a knife, create a decorative pattern on top of the potatoes. Brush with melted butter. Bake at 350 degrees for 1 hour until a golden crust has formed.

ROAST WITH YORKSHIRE PUDDING

Serves 6 to 8
Preparation Time: 20 minutes
Cooking Time: 30 minutes
Intermediate

1 roast

YORKSHIRE PUDDING INGREDIENTS

2 eggs	1 cup whole wheat pastry flour
½ teaspoon salt	1 cup milk
	4 tablespoons oil

GRAVY INGREDIENTS

2 cups water or wheat water	¼ teaspoon black pepper
4 tablespoons chickpea or soy flour	½ teaspoon cumin, ground
	½ teaspoon coriander, ground
2 teaspoons tamari soy sauce	

YORKSHIRE PUDDING

One hour before roast has completed its normal cooking time, prepare pudding.

Preheat oven to 400 degrees.

Blend eggs, salt, flour and milk at high speed for 1 minute in an electric blender or food processor.

Pour oil into a 10-inch-by-15-inch shallow baking pan. Place in oven for 10 minutes until water sizzles when sprinkled onto it. Remove pan from oven. Pour batter into pan with oil. Bake for 15 minutes, then reduce heat to 375 for another 15 minutes until pudding has risen and is crisp and brown.

GRAVY

While pudding is baking, make gravy. In a saucepan, beat together all gravy ingredients with a wire whisk. Cook over medium heat, stirring occasionally to prevent lumps from forming. After 10 minutes, reduce heat to simmer.

SERVING

Place roast on a large serving platter. Cut pudding into serving squares and arrange around the roast. Pour gravy into a gravy boat just before serving.

BRITISH POULTRY RECIPES

POULTRY PIECES AND LEEK PIE

Serves 4 to 6
Preparation Time: 30 minutes
Baking Time: 40 minutes
Intermediate

PASTRY INGREDIENTS

2 cups whole wheat pastry
flour
⅛ teaspoon salt

¼ pound (1 stick) butter, cut
into small bits
4 to 6 tablespoons ice water

FILLING INGREDIENTS

1 tablespoon oil
2 cups poultry pieces, cut in
1-inch cubes
1 cup leeks, chopped
1 celery stalk, chopped
1 sprig parsley, chopped
¼ teaspoon turmeric
1 teaspoon nutritional yeast

2 tablespoons chickpea or soy
flour
⅛ teaspoon salt
¼ teaspoon celery seeds
⅛ teaspoon garlic powder
⅔ cup water or wheat water
1 teaspoon butter, melted
¼ cup heavy cream

PASTRY

To make pastry, combine flour and salt in a bowl. Add butter
and rub together with fingers or a pastry blender until mixture
resembles coarse oatmeal. Add ice water and mix with a fork.
Form into a ball. If mixture does not hold together firmly, add
an additional tablespoon of ice water. Wrap in waxed paper
and refrigerate for 30 minutes before rolling.

FILLING

While pastry chills, prepare filling. In heavy frying pan, heat
oil over medium heat. Sauté poultry until browned. Add leeks
and sauté for 3 minutes. Remove from heat. Stir in celery, parsley, turmeric, flour, nutritional yeast, salt, celery seeds, garlic
powder and water or wheat water. Set aside.

ASSEMBLING

Remove pastry from refrigerator. Divide into 2 pieces. On a floured board, roll into two circles large enough to fit a 9-inch pie plate. Line an oiled pie plate with one piece of pastry. Pour filling into pastry-lined pie plate and cover with top pastry. Trim edges, tuck under and pinch in a decorative manner. With a sharp knife, cut a hole in the center of the top crust about 1 inch in diameter and remove. Brush top with melted butter. Bake at 350 degrees for 40 minutes until top crust is golden brown.

Just before serving heat heavy cream to lukewarm and pour through the hole in the crust.

POULTRY PIECES WITH LEMON AND CREAM SAUCE

Serves 6
Preparation Time: 15 minutes
Cooking Time: 20 minutes
Intermediate

⅓ cup soy flour
pinch each of sage, marjoram, basil, tarragon and thyme
1 egg
1 tablespoon water
⅓ cup corn flour
½ cup oil
12 poultry pieces
1 cup heavy cream

⅓ cup fresh lemon juice
2 teaspoons lemon peel, finely grated
⅛ teaspoon thyme
2 tablespoons butter
2 tablespoons whole wheat pastry flour
1 cup milk

Arrange three bowls in a line within easy reach of cooking surface. In the first bowl, combine flour with a pinch of each herb. In the second, beat egg with water. In the third place corn flour.

In a heavy frying pan, heat oil until water sizzles when sprinkled onto it. Coat poultry pieces first with seasoned soy flour, then with egg and lastly with corn flour. Place in hot oil and fry on both sides until golden and crisp. Remove from oil and place in a baking dish. Cover and place in a 200-degree oven while preparing sauce.

In a saucepan, combine cream, lemon juice, lemon peel and thyme. Simmer for 5 minutes until hot. Strain through a fine mesh sieve. Reserve cream and discard lemon peel and thyme that remain in sieve.

In a frying pan, melt butter over medium heat. Stir in pastry flour. Gradually add milk, stirring constantly to prevent lumps from forming. Bring to a gentle boil, then reduce heat to simmer. When boiling subsides, remove from heat and stir in lemon-flavored cream.

Remove poultry from oven and pour sauce over fried pieces before serving.

BRITISH SPICED LINK AND MIXED WHEAT "MEAT" RECIPES

TOAD-IN-THE-HOLE

Serves 4
Preparation Time: 5 minutes
Standing Time: 1 hour
Baking Time: 30 minutes
Elementary

1 cup whole wheat pastry flour	pinch black pepper
2 eggs	12 spiced links
⅛ teaspoon salt	2 tablespoons oil

In an electric blender or food processor at high speed, blend flour, eggs, salt and black pepper for just 3 seconds. Scrape down the sides of the blender or food processor jar and blend at high speed for one minute longer. Refrigerate for 1 hour.

Preheat oven to 400 degrees. Arrange spiced links in a shallow baking dish. Pour oil evenly over links. Pour batter over links and oil. Bake for 30 minutes until batter is crisp and brown. Cut into squares to serve.

JELLIED WHEAT "MEAT" LOAF

Serves 6 to 8
Preparation Time: 45 minutes
Baking Time: 30 minutes
Chilling Time: 3 hours
Advanced

PASTRY INGREDIENTS

4 cups whole wheat pastry
  flour
¼ teaspoon salt

8 tablespoons butter
4½ tablespoons milk
1½ tablespoons water

FILLING INGREDIENTS

1 tablespoon oil
2 cups cutlets, cut in 1-inch
  cubes
2 cups spiced links, sliced
¼ cup fresh parsley, chopped
2 tablespoons fresh lemon
  juice

1 teaspoon lemon peel, finely
  grated
1 teaspoon sage
¼ teaspoon black pepper
2 cups water or wheat water
1 tablespoon agar powder
4 hard-boiled eggs, sliced

½ cup walnuts

PASTRY

To make pastry, mix flour and salt in a bowl. In a saucepan, heat butter, milk and water until butter melts. Whip with a wire whisk for 3 minutes until butter is well combined with milk. Beat liquid into flour a few tablespoons at a time until a ball can be formed. Turn dough onto a floured board and knead for 3 minutes until smooth. Place in a covered bowl and allow to stand for 30 minutes while preparing filling.

FILLING

To prepare filling, heat oil in a heavy frying pan over medium heat. Sauté cutlet cubes until lightly browned on all sides. Remove from heat and mix in spiced link slices, parsley, lemon juice, lemon peel, sage and black pepper.

In a separate saucepan, place water or wheat water and sprinkle agar powder over water. Bring to a gentle boil for 3 minutes and reduce heat to simmer. Skim off any foam from the surface of the liquid. Continue to simmer while assembling loaf.

ASSEMBLING LOAF

Divide dough into two equal portions. On a floured board, roll into two rectangles, one 20 inches long by 13 inches wide and the other 11 inches long by 6 inches wide. Oil a loaf pan that is 10 inches long, 5 inches wide and 4 inches deep. Drape the larger piece of pastry over the loaf pan. Gently press pastry into the pan, being careful not to tear it. Alternate layers of cutlet–spiced link mixture, sliced eggs and walnuts in the lined loaf pan until all the ingredients are used. Pour agar and water over the filling, allowing it to settle into the filling. Cover filled loaf pan with second pastry. Fold in edges and pinch in a decorative manner. Punch holes in the top crust with a fork.

Bake at 350 degrees for 30 minutes until top crust is lightly browned. Place in a refrigerator to gel for 3 hours.

To remove from mold, place loaf pan in hot water for 3 minutes. Loosen around edges with a knife. Place a serving plate over the loaf pan and turn upside down. Lift off loaf pan. Slice before serving.

STEAK AND CUTLET PIE

Serves 4 to 6
Preparation Time: 45 minutes
Baking Time: 30 minutes
Intermediate

PASTRY INGREDIENTS

1½ cups whole wheat pastry flour	½ teaspoon salt
	½ cup oil
3 tablespoons ice water	

FILLING INGREDIENTS

1¼ cups steak, cut in 1-inch cubes	⅛ teaspoon nutmeg
	1 teaspoon tamari soy sauce
1¼ cups cutlets, cut in 1-inch cubes	¼ teaspoon black pepper
	⅔ cup mushrooms, sliced
2 tablespoons chickpea or soy flour	½ cup onions, chopped
	2 tablespoons parsley, chopped
⅔ cup water or wheat water	

PASTRY

To make pastry, mix flour and salt in a bowl. Blend in oil, using fingers or a fork, until mixture resembles coarse oatmeal. Add water and form into a ball. Refrigerate for 30 minutes before rolling.

FILLING

Combine all filling ingredients and mix thoroughly.

ASSEMBLING

Divide pastry into two balls. Roll on a floured board into two circles large enough to fit in a 9-inch pie plate. Line pie plate with one pastry. Spoon filling into pie plate. Cover with second pastry. Trim edges, fold under and pinch edges together decoratively around the pie plate. Punch holes in the top crust with a fork. Bake at 400 degrees for 30 minutes until crust is lightly browned.

CHAPTER EIGHT

French Wheat "Meat" Cuisine

The French are not noted for simplicity or speed in cooking, but their painstaking methods of preparing dishes give them a wide reputation among gourmet cooks. We have simplified and modified traditional French cuisine to suit the needs of wheat "meats" while maintaining the Continental flair of the food.

Although this cookbook is essentially health oriented, we found it impossible to obtain the flavors and sense of gourmet French cooking without the use of wine in many recipes. However, since many people may not wish to use wine in cooking, we recommend using water or wheat water as a substitute.

For those who are calorie conscious, the heavy cream sauces of French cooking may become accessible in wheat "meat" recipes since calories are saved by substituting it for meat.

FRENCH CUTLET RECIPES

CUTLET CUBE STEW WITH SPRING VEGETABLES

Serves 6 to 8
Preparation Time: 20 minutes
Cooking Time: 1 hour
Intermediate

VEGETABLE INGREDIENTS

6 tablespoons sesame oil
1 teaspoon tamari soy sauce
8 small potatoes
4 turnips, quartered

12 onions, 1 inch in diameter
8 carrots, cut in 3-inch chunks
1 cup fresh peas
1 cup fresh green beans

2 tablespoons melted butter

SAUCE INGREDIENTS

1 tablespoon oil
¼ cup scallions, chopped
2 garlic cloves, minced
2 tablespoons fresh parsley, chopped
2 bay leaves

2 tablespoons miso
2 cups water or wheat water
4 tomatoes, peeled and chopped
2 teaspoons arrowroot starch mixed with 1 tablespoon water

CUTLET INGREDIENTS

¼ cup chickpea or soy flour
1 teaspoon thyme
⅛ teaspoon salt

⅛ teaspoon black pepper
1 teaspoon cumin, ground
½ cup oil

3 cups cutlets, in 1-inch cubes

VEGETABLES

To prepare vegetables, beat sesame oil and soy sauce until they form a light brown milklike solution. Rub on potatoes, turnips, onions and carrots. Place in a covered baking dish and bake at 400 degrees for 35 minutes. Mix peas and green beans with melted butter and sprinkle them over other vegetables. Bake for a final 10 minutes.

SAUCE

In a heavy frying pan, heat oil over medium heat. Sauté scallions, garlic and parsley for 2 minutes. Add bay leaves. In a bowl, combine miso and water or wheat water until thoroughly mixed. Pour into frying pan. Reduce heat to low and add tomatoes. Simmer for 10 minutes. Stir in arrowroot and water mixture. Continue cooking, stirring occasionally, for 10 minutes until sauce thickens.

CUTLETS

To prepare cutlet cubes, combine flour, thyme, salt, pepper and cumin. In a heavy frying pan, heat oil until water sizzles when sprinkled onto it. Coat cutlet cubes thoroughly with seasoned flour. Fry until a crisp crust forms. Remove with a slotted spoon and place in the center of a large serving platter. Arrange baked vegetables around them and pour sauce over cutlets.

OLD-FASHIONED CUTLET STEW
WITH CREAM SAUCE

Serves 4 to 6
Preparation Time: 20 minutes
Cooking Time: 45 minutes
Intermediate

3 cups water or wheat water
1 tablespoon nutritional yeast
½ teaspoon salt
¼ teaspoon sage
¼ teaspoon thyme
¼ teaspoon garlic powder
¼ teaspoon tarragon
¼ teaspoon rosemary, crushed
½ teaspoon turmeric
15 small white onions, peeled
1 cup mushrooms, sliced

⅓ cup butter
3 tablespoons chickpea or soy flour
2 tablespoons cool water
2½ cups cutlets, cut into 1-inch cubes
2 egg yolks
1 cup heavy cream
½ teaspoon lemon juice
2 tablespoons fresh parsley, chopped

In a soup pot, combine water, nutritional yeast, salt, sage, thyme, garlic powder, tarragon, rosemary, turmeric, onions and mushrooms. Bring to a gentle boil. Continue to boil for 15 minutes until onions are tender. Mix half the butter with flour and water to form a paste. Stir into cooking soup. Reduce heat to simmer.

In a frying pan, heat remaining half of butter over medium heat. Sauté cutlet cubes until lightly browned. Add sautéed cutlets to stew. Cook for 20 minutes.

In a small bowl, beat together egg yolks and cream with a wire whisk. Remove stew from heat and stir in cream mixture, one tablespoon at a time, until thoroughly blended. Stir in lemon juice and sprinkle with parsley before serving.

CUTLET STEW WITH
TOMATOES AND MUSHROOMS

Serves 4 to 6
Preparation Time: 20 minutes
Cooking Time: 30 minutes
Intermediate

3 tablespoons butter	½ cup fresh mushrooms
3 onions, finely chopped	2 tablespoons fresh parsley,
1 garlic clove, chopped	chopped
½ cup white wine	4 tablespoons olive oil
1½ cups water or wheat water	¼ cup chickpea or soy flour
1 teaspoon tamari soy sauce	⅛ teaspoon black pepper
5 tomatoes, chopped	⅛ teaspoon salt
2 ¼-inch-wide strips of lemon	1 teaspoon cumin, ground
peel	3 cups cutlets, cut in 1-inch
1 bay leaf	cubes
1 teaspoon dried parsley	

In a heavy-bottomed soup pot, melt 2 tablespoons butter over medium heat. Sauté onions and garlic until transparent. Add wine and boil gently for 10 minutes. Stir in water or wheat water, soy sauce, tomatoes, lemon peel, bay leaf and dried parsley.

In a heavy frying pan, melt remaining tablespoon butter. Sauté fresh parsley and mushrooms until mushrooms have darkened in color and decreased in size. Add to soup pot.

Return frying pan to burner and heat oil. In a bowl, mix flour, pepper, salt and cumin. Toss cutlets in seasoned flour. Sauté in oil until a crisp crust forms. Spoon cutlets into stew just before serving.

CUTLETS WITH CREAM AND MUSTARD SAUCE

Serves 6
Preparation Time: 15 minutes
Cooking Time: 30 minutes
Intermediate

⅓ cup chickpea or soy flour
pinch salt
pinch pepper
 6 cutlets, pounded thin
 3 tablespoons oil
 3 tablespoons butter
 3 onions, thinly sliced
 1 tablespoon wine vinegar

1 tablespoon fresh parsley, chopped
1 bay leaf
¾ cup heavy cream
2 teaspoons prepared mustard
½ teaspoon lemon juice
 6 sprigs of parsley or 6 lemon wedges

In a bowl, mix flour, salt and pepper. Coat cutlets thoroughly with seasoned flour.

In a heavy frying pan, heat oil and butter until water sizzles when sprinkled into pan. Fry floured cutlets on both sides until golden brown and crisp. Remove cutlets and place in a covered casserole dish. Keep warm in a 200-degree oven while preparing sauce.

Add onions to oil and butter. Sauté until transparent. Stir in vinegar and cook for 5 minutes. Remove cutlets from oven and spoon onions over them. Return to oven.

In a saucepan, mix parsley, bay leaf, cream and prepared mustard. Boil gently for 5 minutes until cream has thickened enough to coat the back of a spoon. Remove from heat and stir in lemon juice. Pour sauce over cutlets, garnish with parsley or lemon wedges and serve.

CUTLETS WITH PRUNES AND CREAM SAUCE

Serves 4
Soaking Time: 4 hours
Preparation Time: 10 minutes
Cooking Time: 25 minutes
Intermediate

24 large prunes	3 tablespoons oil
1 cup white wine	½ cup water or wheat water
⅓ cup chickpea or soy flour	½ teaspoon cumin, ground
⅛ teaspoon salt	½ teaspoon tarragon
⅛ teaspoon black pepper	½ cup heavy cream
4 cutlets, pounded thin	2 teaspoons apple butter

½ teaspoon fresh lemon juice

In a saucepan, soak prunes in wine for 4 hours, then cook over medium heat for 10 minutes. Drain prunes and reserve wine.

In a bowl, mix flour, salt and pepper. Coat cutlets thoroughly with seasoned flour.

In a heavy frying pan, heat oil over medium heat. Fry cutlets on both sides until lightly browned. Place cutlets in a covered casserole and keep warm in a 200-degree oven while preparing sauce.

Add wine reserved from soaking prunes to hot oil and cook for 10 minutes until most of the wine has evaporated. Pour in water, cumin, tarragon and heavy cream. Boil mixture for 5 minutes until it is thick enough to coat a spoon. Reduce heat to simmer. After 10 minutes, when temperature of cream sauce is low enough so as not to curdle, stir in prunes, apple butter and lemon juice. Simmer for 5 minutes.

Remove cutlets from oven and place on a serving platter. Arrange prunes around cutlets and pour sauce over them.

CUTLETS WITH CABBAGE

Serves 4
Preparation Time: 15 minutes
Precooking Time: 25 minutes
Baking Time: 30 minutes
Intermediate

2 quarts water or wheat water
4 cups cabbage, grated
3 tablespoons butter
2 onions, chopped
2 garlic cloves, minced
pinch black pepper
3 tablespoons oil

1 teaspoon cumin, ground
4 cutlets, pounded thin
1 cup heavy cream
4 tablespoons Parmesan cheese, grated
4 tablespoons whole wheat breadcrumbs

1 bay leaf

In a large soup pot, boil water or wheat water. Add cabbage and reduce heat to medium-low. Cover and cook cabbage for 5 minutes until tender. Drain cabbage and set aside.

In a heavy frying pan, melt butter over medium heat. Sauté onions and garlic until transparent. Pour in cabbage and cook 5 minutes while stirring. When all moisture has evaporated, pour into a bowl. Sprinkle with pepper.

Return pan to burner and increase heat to medium-high. Add oil and heat for 30 seconds. Stir in cumin. Fry cutlets on both sides until golden brown. Remove from heat.

In a shallow baking dish, spread a layer of one third of the cabbage mixture. Place cutlets on top in a single layer. Cover with remaining cabbage.

In a saucepan, scald cream and pour over casserole. Allow to stand 5 minutes until cream has seeped into cabbage mixture.

In a bowl, mix cheese and breadcrumbs. Sprinkle over the casserole. Tuck bay leaf into the side of the casserole.

Bake for 30 minutes in a 350-degree oven until top is lightly browned.

BRAISED CUTLETS WITH CARROT-CURRANT SAUCE AND PARSLEY TOPPING

Serves 4
Preparation Time: 20 minutes
Cooking Time: 25 minutes
Intermediate

1½ cups water or wheat water
2 tablespoons currants
¼ cup carrot, finely grated
½ teaspoon onion, minced
½ teaspoon basil
⅛ teaspoon salt
pinch black pepper
½ teaspoon lemon juice
3 tablespoons oil

1 teaspoon cumin, ground
4 cutlets, pounded thin
3 tablespoons chickpea or soy flour
1 tablespoon butter
¾ cup whole wheat bread-crumbs
2 tablespoons fresh parsley, finely chopped

In a saucepan, bring water to a boil and reduce heat to medium. When boiling subsides, add currants, carrot, onion, basil, salt, pepper and lemon juice. Continue cooking for 15 minutes while preparing cutlets.

In a heavy frying pan heat oil over medium heat. Stir in cumin. Brown cutlets on both sides in seasoned oil. Remove from pan and set aside.

Stir flour into oil. Gradually add currant-carrot mixture, stirring constantly to prevent lumps from forming. Return cutlets to pan and reduce heat to simmer.

In a separate frying pan, melt butter. Sauté breadcrumbs in butter until brown and crisp. Stir in parsley.

Turn cutlets and sauce onto a serving platter and top with breadcrumb and parsley mixture.

FRENCH STEAK RECIPES

SAUTÉED STEAK WITH MUSTARD SAUCE

Serves 4 to 6
Preparation Time: 10 minutes
Cooking Time: 15 minutes
Elementary

⅓ cup butter
2½ cups steak, cut in 1-inch cubes
2 tablespoons scallions, finely chopped
¾ cup white wine

2 tablespoons prepared mustard
⅛ teaspoon salt
pinch black pepper
2 teaspoons lemon juice
3 tablespoons chopped parsley

In a frying pan, melt 3 tablespoons butter over medium heat. Sauté steak cubes until lightly browned and remove with a slotted spoon. Add scallions and sauté for 2 minutes until darkened in color. Pour in wine and boil gently for 5 minutes until liquid is reduced.

In a bowl, mix mustard with remaining butter to form a smooth paste. Season with salt and pepper.

Remove wine and scallions from heat and stir in mustardbutter paste one tablespoon at a time. Add steak cubes, lemon juice and parsley. Return to heat and simmer for 5 minutes until reheated.

SAUTÉED STEAK IN WINE SAUCE

Serves 6
Preparation Time: 10 minutes
Cooking Time: 20 minutes
Intermediate

SAUCE INGREDIENTS

2 tablespoons butter	1 tablespoon fresh parsley,
½ cup scallions, finely	chopped
chopped	3 tablespoons hot water
1½ cups red wine	1 tablespoon lemon juice
¼ teaspoon tarragon	1 teaspoon arrowroot starch
1 bay leaf	mixed with 2 teaspoons water
1 teaspoon miso	

STEAK INGREDIENTS

1 tablespoon butter	6 steaks
2 tablespoons oil	pinch black pepper

6 sprigs of parsley or 6 lemon wedges

SAUCE

In a saucepan, melt butter. Sauté scallions for 2 minutes. Add wine, tarragon, bay leaf and parsley. Cook for 10 minutes over medium heat until reduced to 1 cup. In a small bowl, cream miso, hot water and lemon juice. Stir into wine mixture. Add starch and water combination while stirring. Continue to stir for 2 minutes until sauce has thickened slightly. Reduce heat to simmer.

STEAK

In a heavy frying pan, heat butter and oil over medium heat. Brown steak on both sides. Sprinkle with pepper and place on a serving platter. Pour wine sauce over steaks and garnish with parsley or lemon wedges before serving.

FRENCH SPICED LINK AND MIXED WHEAT "MEAT" DISHES

BRAISED SAUERKRAUT WITH SPICED LINKS

Serves 6 to 8
Preparation Time: 15 minutes
Cooking Time: 25 minutes
Elementary

¼ cup olive oil
6 onions, chopped
2 garlic cloves, minced
2 apples, chopped
3 cups sauerkraut
1½ cups water or wheat water
1 tablespoon nutritional yeast
½ teaspoon salt
½ teaspoon celery seeds
¼ teaspoon thyme
¼ teaspoon tarragon
¼ teaspoon rosemary

½ teaspoon turmeric
⅛ teaspoon black pepper
1 bay leaf
¼ cup raisins
¼ cup fresh parsley, chopped
¼ cup spiced links, crumbled
4 potatoes, sliced
2 tablespoons butter
12 spiced links, sliced
8 sprigs of parsley
1 apple, in wedges

In a flameproof casserole, heat olive oil over medium-high heat. Sauté onions and garlic until transparent. Add apples and sauerkraut and cook for 10 minutes. Stir in water or wheat water, nutritional yeast, salt, celery seeds, thyme, tarragon, rosemary, turmeric, black pepper, bay leaf, raisins, parsley and crumbled spiced links. Reduce heat and simmer for 20 minutes, uncovered.

In a pot, cover potatoes with 2 cups of water and boil for 15 minutes until tender.

In a frying pan, melt butter and sauté spiced links until lightly browned.

To serve, spoon sauerkraut mixture into the center of a serving platter. Surround with spiced link slices, potato slices, parsley sprigs and apple wedges.

WHITE BEAN CASSEROLE WITH CUTLETS AND SPICED LINKS

Serves 4 to 6
Precooking Time: 2 hours (for beans)
Preparation Time: 15 minutes
Baking Time: 45 minutes
Elementary

CASSEROLE INGREDIENTS

1 cup white beans, soaked overnight
3 cups water or wheat water
½ cup spiced links, crumbled
1 garlic clove, minced
1 teaspoon thyme

½ teaspoon salt
⅛ teaspoon black pepper
4 tablespoons butter
1 cup cutlets, cut in 1-inch cubes
6 spiced links, sliced

4 unpeeled tomatoes, chopped

TOPPING INGREDIENTS

1 cup dried whole wheat breadcrumbs

3 tablespoons butter, melted
¼ cup parsley, chopped

CASSEROLE

Drain soaked beans. Bring to a boil with water or wheat water in a covered pot. Boil for 10 minutes and reduce heat to medium-low. Cook for 90 minutes until tender. Add crumbled links, garlic, thyme, salt and black pepper.

In a heavy frying pan, melt butter over medium heat. Sauté cutlet cubes until lightly browned. Remove from heat and stir in spiced link slices.

In an oiled casserole dish, alternate layers of wheat "meat" mixture, cooked beans and chopped tomatoes. Begin with a layer of wheat "meats" and end with a layer of cooked beans.

TOPPING

In a bowl, combine breadcrumbs, butter and parsley. Sprinkle over casserole. Bake at 325 degrees for 45 minutes until topping is browned.

CHAPTER NINE

Spanish Cooking with Wheat "Meat"

The foods of Spain have the wonderful spicing characteristic of ethnic cooking but the delicacy of French cuisine. Spanish food is simpler to prepare than French, but the flavors of garlic, pepper and wine give wheat "meats" a gourmet touch. Again, wine is often used in Spanish recipes, but for those who prefer to use no alcohol, we suggest substituting water or wheat water.

SPANISH CUTLET RECIPES

CUTLETS IN ORANGE SAUCE

Serves 4 to 6
Preparation Time: 20 minutes
Cooking Time: 10 minutes
Elementary

2 tablespoons olive oil
6 cutlets, pounded thin
1 onion, chopped
1 garlic clove, minced
½ cup fresh orange juice
1 teaspoon orange rind, finely grated

¼ teaspoon cinnamon
⅓ cup almonds, chopped
½ cup cooking sherry
½ cup water or wheat water
1 teaspoon arrowroot starch mixed with 1 teaspoon water

In a heavy frying pan, heat oil over medium-high heat. Brown cutlets on both sides. Remove and set aside.

In same oil, sauté onion until transparent. Add garlic, orange juice, orange rind, cinnamon, almonds and sherry. Reduce heat to simmer and cook for 1 minute. Stir in water or wheat water. Return cutlets to pan. Simmer, uncovered, for 10 minutes. Place cutlets on a serving platter. Bring sauce to a gentle boil and stir in starch and water mixture. Continue stirring for 2 minutes until sauce thickens. Pour sauce over cutlets before serving.

SCALLOPPINE WITH ZUCCHINI

Serves 6
Preparation Time: 15 minutes
Cooking Time: 25 minutes
Intermediate

½ cup chickpea flour
½ teaspoon salt
4 tablespoons milk
2 eggs, beaten
½ cup whole wheat breadcrumbs

6 cutlets, pounded thin
¼ cup olive oil
2 zucchini squash, thinly sliced
2 teaspoons lemon juice
4 tablespoons tomato juice

Arrange three bowls in a row within easy reach of cooking surface. In the first, combine flour and salt. In the second, beat milk and eggs. In the third, place breadcrumbs. Coat cutlets first with seasoned flour, next with milk and egg and lastly with breadcrumbs.

In a heavy frying pan, heat oil until water sizzles when sprinkled onto it. Fry breaded cutlets on both sides until golden brown and crisp. Remove from oil and place in a shallow covered baking dish. Place in a 200-degree oven, covered, while preparing zucchini and sauce.

In same oil, fry zucchini until slightly browned but still crisp. Spoon zucchini over cutlets and return to oven.

Add lemon juice and tomato juice to remaining oil. Scrape free all bits of brown breading and boil for 3 minutes.

Remove cutlets and zucchini from oven and pour sauce over them just before serving.

CUTLETS IN SHERRY SAUCE

Serves 4
Preparation Time: 10 minutes
Cooking Time: 25 minutes
Intermediate

1 teaspoon cumin, ground	½ cup water or wheat water
½ cup chickpea or soy flour	⅛ teaspoon thyme
6 cutlets, pounded thin	¼ teaspoon basil
¼ cup olive oil	¼ teaspoon cumin seeds
4 tablespoons butter	⅛ teaspoon rosemary, ground
2 onions, chopped	¾ teaspoon arrowroot starch
½ cup dry cooking sherry	mixed with 1 teaspoon water

In a bowl, mix cumin and flour. Coat cutlets with seasoned flour.

In a heavy frying pan, heat oil over medium-high heat until water sizzles when sprinkled onto it. Fry cutlets on both sides until lightly browned.

In a separate frying pan, melt butter over medium heat while cutlets are frying. Sauté onions until transparent. Add sherry, water or wheat water, thyme, basil, cumin seeds and rosemary. Reduce heat to simmer for 1 minute. Stir in starch and water mixture. Continue stirring for 2 minutes until sauce thickens.

Place cutlets on a serving platter and top with sauce.

SPANISH STEAK RECIPES

CINNAMON TOMATO STEW

Serves 4 to 6
Preparation Time: 10 minutes
Cooking Time: 20 minutes
Elementary

3 tablespoons olive oil	1 bay leaf
¾ cup onion, chopped	½ teaspoon cinnamon
1 garlic clove, minced	¼ teaspoon black pepper
2 green peppers, chopped	2 tablespoons butter
5 unpeeled tomatoes, chopped	¾ cup whole wheat bread-
2 cups steak, in 1-inch cubes	crumbs
½ teaspoon salt	

In a frying pan, heat oil over medium heat. Sauté onions until transparent. Add garlic and green peppers and sauté until peppers have deepened in color and are still crisp. Add tomatoes, steak cubes, salt, bay leaf, cinnamon and black pepper. Reduce heat to simmer. Cover and cook for 10 minutes.

In a separate frying pan, melt butter. Sauté breadcrumbs until browned and crisp. Sprinkle hot breadcrumbs over stew before serving.

STEAK STEW WITH PEAS AND LIMA BEANS

Serves 4 to 6
Preparation Time: 25 minutes
Cooking Time: 1 hour
Intermediate

¼ cup olive oil
2½ cups steak, cut in 1-inch cubes
1 garlic clove, minced
6 small onions, peeled
3 carrots, cut in 1-inch chunks
4 unpeeled tomatoes, chopped

½ teaspoon tarragon
½ teaspoon rosemary
½ teaspoon thyme
½ teaspoon cumin, ground
½ teaspoon salt
¾ cup water or wheat water
¾ cup red wine
1 cup fresh peas

1 cup fresh lima beans

In a heavy frying pan, heat olive oil until water sizzles when sprinkled onto it. Fry steak cubes until lightly browned. Remove with a slotted spoon and place in a covered casserole dish.

In the same oil, fry garlic and onions until lightly browned. Remove with a slotted spoon and add to casserole.

To the same frying pan, add carrots, tomatoes, tarragon, rosemary, thyme, cumin, salt, water and wine. Cook for 3 minutes. Pour over steak cubes, onions and garlic. Stir in peas and lima beans and bake for 30 minutes before serving.

BULLFIGHTER'S STEAK

Serves 6
Preparation Time: 20 minutes
Marinating Time: 4 hours
Cooking Time: 15 minutes
Intermediate

½ cup olive oil
1 lemon, quartered
1 orange, quartered

2 garlic cloves, crushed
4 whole cloves
6 steaks

Place oil, lemon, orange, garlic and cloves in a heavy frying pan and heat over low heat. Simmer for 15 minutes until the lemon and orange rinds have turned brown. Remove fruit and squeeze the juice into oil. Discard fruit. Pour mixture over steaks while still hot. Allow to marinate for 4 hours.

Place steaks with marinade liquid in a heavy frying pan. Allow to cook on both sides until browned.

STEAK CUBES SMOTHERED IN JUICE

Serves 4
Preparation Time: 10 minutes
Cooking Time: 40 minutes
Elementary

2 tablespoons olive oil
1 tablespoon butter
2½ cups steak, cut in 1-inch cubes
⅛ teaspoon cloves

1 teaspoon lemon juice
¼ teaspoon cumin, ground
1 tablespoon fresh parsley, chopped
½ cup raisins

1 cup tomato juice

In a frying pan, heat oil and butter over medium heat. Brown steak cubes. Add cloves, lemon juice, cumin, parsley, raisins and tomato juice. Reduce heat and simmer for 20 minutes.

SPANISH HASH

Serves 4 to 6
Preparation Time: 15 minutes
Cooking Time: 10 minutes
Elementary

1 tablespoon olive oil
1 onion, chopped
2 green peppers, chopped

1 tomato, chopped
2 cups steak, finely diced
¼ teaspoon marjoram

pinch salt

In a heavy frying pan, heat olive oil over medium heat. Sauté onion until transparent. Sauté peppers until darkened in color but still crisp. Stir in tomato, steak, marjoram and salt. Reduce heat and simmer for 10 minutes before serving.

CHICKPEA STEW

Serves 4 to 6
Preparation Time: 20 minutes
Cooking Time: 50 minutes
Elementary

¼ cup olive oil
2 cups steak, cut in 1-inch
  cubes
1 onion, chopped
½ cup water or wheat water

3 sweet potatoes, diced
2 carrots, in 1-inch chunks
2 cups cooked chickpeas
2 tomatoes, chopped
4 scallions, chopped

In a heavy frying pan, heat oil over medium heat. Sauté steak cubes in oil until lightly browned. Remove with a slotted spoon and set aside. In the same oil, sauté onions until transparent. Add water, sweet potatoes, carrots and chickpeas. Cook for 30 minutes until vegetables are tender. Stir in steak cubes, tomatoes and scallions. Reduce heat and simmer for 10 minutes before serving.

SPANISH ROAST RECIPES

ROAST IN RED WINE

Serves 6 to 8
Preparation Time: 10 minutes
Cooking Time: 4 hours in a Crock-Pot,
1 hour in an oven
Elementary

1 roast
¼ teaspoon marjoram
2 bay leaves
1 onion, minced
1 green pepper, chopped
1 garlic clove, minced
4 tablespoons olive oil

4 tomatoes, chopped
¼ teaspoon cinnamon
⅛ teaspoon cloves, ground
1 cup red wine
2 teaspoons arrowroot starch
  mixed with 2 teaspoons
  water

Four hours before the normal cooking time for a roast is completed in a Crock-Pot, or one hour before it is completed in an oven, add marjoram, bay leaves, onion, green pepper, garlic, olive oil, tomatoes, cinnamon, cloves and wine. Allow roast to finish cooking as usual.

Place roast on a serving platter and pour liquid and chopped vegetables into a saucepan. Bring to a gentle boil. Stir in starch and water mixture. Continue stirring until sauce thickens.

Slice roast in thin slices and pour sauce over them just before serving.

ROAST WITH SPANISH SPICES

Serves 4 to 6
Preparation Time: 10 minutes
Cooking Time: 15 minutes
Elementary

1 roast	1 teaspoon cumin, ground
¼ cup olive oil	1 teaspoon rosemary, ground
1 teaspoon paprika	⅛ teaspoon oregano
1 garlic clove, crushed	1 lemon, cut in wedges

Slice roast into ⅛-inch slices. In a mixing bowl, beat together oil, paprika, garlic, cumin, rosemary and oregano. Rub mixture onto roast slices and arrange in a shallow baking dish. Bake at 325 degrees for 15 minutes. Garnish with lemon wedges before serving.

SPANISH POULTRY RECIPES

POULTRY PIECES, ARTICHOKE HEARTS AND OLIVES

Serves 4 to 6
Preparation Time: 15 minutes
Cooking Time: 25 minutes
Elementary

3 tablespoons olive oil	¼ teaspoon salt
3 cups poultry pieces, cut in 1-inch chunks	⅛ teaspoon fennel
	⅛ teaspoon thyme
1 onion, chopped	⅛ teaspoon marjoram
½ cup water or wheat water	½ teaspoon nutritional yeast
1 tomato, finely chopped	½ cup cooked artichoke hearts

In a heavy frying pan, heat oil over medium heat. Sauté poultry until lightly browned. Add onion and sauté until transparent. Stir in water or wheat water, tomato, salt, fennel, thyme, marjoram and nutritional yeast. Reduce heat, add artichoke hearts, and simmer for a final 5 minutes before serving.

POULTRY PIECES WITH ORANGES

Serves 4 to 6
Preparation Time: 15 minutes
Cooking Time: 20 minutes
Intermediate

¼ cup olive oil
2½ cups poultry pieces, cut in
    1-inch cubes
1 onion, chopped
½ cup water or wheat water
¼ teaspoon cumin, ground
¼ teaspoon rosemary
¼ teaspoon thyme
¼ teaspoon cinnamon

1 teaspoon nutritional yeast
1 cup fresh orange sections
    with the membranes removed
½ cup raisins
¼ cup almonds
⅛ teaspoon cloves
½ teaspoon arrowroot starch
    mixed with 1 teaspoon water
1 orange, halved and sliced

In a heavy frying pan, heat oil. Sauté poultry chunks until golden brown. Add onion and sauté until transparent. Stir in water or wheat water, cumin, rosemary, thyme, cinnamon, nutritional yeast, orange sections, raisins, almonds and cloves. Reduce heat and simmer for 10 minutes. Add starch and water mixture, stirring constantly for 3 minutes until sauce thickens slightly. Garnish with orange slices.

POULTRY SLICES IN ALMOND SAUCE

Serves 4 to 6
Preparation Time: 15 minutes
Cooking Time: 25 minutes
Intermediate

⅓ cup chickpea flour or soy
    flour
¼ teaspoon salt
2 eggs
1 tablespoon water or wheat
    water
½ cup corn meal

8 poultry pieces, sliced
¼ cup oil
½ cup chopped almonds
2 tablespoons whole wheat
    pastry flour
1 cup milk
¼ cup heavy cream

¼ cup black olives, chopped

Arrange three bowls in a line near your stove. In the first mix chickpea or soy flour with salt. In the second, beat eggs with water or wheat water. In the third, place corn meal. Coat each poultry slice first in flour, then in egg and lastly in corn meal.

In a frying pan, heat oil until water sizzles when sprinkled onto it. Fry poultry slices on both sides until golden and crisp. Drain on paper towels.

Add almonds to the same oil and fry for 30 seconds. Stir in pastry flour. When blended, slowly add milk and cream, stirring constantly to prevent lumps from forming. When gravy has thickened, remove from heat and stir in olives.

Arrange poultry slices on a serving platter and pour gravy over them just before serving.

SPANISH MIXED WHEAT "MEAT" DISHES

SCALLOPPINE GYPSY STYLE

Serves 6
Preparation Time: 15 minutes
Cooking Time: 40 minutes
Intermediate

⅓ cup soy or chickpea flour	1 green pepper, finely chopped
¼ teaspoon salt	⅔ cup spiced links, crumbled
½ teaspoon cumin, ground	¾ cup mushrooms, chopped
2 tablespoons butter	¼ cup cooking sherry
3 tablespoons olive oil	1 cup water or wheat water
6 cutlets, pounded thin	1 teaspoon arrowroot starch
1 onion, chopped	mixed with 2 teaspoons water

In a bowl, combine flour, salt and cumin. Rub seasoned flour into cutlets. In a heavy frying pan heat butter and oil. Fry cutlets on both sides until lightly browned. Remove and place in a shallow baking dish.

In the same frying pan, sauté onion, green pepper, crumbled links and mushrooms, stirring constantly, for 5 minutes. If mixture begins to stick to the pan, add 1 tablespoon water. Spoon a portion of this mixture onto each cutlet. Add sherry to frying pan and bring to a gentle boil. Stir in water and reduce heat to simmer for 5 minutes. Add starch and water mixture. Stir constantly for 3 minutes until sauce thickens. Pour sauce over cutlets and bake at 325 degrees for 10 minutes.

STUFFED ROAST SLICES

Serves 6
Preparation Time: 15 minutes
Precooking Time: 20 minutes
Baking Time: 30 minutes
Advanced

STUFFING INGREDIENTS

1 cup spiced links, crumbled	pinch nutmeg
1 cup mushrooms, chopped	¼ teaspoon salt
2 hard-boiled eggs, chopped	1 egg, beaten
⅓ cup ripe olives, chopped	½ cup whole grain bread-
2 garlic cloves, minced	crumbs or cracker crumbs
2 tablespoons dried parsley	

CASSEROLE INGREDIENTS

1 roast	4 unpeeled tomatoes, chopped
¼ cup olive oil	¼ cup dry cooking sherry
1 onion, chopped	¼ teaspoon salt

STUFFING

In a bowl, mix crumbled spiced links, mushrooms, chopped eggs, olives, garlic, parsley, nutmeg, salt, beaten egg and bread or cracker crumbs.

CASSEROLE

Cut roast horizontally into 6 thin ⅛-inch slices. Place equal servings of stuffing in the center of each slice. Roll up slices with stuffing inside and secure with toothpicks.

In a heavy frying pan, heat oil over medium heat. Brown stuffed roast rolls on all sides. Remove from oil and place in a casserole dish.

In the same oil, sauté onion until transparent. Add tomatoes, sherry and salt. Cook for 3 minutes. Pour over stuffed roast rolls. Bake casserole for 30 minutes at 300 degrees, covered.

CHAPTER TEN

Italian Wheat "Meat" Recipes

The large Italian population in the United States has had its influence on American eating habits. Spaghetti and pizza are everyday dishes. We've included these favorites in this chapter, but we've added some more exotic Italian delicacies fit for a special feast. If you've never made your own pasta and didn't think you could with whole wheat flour, you'll be surprised by our pasta recipes. Making ravioli and manicotti is both an exciting cooking adventure and a very special taste treat. Italian food provides a very good way to serve wheat "meats" without anyone's knowing that something has been substituted.

ITALIAN CUTLET RECIPES

CUTLET PARMIGIANA

Serves 4
Preparation Time: 15 minutes
Precooking Time: 25 minutes
Baking Time: 20 minutes
Intermediate

SAUCE INGREDIENTS

2 tablespoons olive oil
1 12-ounce can tomato paste
1½ cups water or wheat water
½ teaspoon allspice

3 garlic cloves, minced
1 teaspoon tamari soy sauce
1 teaspoon oregano

CUTLET INGREDIENTS

⅓ cup soy or chickpea flour
½ teaspoon salt
¼ teaspoon black pepper
1 egg

1 tablespoon milk
¾ cup whole wheat bread-
crumbs
4 cutlets, pounded thin

ASSEMBLING INGREDIENTS

2 tablespoons scallions,
chopped fine
2 tablespoons butter
⅔ cup mozzarella cheese,
grated

4 tablespoons Parmesan
cheese, grated

SAUCE

In a saucepan, combine all sauce ingredients. Bring to a gentle boil, then reduce heat to low. Simmer while preparing cutlets.

CUTLETS

Arrange three bowls in a line near your stove. In the first, mix flour, salt and pepper. In the second, beat egg with milk. In the third, place breadcrumbs. Coat cutlets first in seasoned flour, next with egg-milk mixture and last with breadcrumbs. Set aside.

In a frying pan, heat oil until water sizzles when sprinkled onto it. Fry cutlets on both sides until golden brown and crisp. Remove from oil.

ASSEMBLING

Pour a thin layer of sauce in a baking dish. Lay cutlets in a single layer over sauce. Cream scallions and butter together and place 1 tablespoon on each cutlet. Sprinkle grated mozzarella cheese over cutlets. Pour remaining sauce over cutlets and top with grated Parmesan cheese. Bake for 20 minutes at 375 degrees before serving.

SCALLOPPINE WITH ITALIAN SPICES

Serves 4
Preparation Time: 10 minutes
Cooking Time: 15 minutes
Elementary

⅓ cup soy or chickpea flour
¼ teaspoon salt
¼ teaspoon black pepper
4 cutlets, pounded thin
¼ cup butter
2 tablespoons olive oil

1 garlic clove, minced
1 teaspoon rosemary, crumbled
1 teaspoon tamari soy sauce
6 tablespoons cooking sherry
2 cups peas
2 tablespoons parsley, chopped

In a bowl, mix flour, salt and pepper. Coat cutlets with seasoned flour. In a frying pan, heat butter and oil over medium heat. Brown cutlets on both sides.

In a small bowl, combine garlic, rosemary, soy sauce, sherry, peas and parsley. Pour into frying pan with cutlets. Reduce heat to simmer, cover and cook for 10 minutes until peas are darkened in color yet still crisp.

ITALIAN STEAK DISHES

CORN MEAL STEW

Serves 6
Preparation Time: 15 minutes
Cooking Time: 20 minutes
Intermediate

STEW INGREDIENTS

3 tablespoons olive oil
2 tablespoons butter
1 cup mushrooms, sliced
3 onions, chopped
1½ cups steak, cut in 1-inch cubes
2 garlic cloves, minced
3 tablespoons fresh parsley, chopped

¼ teaspoon black pepper
1 bay leaf, crumbled
½ cup water or wheat water
¼ cup celery, diced
¼ cup carrot, grated
1 tomato, chopped
½ cup tomato juice
pinch nutmeg

CORN MEAL INGREDIENTS

1 cup corn meal
5 cups water
½ teaspoon salt

2 tablespoons butter
⅓ cup butter, melted
¾ cup Parmesan cheese, grated

STEW

In a heavy frying pan, heat oil and butter over medium heat. Sauté mushrooms and onions until mushrooms have darkened in color and decreased in size and onions are transparent. Stir in the rest of stew ingredients and reduce heat to simmer. Continue to simmer while preparing corn meal.

CORN MEAL

In a saucepan, combine corn meal, water and salt. Bring to a boil, then reduce heat and simmer for 15 minutes. Stir in butter and remove from heat.

Spoon corn meal into individual serving bowls. Pour melted butter over each serving, sprinkle with cheese and top with stew.

OLIVES AND STEAK

Serves 4
Preparation Time: 10 minutes
Cooking Time: 20 minutes
Elementary

3 tablespoons olive oil
2 tablespoons butter
4 steaks, pounded thin
3 onions, chopped
2 garlic cloves, minced
½ teaspoon oregano

½ teaspoon black pepper
¼ cup red wine
½ cup olives, chopped
1 loaf whole wheat Italian
   bread

In a heavy frying pan, heat butter and olive oil over medium heat. Cut steaks into 1-inch-wide strips. Sauté strips for 3 minutes on each side until browned. Add onions and sauté until transparent. Reduce heat to low. Mix in garlic, oregano, black pepper, wine and olives. Simmer for 10 minutes.

Toast bread in an oven broiler for 2 minutes on each side until lightly browned. Place toasted Italian bread on individual plates and pour steak mixture over it.

ITALIAN GROUND GLUTEN RECIPES

GROUND GLUTEN SAUCE ON PASTA SHELLS

Serves 4 to 6
Preparation Time: 10 minutes
Cooking Time: 40 minutes
Elementary

6 tablespoons olive oil
1½ cups ground gluten
¼ teaspoon salt
2 garlic cloves, minced
½ teaspoon allspice
3 tablespoons fresh parsley,
   finely chopped
1 teaspoon oregano

8 tomatoes, chopped
3 tablespoons tomato paste
⅔ cup water or wheat water
2 quarts water
2½ cups whole wheat pasta
   shells
½ cup Parmesan cheese,
   grated

In a heavy frying pan, heat olive oil over medium heat. Sauté ground gluten until lightly browned. Add salt, garlic, allspice, parsley and oregano. Continue to sauté for 5 minutes. If mixture sticks to pan, add 1 tablespoon water.

Purée tomatoes, tomato paste and water or wheat water in an electric blender or food processor. Add tomato purée to ground gluten. Reduce heat and simmer for 30 minutes.

Bring 2 quarts water to a boil in a pot. Add pasta shells and boil for 10 to 15 minutes until tender. Drain.

In a serving bowl, mix pasta shells with ½ cup of the tomato-gluten sauce and the grated cheese. Top with remaining sauce before serving.

SPAGHETTI WITH GROUND GLUTEN AND EGGPLANT SAUCE

Serves 4 to 6
Preparation Time: 15 minutes
Cooking Time: 1 hour
Elementary

3 tablespoons olive oil	½ teaspoon salt
2 onions, chopped	¼ teaspoon black pepper
⅔ cup ground gluten	3 green peppers, thinly sliced
3 garlic cloves, minced	8 tomatoes, chopped
1 eggplant, diced	⅔ cup water or wheat water
¼ cup fresh parsley, chopped	2 quarts water
½ teaspoon oregano	1 pound whole grain spaghetti

2 cups mozzarella cheese, grated

In a heavy frying pan, heat olive oil over medium heat. Sauté onions until transparent. Add ground gluten and fry until browned lightly. Stir in garlic, eggplant, parsley, oregano, salt, pepper and green peppers and sauté for an additional 5 minutes. If mixture sticks to pan, add 1 tablespoon water.

Purée tomatoes and water in an electric blender or food processor until smooth. Add puréed tomatoes to ground gluten mixture and simmer for 40 minutes.

In a pot bring 2 quarts water to a boil. Add spaghetti and boil for 10 to 12 minutes until tender. Drain spaghetti. Pour into a serving platter and top with grated cheese.

A NOTE ABOUT USING EGGPLANT

If eggplant has been sitting on a grocery store shelf for a length of time, it will acquire a bitter taste. This unpleasant taste can be eliminated by placing the diced eggplant in a mixing bowl and tossing it with ½ teaspoon salt, then allowing it to sit for 2 hours. The eggplant will seem to "sweat." Pour off the liquid that accumulates in the bottom of the bowl and press diced eggplant between paper towels before adding to sauce.

GROUND GLUTEN TARTARE

Serves 4
Preparation Time: 20 minutes
Cooking Time: 2 minutes
Intermediate

2 cups ground gluten	1 teaspoon tamari soy sauce
4 eggs	2 tablespoons lemon juice
¼ cup black pepper	1 teaspoon cider vinegar
1 garlic clove, crushed	⅛ teaspoon dry mustard
2 tablespoons olive oil	10 ripe Greek olives, finely
4 scallions, finely chopped	chopped
3 tablespoons fresh parsley, finely chopped	

Place ½ cup of ground gluten on each of 4 bread plates. Boil eggs for 2 minutes and then leave in hot water for 1 minute. Carefully open shells and remove yolks, taking care not to break yolks. Place 1 yolk in the center of each bed of ground gluten. Sprinkle with black pepper.

To make dressing, mince egg whites and place in a small mixing bowl. Beat in the rest of the ingredients one at a time. Pour dressing over ground gluten and egg yolks just before serving.

QUICK GROUND GLUTEN SPAGHETTI

Serves 4 to 6
Preparation Time: 5 minutes
Cooking Time: 15 minutes
Elementary

2 tablespoons olive oil	1 teaspoon tamari soy sauce
⅔ cup ground gluten	1 teaspoon oregano
1 12-ounce can tomato paste	½ teaspoon allspice
1½ cups water or wheat water	2 quarts water
3 garlic cloves, minced	1 pound whole grain spaghetti
1 cup mozzarella cheese, grated	

In a frying pan, heat oil over medium heat. Sauté ground gluten for 5 minutes until lightly browned. Add tomato paste, water or wheat water, garlic, soy sauce, oregano and allspice. Beat with a wire whisk until water and tomato paste are thoroughly combined. Cook over medium heat for 15 minutes while preparing spaghetti.

Bring 2 quarts water to a boil in a pot. Add spaghetti and boil for 10 to 12 minutes until tender. Drain and place in a serving bowl; top with sauce and grated cheese.

BURGER CASALINGA

Serves 4 to 6
Preparation Time: 20 minutes
Cooking Time: 20 minutes
Elementary

3 cups ground gluten	1 tablespoon olive oil
1 cup chickpea or soy flour	¼ teaspoon black pepper
1 tablespoon miso	⅓ cup tomato paste
2 onions, finely chopped	1 cup water or wheat water
1 tablespoon dried chives	

Combine ground gluten, flour, miso and half the chopped onions. With moistened hands, shape into patties. If mixture does not hold its shape easily, add more flour. Set patties aside.

In a frying pan, heat oil over medium heat. Sauté remaining chopped onions until transparent. Add black pepper, tomato paste, water or wheat water and dried chives. Stir until well combined. Bring to a gentle boil. Add patties to sauce, cover and continue to boil gently for 15 minutes until burgers are firm. Serve burgers topped with sauce.

ITALIAN WHEAT "MEAT" BALL SAUCE

Serves 6
Preparation Time: 15 minutes
Cooking Time: 25 minutes
Elementary

WHEAT "MEAT" BALL INGREDIENTS

1 cup soy or chickpea flour
½ teaspoon oregano
1 teaspoon dried chives
2 garlic cloves, minced
⅓ cup Parmesan cheese, finely grated

pinch black pepper
pinch salt
½ teaspoon rosemary
3 cups ground gluten
3 onions, finely chopped
⅔ cup water or wheat water

1 teaspoon oil

SAUCE INGREDIENTS

2 tablespoons olive oil
1 12-ounce can tomato paste
1½ cups water
3 garlic cloves, minced

1 teaspoon tamari soy sauce
1 teaspoon oregano
½ teaspoon rosemary
½ teaspoon allspice

WHEAT "MEAT" BALLS

In a mixing bowl, combine flour, oregano, chives, garlic, Parmesan cheese, pepper, salt, rosemary, ground gluten and onions. If mixture is sticky, add more flour. Form into balls and set aside.

Pour water or wheat water into a frying pan. Add oil and bring to a gentle boil. Add wheat "meat" balls and cover. Cook for 15 minutes until firm.

SAUCE

In a saucepan, combine all sauce ingredients. Mix well until thoroughly combined. Add wheat "meat" balls and cook over medium heat for 10 minutes.

Wheat "meat" ball sauce can be served with pasta or on top of whole wheat Italian bread.

ITALIAN SPICED LINK RECIPES

SPICED LINK SAUCE WITH SPAGHETTI

Serves 6 to 8
Preparation Time: 15 minutes
Cooking Time: 50 minutes
Elementary

2 cups spiced links, cut in ½-inch chunks	3 tablespoons tomato paste
3 garlic cloves, minced	1 cup water or wheat water
¼ cup fresh parsley, minced	2 quarts water
½ cup mushrooms, sliced	½ teaspoon salt
1 tablespoon butter	1½ pounds whole grain spaghetti
8 tomatoes, chopped	¼ cup light cream

In a bowl combine spiced links, garlic, parsley and mushrooms. In a frying pan, heat butter over medium heat. Sauté link mixture until browned. If it sticks to the pan, add 1 tablespoon water.

Purée tomatoes, tomato paste and water or wheat water in an electric blender or food processor. Add purée to link mixture, reduce heat and simmer for 15 minutes while preparing spaghetti.

To cook spaghetti, bring 2 quarts of water to a boil. Add salt and spaghetti. Boil for 12 minutes until spaghetti is tender. Drain and pour into a serving bowl.

Remove sauce from heat and stir in cream. Pour over spaghetti just before serving.

SPICED LINKS WITH EGGPLANT

Serves 4 to 6
Preparation Time: 15 minutes
Cooking Time: 40 minutes
Intermediate

1 eggplant, peeled and diced	1 onion, minced
12 spiced links, sliced	2 garlic cloves, minced
2 green peppers, sliced	3 tablespoons parsley,
2 tomatoes, sliced	chopped
¼ cup olive oil	2 hot peppers, seeded and
1 teaspoon oregano	minced
1 teaspoon rosemary	¼ cup Parmesan cheese, grated
¼ teaspoon salt	¼ cup whole wheat
¼ teaspoon black pepper	breadcrumbs
¼ cup scallions, chopped	¼ cup butter, melted

In an oiled baking dish, make layers of eggplant, spiced links, green peppers and tomatoes. Pour oil over casserole, then sprinkle with oregano, rosemary, salt, pepper, scallions and onion. Bake at 375 degrees for 15 minutes. Stir in garlic, parsley and hot peppers. Return to oven and bake for 15 minutes longer. Sprinkle with cheese and breadcrumbs, then pour melted butter over topping. Bake for a final 10 minutes until top is lightly browned before serving.

SPICED LINK PIZZA

Serves 4 to 6
Preparation Time: 45 minutes
Cooking Time: 15 minutes
Intermediate

DOUGH INGREDIENTS

⅔ cup water or wheat water, lukewarm	¼ teaspoon salt
2 teaspoons liquid barley malt	2 tablespoons oil
	2 teaspoons baking yeast
	2⅓ cups whole wheat flour

SAUCE INGREDIENTS

2 tablespoons olive oil
1 onion, chopped
1 cup water or wheat water
⅔ cup tomato paste
1 garlic clove, minced
1 teaspoon oregano

½ teaspoon black pepper
⅛ teaspoon allspice
¼ teaspoon basil
1 bay leaf
¼ teaspoon rosemary, crushed
¼ teaspoon salt

TOPPINGS

1 onion, sliced
1 green pepper, sliced
¼ cup olives, chopped
½ cup mushrooms, sliced

1 cup spiced links, sliced
1½ cups mozzarella cheese, grated

DOUGH

In a bowl, combine lukewarm water or wheat water with malt, salt and oil. Sprinkle yeast over and allow to rest for 5 minutes until yeast begins to foam. Mix in flour. Turn dough onto a floured board and knead for 10 minutes until smooth and elastic. Place in an oiled bowl, cover and let rise for 30 minutes while preparing sauce.

SAUCE

In a heavy frying pan, heat oil over medium heat. Sauté onion until transparent. Mix in remaining sauce ingredients. Reduce heat to simmer and cook for 20 minutes.

ASSEMBLING

On a floured board, roll dough into a circle. Place on an oiled pizza tray and pinch up a raised edge to prevent sauce from escaping. Spread sauce evenly over dough. Arrange vegetables and sliced spiced links on top of sauce. Sprinkle with grated cheese. Bake at 450 degrees for 15 minutes before slicing to serve.

ITALIAN MIXED WHEAT "MEAT" DISHES

BAKED LASAGNE

Serves 6 to 8
Preparation Time: 10 minutes
Precooking: 1 hour
Baking Time: 40 minutes
Intermediate

TOMATO SAUCE INGREDIENTS

1 cup ground gluten
1 cup spiced links, crumbled
3 tablespoons fresh parsley, chopped
2 garlic cloves, minced
¼ cup olive oil
4 onions, chopped
½ teaspoon black pepper

8 fresh tomatoes, peeled and chopped
1 green pepper, chopped
3 tablespoons tomato paste
½ teaspoon oregano
½ cup water or wheat water
½ teaspoon salt

TOPPING INGREDIENTS

1 tablespoon butter
2 tablespoons heavy cream
2 tablespoons tomato paste
2 tablespoons chickpea or soy flour

4 tablespoons water or wheat water

ASSEMBLING INGREDIENTS

1 pound lasagne noodles
2 quarts water

1½ cups mozzarella cheese, grated

2 pounds ricotta cheese

SAUCE

In a bowl, mix ground gluten, spiced links, parsley and garlic. In a heavy frying pan, heat oil over medium heat. Add wheat "meat" mixture and sauté until browned. Add onions and sauté until onions are transparent. If mixture begins to stick to the pan, add 1 tablespoon water. Stir in black pepper, tomatoes, green pepper, tomato paste, oregano, water or wheat water and salt. Reduce heat and simmer for 1 hour.

TOPPING

In a saucepan, melt butter. Stir in cream, tomato paste, flour and water or wheat water. Continue to cook, stirring constantly for 5 minutes, until topping thickens.

ASSEMBLING

To cook lasagne noodles, bring 2 quarts water to a boil. Add noodles and boil for 15 minutes until tender. Drain and rinse with cold water.

To assemble lasagne, pour a thin layer of tomato sauce into a rectangular pan or baking dish. Cover with strips of lasagne noodles in a single layer. Add 2 more tablespoons of sauce. Add a layer of ricotta, then one of grated mozzarella cheese. Cover with lasagne noodles and repeat layers, starting with sauce, until all ingredients are used. End with a layer of noodles topped with cream-and-tomato-paste topping.

Cover with foil and bake at 350 degrees for 20 minutes. Remove foil and bake for a final 20 minutes. Cut into squares before serving.

RAVIOLI

Serves 6 to 8
Preparation Time: 1½ hours
Cooking Time: 40 minutes
Advanced

PASTA INGREDIENTS

3½ cups whole wheat pastry   ½ teaspoon salt
    flour   4 eggs
              4 to 5 teaspoons cold water

FILLING INGREDIENTS

1 10-ounce package spinach,   1 cup Parmesan cheese, grated
  stemmed and chopped   1 egg
1 cup ground gluten   ⅛ teaspoon black pepper
1 cup spiced links, crumbled   pinch nutmeg

SAUCE INGREDIENTS

2 tablespoons olive oil

2 tablespoons butter

2 onions, chopped

3 garlic cloves, minced

1 teaspoon rosemary

2 bay leaves, crumbled

pinch allspice

½ teaspoon black pepper

½ cup red wine

7 fresh tomatoes, peeled and chopped

1 cup water or wheat water

⅓ cup tomato paste

1½ cups ground gluten

1 cup spiced links, crumbled

2 quarts water for boiling pasta

PASTA

To make pasta dough, mix flour and salt in a large bread bowl. Make a well in the flour and drop eggs into well. Add water by teaspoonfuls. Mix with hands to form a dough. Turn onto a floured board and knead for 5 minutes until smooth and elastic. Cover and allow to stand for 30 minutes.

FILLING

To make filling, steam spinach until tender. Place in a mixing bowl. Add ground gluten, spiced links, cheese, egg, pepper and nutmeg. Mix thoroughly.

ASSEMBLING RAVIOLI

Divide dough into 6 equal parts. On a floured board, roll each piece of dough into 4-inch-by-16-inch rectangle.

Place portions of filling, 2 tablespoons each, in a row on rolled out dough. Portions should be 2 inches apart and ¾ inch from the edge of the pasta dough. When one row is finished, fold dough over the top of the mounds. Press the edges together with the side of your hand and also use the side of your hand to press the dough together between the mounds of filling. Repeat with each piece of dough. Allow assembled ravioli to stand for 40 minutes. Before boiling, cut ravioli mounds apart by running a sharp knife or pizza cutter along the seams made by pressing with the sides of your hands.

SAUCE

To make sauce, heat olive oil and butter in a heavy frying pan. Pour off ¼ cup to be used later. Sauté onions until brown. Add garlic, rosemary, bay leaves, allspice, black pepper and wine. Cook, covered, for 3 minutes. Add tomatoes, water or wheat water and tomato paste. Simmer for 20 minutes.

Spread ground gluten and crumbled links on an oiled cookie sheet and bake at 300 degrees for 15 minutes. Stir into sauce. Continue to simmer while cooking ravioli.

COOKING RAVIOLI

Bring 2 quarts of water to a boil in a large pot. Place 8 ravioli in water at one time. Cook for 10 minutes and remove with a slotted spoon. Place in a covered casserole dish in a 200-degree oven until all ravioli are cooked. Before serving, pour sauce over ravioli.

MANICOTTI

Serves 6 to 8
Preparation Time: 2 hours
Baking Time: 20 minutes
Advanced

SAUCE INGREDIENTS

2 tablespoons olive oil
2 tablespoons butter
3 onions, chopped
1 cup ground gluten
1 cup spiced links, crumbled
½ cup water or wheat water

5 fresh tomatoes, peeled and chopped
1 tablespoon tomato paste
2 bay leaves
2 garlic cloves, minced
½ teaspoon oregano
½ teaspoon salt
¼ teaspoon black pepper

MANICOTTI PASTA INGREDIENTS

3½ cups whole wheat pastry flour
pinch salt
4 eggs

3⅓ tablespoons ice water
4 quarts water mixed with ½ teaspoon salt
1 tablespoon olive oil

STUFFING INGREDIENTS

1½ cups ricotta cheese
1½ cups mozzarella cheese, grated
1 egg

3 tablespoons Parmesan cheese, grated
¼ teaspoon salt
⅛ teaspoon black pepper

¼ cup Parmesan cheese, grated, for topping

SAUCE

In a heavy frying pan, heat oil and butter. Sauté onions until transparent. Add ground gluten and links and fry until browned. Stir in water or wheat water, tomatoes, tomato paste, bay leaves, garlic, oregano, salt and black pepper. Reduce heat to simmer and cook while preparing manicotti.

PASTA

To make manicotti pasta, mix flour and salt in a large bread bowl. Make a well in the center of the flour. Break eggs into well and gradually add water. Mix with hands to form a dough. Turn dough onto a floured bread board and knead for 5 minutes until smooth and elastic. Cover and let stand for 45 minutes.

Divide dough into 4 equal pieces. Place each piece on a floured board and roll out as thin as possible. Cut into rectangles 4 inches wide by 6 inches long.

Bring 4 quarts of water to a boil in a large pot. Add salt and olive oil. Boil half the manicotti pasta at a time for 5 minutes. Remove with a slotted spoon and drain well. Place between cloth towels to remove all excess water.

STUFFING

In a bowl, combine all stuffing ingredients and mix well.

ASSEMBLING

Place 2 tablespoons stuffing in the center of each piece of pasta. Fold pasta over stuffing from both sides, overlapping pasta.

Spread a thin layer of sauce on the bottom of a baking dish. Arrange stuffed manicotti in baking dish. Pour remaining sauce over manicotti. Sprinkle with grated Parmesan cheese. Bake at 300 degrees for 20 minutes.

CHAPTER ELEVEN

Austrian Wheat "Meat" Cooking

Michael's mother is Austrian. When we met, he would mention over and over again that his favorite childhood food was Wiener schnitzel, breaded veal. We were both vegetarians, but he would tell me that if he ever ate meat again, it would be to taste his mother's Wiener schnitzel once again. Naturally, the first thing I did when we perfected the recipe for cutlets was make breaded "veal." It worked so well that Michael's nagging craving for his mother's cooking has ceased. We highly recommend this simple European way of preparing cutlets. In addition, we have found that cutlets, which are quick and simple to prepare, are well suited to Austrian food since the sauces, spices and cooking methods enhance the flavor of wheat "meat."

Like French food, Austrian food uses cream to make many sauces. However, the calorie- or cholesterol-conscious person who could not eat such dishes may well be able to enjoy them occasionally since wheat "meat" is lower in calories than meat and is cholesterol-free.

Perhaps the greatest deterrent these days to eating veal is its extraordinarily high price. It is by far the most expensive of meats, a full twice the price of a top grade of steak. For this reason alone, many people who enjoy the delicate tenderness of veal may have been deprived of its taste. Cutlets are a very good likeness at a price that takes only pennies out of the pocketbook.

AUSTRIAN CUTLET RECIPES

MARINATED CUTLETS

Serves 6
Preparation Time: 10 minutes
Marinating Time: 6 hours
Cooking Time: 25 minutes
Elementary

3 cups cutlets, cut in 1-inch
  cubes
¼ teaspoon salt
½ cup cider vinegar
2 cups water or wheat water
3 bay leaves

6 onions, chopped
6 peppercorns
½ teaspoon thyme
2 tablespoons oil
4 fresh tomatoes, chopped
¼ cup fresh parsley, chopped

In a mixing bowl, toss cutlet cubes with salt. In a saucepan, combine vinegar, water or wheat water, bay leaves, onions, peppercorns and thyme. Bring to a boil and pour over cutlets. Allow to marinate for 6 hours.

In a heavy frying pan, heat oil over medium heat. Remove cutlet cubes from marinade and brown in oil. Add marinade, tomatoes and parsley to frying pan. Reduce heat and simmer for 10 minutes before serving.

CUTLETS IN DILL AND PAPRIKA SAUCE

Serves 4
Preparation Time: 10 minutes
Cooking Time: 20 minutes
Elementary

1 tablespoon butter
3 onions, chopped
1 garlic clove, minced
3 tablespoons paprika
½ cup water or wheat water
½ cup sour cream

⅓ cup heavy cream
2 tablespoons chickpea or soy
  flour
1 tablespoon dill weed
3 tablespoons oil
1 teaspoon cumin, ground

4 cutlets, pounded thin

In heavy frying pan, melt butter over medium heat. Sauté onions until transparent. Add garlic and sauté until browned. Remove from heat and stir in paprika until onions are well coated. Add water or wheat water and replace on low heat.

In a bowl, mix sour cream, cream, flour and dill. Stir into cooking onions and simmer for 10 minutes while preparing cutlets.

In a separate frying pan, heat oil over medium heat. Stir in cumin and fry cutlets on both sides until browned. Place cutlets on a serving platter and pour sauce over them.

KETTLE GOULASH

Serves 4 to 6
Preparation Time: 20 minutes
Cooking Time: 1 hour
Elementary

3 cups water	⅛ teaspoon black pepper
3 potatoes, diced	1 teaspoon soy sauce
2 tablespoons oil	5 fresh tomatoes, chopped
3 onions, chopped	2 green peppers, chopped
1 garlic clove, minced	½ teaspoon marjoram
3 tablespoons paprika	2 tablespoons butter
½ teaspoon caraway seeds	1 teaspoon cumin, ground
3 cups water or wheat water	2 cups cutlets, cut in 1-inch cubes

Bring water to a boil. Add potatoes and boil for 10 minutes until easily pierced with a fork. Remove from heat, drain and set aside.

In a heavy frying pan, heat oil over medium heat. Sauté onions and garlic until transparent. Remove from heat and stir in paprika until onions are coated. Set aside.

In a large kettle, combine caraway seeds, water or wheat water, black pepper, soy sauce, tomatoes, green peppers, marjoram, parboiled potatoes and sautéed onions and garlic. Cook over medium heat without boiling for 30 minutes.

While goulash is cooking, heat butter in a heavy frying pan over medium-high heat. Stir in cumin and brown cutlets in seasoned oil. Stir into goulash just before serving.

CUTLETS IN MARJORAM SAUCE

Serves 6
Preparation Time: 20 minutes
Cooking Time: 40 minutes
Intermediate

SAUCE INGREDIENTS

2 tablespoons butter
2 tablespoons whole wheat
   pastry flour
¼ teaspoon marjoram

1 teaspoon tamari soy sauce
1 teaspoon lemon juice
2 cups water or wheat
   water

VEGETABLE INGREDIENTS

2 quarts water
3 potatoes, cut in julienne strips
3 parsnips, cut in julienne strips

5 carrots, cut in julienne strips
3 celery stalks, cut in julienne
   strips

CUTLET INGREDIENTS

2 tablespoons oil
1 teaspoon cumin, ground

6 cutlets, pounded thin
3 onions, thinly sliced

SAUCE

To make sauce, melt butter in a saucepan. Stir in flour and cook until browned. Add marjoram, soy sauce and lemon juice. Combine thoroughly to form a paste. Gradually add water or wheat water, stirring constantly to prevent lumps from forming. Reduce heat to simmer and prepare vegetables.

VEGETABLES

Bring water to a boil and add potatoes. Boil for 5 minutes. Reduce heat to medium and add parsnips and carrots. Cook for 15 minutes until tender but not soft. Add celery. Cook for 1 minute and remove from heat. Drain vegetables, cover and set aside.

CUTLETS

To prepare cutlets, heat oil in a heavy frying pan over medium heat. Stir in cumin. Brown cutlets on both sides in seasoned oil. Add onions and sauté until transparent.

Arrange cutlets on a serving platter. Spoon onions and sauce over cutlets and surround with vegetables.

CUTLETS WITH PAPRIKA

Serves 4
Preparation Time: 10 minutes
Cooking Time: 20 minutes
Elementary

3 tablespoons butter
3 onions, grated
1½ tablespoons paprika
½ cup water or wheat water
1 teaspoon nutritional yeast
2 tablespoons whole wheat
  pastry flour

1 cup sour cream
⅓ cup soy or chickpea flour
½ teaspoon salt
¼ teaspoon black pepper
1 teaspoon cumin, ground
4 cutlets, pounded thin
3 tablespoons oil

1 tablespoon lemon juice

In a heavy frying pan, melt butter over medium heat. Sauté onions until lightly browned. Remove from heat and stir in paprika until onions are evenly coated. Return to heat and add water or wheat water and nutritional yeast. Reduce heat to low.

In a bowl, mix pastry flour with sour cream. Beat one teaspoon at a time into simmering onion mixture. Continue to simmer, stirring occasionally, while frying cutlets.

In another bowl, mix chickpea or soy flour with salt, black pepper and cumin. Coat cutlets with seasoned flour.

In a frying pan, heat oil over medium heat. Fry cutlets on both sides until lightly browned. Arrange cutlets on a serving platter, sprinkle lemon juice over them and serve with sauce.

WIENER SCHNITZEL: BREADED CUTLETS

Serves 4
Marinating Time: 1 hour
Preparation Time: 15 minutes
Cooking Time: 15 minutes
Elementary

4 cutlets, pounded thin
1 cup fresh lemon juice
⅓ cup chickpea flour or soy flour
¼ teaspoon salt
pinch black pepper

2 eggs
2 tablespoons milk
1 cup whole grain breadcrumbs
1 cup oil
8 lemon wedges

Place cutlets in a bowl. Pour lemon juice over them and marinate for 1 hour.

Arrange three bowls in a line near your stove. In the first, mix chickpea or soy flour, salt and pepper. In the second, beat eggs and milk. In the third, place breadcrumbs. Coat each cutlet, first in seasoned flour, next in egg-milk mixture and lastly in breadcrumbs.

In a heavy frying pan, heat oil until water sizzles when sprinkled onto it. Fry cutlets on both sides until golden brown and crisp. Garnish with lemon wedges just before serving.

CUTLETS WITH MUSHROOMS

Serves 4
Marinating Time: 1 hour
Preparation Time: 10 minutes
Cooking Time: 25 minutes
Elementary

4 cutlets, pounded thin	⅓ cup soy or chickpea flour
1 cup lemon juice	4 tablespoons butter
1 teaspoon cumin, ground	4 tablespoons oil
½ teaspoon salt	1 cup mushrooms, sliced
¼ teaspoon black pepper	½ cup heavy cream

Place cutlets in a bowl. Pour lemon juice over them and marinate for 1 hour.

In another bowl, mix cumin, salt, black pepper and soy or chickpea flour. Coat cutlets with seasoned flour. In a frying pan, heat butter and oil over medium heat until water sizzles when sprinkled onto them. Fry cutlets on both sides until golden brown. Place fried cutlets in a covered baking dish and place in a 200-degree oven to keep warm.

Pour grease out of frying pan, leaving only a thin film. Return to heat and sauté mushrooms until darkened in color and decreased in size. Stir in heavy cream and bring to a gentle boil. Allow to boil for 3 minutes until thickened enough to coat the back of a spoon. Pour mushroom sauce over cutlets just before serving.

BRAISED CUTLETS WITH PAPRIKA AND CARAWAY

Serves 6
Preparation Time: 15 minutes
Cooking Time: 30 minutes
Elementary

1 tablespoon butter	1 tablespoon caraway seeds
3 onions, chopped	2 tablespoons oil
¾ cup carrot, grated	pinch black pepper
1 teaspoon paprika	¼ teaspoon salt
1 cup water or wheat water	½ teaspoon cumin, ground
1 teaspoon tamari soy sauce	6 cutlets, pounded thin
1 cup sour cream	2 tablespoons fresh parsley,
2 tablespoons whole wheat pastry flour	chopped

In a heavy frying pan, melt butter over medium heat. Sauté onions until transparent. Add carrot and sauté for 3 minutes. Stir in paprika. Add water and soy sauce.

In a bowl, mix sour cream and flour. Reduce heat to low and mix in sour cream–flour combination 1 teaspoon at a time. Add caraway seeds and continue to simmer while preparing cutlets.

In a separate frying pan, heat oil over medium heat. Stir in pepper, salt and cumin. Brown cutlets on both sides. Arrange on a serving platter and pour sauce over cutlets. Sprinkle with parsley just before serving.

CUTLETS IN SOUR CREAM

Serves 6
Preparation Time: 20 minutes
Cooking Time: 30 minutes
Intermediate

CUTLET INGREDIENTS

½ teaspoon salt	¼ cup soy or chickpea flour
⅛ teaspoon black pepper	6 cutlets, pounded thin
½ teaspoon cumin, ground	4 tablespoons oil

GARNISH VEGETABLES

3 parsnips, cut into julienne strips

3 carrots, cut into julienne strips

SAUCE INGREDIENTS

3 tablespoons butter
4 onions, chopped
2 garlic cloves, minced
½ cup carrot, grated
2 tablespoons chickpea or soy flour
2 cups water or wheat water
1 teaspoon tamari soy sauce

⅛ teaspoon allspice
3 bay leaves
⅛ teaspoon black pepper
⅛ teaspoon thyme
¼-inch-wide strip lemon peel
2 tablespoons parsley, chopped
3 tablespoons lemon juice
¾ cup heavy cream

CUTLETS

In a bowl, mix salt, pepper, cumin and soy or chickpea flour. Coat cutlets with seasoned flour. In a heavy frying pan, heat oil over medium heat. Fry cutlets on both sides until lightly browned. Place in a covered casserole in a 200-degree oven to keep warm.

VEGETABLES

Steam vegetables for 15 minutes until cooked yet still crisp. Arrange vegetables around cutlets in casserole.

SAUCE

In a heavy frying pan, heat butter over medium heat. Sauté onions and garlic until transparent. Add grated carrot and sauté for 3 minutes. Remove pan from heat and stir in chickpea or soy flour. Gradually add water or wheat water, stirring constantly to prevent lumps from forming. Reduce heat to low and return pan to burner. Add soy sauce, allspice, bay leaves, pepper, thyme, lemon peel and parsley. Simmer, stirring constantly, for 10 minutes until sauce thickens and there is no taste of raw flour. Remove sauce from heat and stir in lemon juice and cream.

Remove casserole from oven and pour sauce over cutlets before serving.

AUSTRIAN STEAK RECIPES

STEAK WITH CARAWAY SEEDS

Serves 4 to 6
Preparation Time: 10 minutes
Cooking Time: 15 minutes
Elementary

STEAK INGREDIENTS

1 tablespoon oil
1 tablespoon butter

4 to 6 steaks
2 tablespoons lemon juice

CARAWAY TOPPING INGREDIENTS

1 tablespoon butter
1 tablespoon oil
4 onions, chopped

1 garlic clove, minced
1 teaspoon caraway seeds
⅛ teaspoon marjoram

SAUCE INGREDIENTS

1 tablespoon whole wheat
   pastry flour

1 cup sour cream

STEAK

In a heavy frying pan, heat oil and butter over medium heat. Brown steaks on both sides. Place in a covered casserole, sprinkle with lemon juice and place in a 200-degree oven to keep warm.

CARAWAY TOPPING

In the same frying pan, heat butter and oil over medium heat. Sauté onions, garlic, caraway seeds and marjoram until onions are browned. Spoon mixture on top of steaks and return casserole to oven.

SAUCE

To make sauce, beat flour and sour cream together in a saucepan. Simmer for 10 minutes. Spoon sauce over steaks just before serving.

STEAK STRIPS WITH ONIONS AND PEPPERS

Serves 6
Preparation Time: 10 minutes
Cooking Time: 20 minutes
Elementary

2 tablespoons oil
4 onions, thinly sliced
1 teaspoon paprika

1 cup mushrooms, sliced
3 green peppers, sliced
2 tablespoons butter

6 steaks, cut in 1-inch strips

In a heavy frying pan, heat oil over medium heat. Sauté onions until transparent. Stir in paprika to coat onions. Add mushrooms and sauté until decreased in size and darkened in color. If mixture begins to stick to the pan, add 1 tablespoon water. Add green peppers and sauté for 3 minutes until darkened in color and still crisp.

Push all vegetables to one side and add butter. When butter has melted, brown steak strips on both sides. Arrange fried strips on a serving platter and top with sautéed vegetables.

AUSTRIAN MIXED WHEAT "MEAT" AND GROUND GLUTEN RECIPES

CUTLETS WITH SPICED LINKS AND PICKLES

Serves 4
Preparation Time: 10 minutes
Cooking Time: 20 minutes
Elementary

1 tablespoon oil
3 onions, chopped
1 garlic clove, minced
1 tablespoon paprika
½ cup water or wheat water
1 teaspoon whole wheat pastry
   flour
1 cup sour cream

1 tablespoon tomato paste
8 spiced links, sliced
½ cup dill pickles, sliced
¼ cup chickpea or soy flour
½ teaspoon salt
⅛ teaspoon black pepper
4 cutlets, pounded thin
3 tablespoons butter

In a frying pan, heat oil over medium heat. Sauté onions until transparent. Stir in garlic and paprika. Reduce heat to low.

In a bowl, mix water, pastry flour, sour cream and tomato paste. Stir into frying pan a teaspoon at a time. Add links and pickles and continue to simmer while preparing cutlets.

In a bowl, mix flour, salt and pepper. Coat cutlets in seasoned flour. In a frying pan, melt butter over medium heat. Brown cutlets on both sides. Pour sauce over fried cutlets before serving.

STEAK ROULADES

Serves 4
Preparation Time: 20 minutes
Cooking Time: 15 minutes
Intermediate

STUFFING INGREDIENTS

¾ cup spiced links, crumbled	½ cup bread or cracker crumbs
¾ cup onion, grated	⅛ teaspoon black pepper
1 garlic clove, minced	2 tablespoons paprika
1 cup ground gluten	⅛ teaspoon marjoram

2 eggs, lightly beaten

STEAK INGREDIENTS

3 tablespoons oil	4 steaks, pounded thin

SAUCE INGREDIENTS

3 onions, chopped	1 teaspoon tamari soy sauce
1 garlic clove, minced	3 tablespoons tomato paste
1 tablespoon paprika	2 bay leaves
1 cup water or wheat water	¼ teaspoon black pepper

STUFFING

Mix all stuffing ingredients in a bowl and set aside.

STEAKS

To prepare steaks, heat oil in a heavy frying pan over medium heat. Brown steaks on both sides and set aside.

SAUCE

To make sauce, sauté onions in the same pan used to fry steaks. Stir in garlic, paprika, water or wheat water, soy sauce, tomato paste, bay leaves and black pepper. Simmer while assembling roulades.

ASSEMBLING

Place 2 tablespoons of stuffing in the center of each steak. Roll up and secure with a toothpick. Stir remaining stuffing into simmering sauce. Add roulades to sauce. Continue simmering for 10 minutes until thoroughly heated.

LAYERED SAUERKRAUT

Serves 4 to 6
Preparation Time: 20 minutes
Baking Time: 1 hour
Elementary

3 cups water	5 onions, chopped
1 cup brown rice	2 garlic cloves, minced
3 tablespoons oil	2 tablespoons paprika
1 teaspoon cumin, ground	4 cups sauerkraut
2½ cups cutlets, cut in 1-inch cubes	1 cup water or wheat water
	⅛ teaspoon salt
8 spiced links, sliced	1½ cups sour cream
¾ cup milk	

In a covered pot, bring 3 cups water to a boil and add rice. Cook, covered, for 15 minutes and drain. Set aside.

In a frying pan, heat oil over medium heat. Stir in cumin. Brown cutlet cubes in seasoned oil. Remove cubes from pan and place in a bowl with spiced links.

To the same frying pan, add onions and garlic. Sauté until browned. Remove from heat, stir in paprika and set aside.

In an oiled casserole, spread a layer of sauerkraut. Follow with a layer of cutlet-link mixture, then a layer of onions and a layer of rice. Repeat layers, ending with rice.

In a bowl, mix water or wheat water, salt, sour cream and milk. Pour over casserole. Bake at 300 degrees for one hour until rice is soft.

WHEAT "MEAT" STRUDEL

Serves 5 to 7
Preparation Time: 45 minutes
Baking Time: 30 minutes
Advanced

STRUDEL DOUGH INGREDIENTS

¾ cup lukewarm water
1 egg, lightly beaten
¼ teaspoon vinegar
3 tablespoons melted butter

½ teaspoon salt
2½ cups whole wheat pastry flour

FILLING INGREDIENTS

1 tablespoon oil
4 onions, chopped
2 tablespoons paprika
1 egg, lightly beaten
2 tablespoons fresh parsley, chopped

4 cups ground gluten
1 cup soy milk powder
2 tablespoons butter, melted
3 tablespoons water or wheat water

ASSEMBLING INGREDIENTS

½ cup butter, melted

1 cup whole wheat breadcrumbs, fine

STRUDEL DOUGH

In a bowl, mix water, egg, vinegar and melted butter. In another large bowl, combine salt and flour. Pour liquids into flour and beat with a wooden spoon for 5 minutes. Turn dough onto a floured board and knead for 10 minutes until smooth and elastic. If dough becomes sticky, add 3 tablespoons more whole wheat pastry flour. Place dough in an oiled bowl, cover and allow to stand for 30 minutes.

FILLING

While dough is sitting, filling can be made. In a heavy frying pan, heat oil over medium heat. Sauté onions until transparent. Remove from heat and pour into a mixing bowl. Stir in paprika, egg, parsley, ground gluten, soy milk powder, melted butter and water or wheat water. Set aside.

ASSEMBLING

Preheat oven to 450 degrees.

Cover a table with a cotton sheet or tablecloth. Sprinkle the entire surface generously with flour. Place the dough in the center of the table and brush generously with butter. Roll dough out to a paper-thin rectangle 4 feet by 6 feet. Brush the whole surface of the dough with butter and sprinkle lightly with fine breadcrumbs.

Spoon cooled filling along the 4-foot edge of the pastry to form a line 3 inches wide. Carefully lift the tablecloth on the side where the filling has been placed. By lifting the cloth higher and higher, the entire strudel will roll over and over to form a delicate, many-layered strudel dough.

Cut the long strudel into 4 1-foot sections. Press the sides of each section together to form a seam. Transfer sections to 2 well-oiled baking sheets. Brush the top of the sections with butter and sprinkle with breadcrumbs.

Bake in preheated 450-degree oven for 10 minutes. Reduce heat to 400 and bake a final 20 minutes until strudel is crisp and brown.

CHAPTER TWELVE

Greek Wheat "Meat" Recipes

Food combining yogurt, feta cheese, beans, eggplant and tomatoes with wheat "meats" and the ever-pervasive flavor of garlic are among the most enjoyable ways to eat grain-based meats. The yogurt, feta cheese and chickpeas used regularly in these recipes serve as perfect complementary proteins for wheat "meats" while complementing their taste as well.

Although unusual, the basic ingredients for Greek cooking can be found in most supermarkets. Therefore, no special trips to out-of-the-way little food shops will be necessary to enjoy these dishes.

GREEK CUTLET RECIPES

CUTLET PIE WITH FETA CHEESE

Serves 4 to 6
Preparation Time: 45 minutes
Baking Time: 40 minutes
Intermediate

PASTRY INGREDIENTS

¼ cup water, lukewarm
1 egg, beaten
⅛ teaspoon vinegar

2 tablespoons melted butter
1¼ cups whole wheat pastry
flour
¼ teaspoon salt

FILLING INGREDIENTS

3 tablespoons oil
4 cutlets, cut in 1-inch cubes
1½ cups brown rice, cooked
2 tablespoons milk
1 cup feta cheese, crumbled
3 tablespoons butter, melted
3 tablespoons fresh mint or
1 teaspoon dried mint

2 garlic cloves, minced
½ teaspoon salt
¼ teaspoon black pepper
pinch cinnamon
3 onions, grated
4 eggs, hard-boiled and
sliced

PASTRY

In a bowl, beat together warm water, egg, vinegar and 1 tablespoon melted butter. Reserve the second tablespoon for brushing crust before baking. In a separate bowl, mix flour and salt. Add liquids to flour and beat with a wooden spoon for 5 minutes. Turn onto a floured board and knead for 10 minutes, adding flour as dough becomes sticky. When dough is smooth and elastic, place in an oiled bowl, cover and allow to stand while preparing filling.

FILLING

In a heavy frying pan, heat oil over medium heat. Brown cutlet cubes. Remove from heat and mix with rice, milk, feta cheese, melted butter, mint, garlic, salt, pepper, cinnamon, onions and eggs.

ASSEMBLING

Divide dough in half and roll into 2 circles large enough to fit a 9-inch pie plate. Line a well-oiled pie plate with one crust. Spoon filling into lined pie plate. Cover with second crust. Trim edges, tuck under and pinch around the rim. Prick top with the prongs of a fork. Brush with remaining butter and bake at 350 degrees for 40 minutes until top crust is golden brown.

CUTLET PILAF

Serves 4
Marinating Time: 1 hour
Preparation Time: 15 minutes
Cooking Time: 1 hour and 15 minutes
Elementary

4 cutlets
½ cup lemon juice mixed with
  ½ cup water
1 tablespoon olive oil
1½ cups brown rice
2 cups water or wheat water

3 tablespoons butter
1 teaspoon cumin, ground
3 onions, chopped
2 garlic cloves, minced
3 tablespoons tomato paste
½ teaspoon salt
⅛ teaspoon black pepper

Place cutlets in a bowl. Pour lemon juice–water mixture over them and allow to marinate for 1 hour.

In a saucepan, combine oil, rice and water or wheat water. Bring to a boil and reduce heat to low. Simmer, covered, for 50 minutes until rice is tender.

In a heavy frying pan, melt butter over medium heat. Stir in cumin. Remove cutlets from marinade and dry between paper towels. Reserve lemon water. Brown cutlets on both sides. Place in a covered casserole and keep warm in a 200-degree oven.

To same butter, add onions and garlic. Sauté until browned. Dissolve tomato paste in lemon water. Add to cooking onions and garlic. Stir in cooked rice, salt and pepper. Spoon rice onto a platter and top with cutlets.

EGGPLANT PURÉE WITH CUTLETS

Serves 4 to 6
Preparation Time: 10 minutes
Cooking Time: 1 hour
Intermediate

5 eggplants
4 tablespoons butter, melted
3 tablespoons tahini (ground, hulled sesame seeds)
3 garlic cloves, crushed
¼ teaspoon salt
¼ teaspoon black pepper
3 tablespoons olive oil

1 teaspoon cumin, ground
5 cutlets, cut in 1-inch cubes
3 onions, chopped
¼ cup tomato paste mixed with 1 cup water
⅛ teaspoon allspice
⅛ teaspoon cinnamon
⅛ teaspoon nutmeg

In a 400-degree oven, bake eggplants for 30 minutes until soft, or char them directly over a gas flame until soft. Remove skins and purée the pulp in an electric blender or food processor. Mix purée with melted butter, tahini, garlic, salt and pepper. Set aside.

In a frying pan, heat oil over medium heat. Add cumin. Fry cutlet cubes until lightly browned. Add onions and sauté until onions are transparent. Stir in tomato paste and water, allspice, cinnamon and nutmeg. Reduce heat and simmer for 10 minutes.

Spoon cutlets in tomato sauce into the center of a serving platter and surround with eggplant purée.

CUTLETS WITH GREEN PEPPERS

Serves 4
Preparation Time: 20 minutes
Baking Time: 30 minutes
Elementary

2½ cups fresh green beans, sliced
3 tablespoons olive oil
2½ cups cutlets, cut in 1-inch cubes
4 onions, peeled and chopped

5 unpeeled tomatoes, chopped
½ teaspoon salt
⅛ teaspoon black pepper
¼ teaspoon nutmeg
½ teaspoon allspice
½ cup feta cheese, crumbled

Place green beans in a layer on the bottom of an oiled casserole. In a heavy frying pan, heat oil over medium heat. Brown cutlet cubes and spoon over beans. To the same frying pan, add onions and sauté until transparent. Spoon onions over cutlet cubes. Spread chopped tomatoes over onions. Sprinkle with spices. Top with feta cheese and bake at 325 degrees, covered, for 30 minutes.

CUTLETS WITH KIDNEY BEANS

Serves 6
Preparation Time: 15 minutes
Cooking Time: 3 hours
Elementary

½ teaspoon salt	2 tablespoons fresh dill weed
4 cups water or wheat water	or 1 tablespoon dried dill
1 cup dry kidney beans	weed
¼ cup olive oil	3 tablespoons fresh mint or
3 cups cutlets, cut in	1 teaspoon dried mint
1-inch cubes	1 teaspoon fenugreek, ground
2 onions, chopped	1 teaspoon turmeric
1 cup fresh parsley, chopped	1 teaspoon oregano
¼ cup leeks, finely chopped	pinch black pepper
½ cup lemon juice	¼ teaspoon salt

In a pot, combine salt and water. Bring to a boil. Add kidney beans and continue to boil for 5 minutes. Reduce heat to medium and cook for 2½ hours until soft.

In a frying pan, heat oil over medium heat. Brown cutlet cubes. Add onions and sauté until transparent. If mixture sticks to pan, add 1 tablespoon water. Stir in parsley, leeks, dill, mint, fenugreek, turmeric, oregano, pepper, salt, cooked beans and lemon juice. Cook for 5 minutes before serving.

GREEK GROUND GLUTEN RECIPES

POTATO MOUSSAKA WITH GROUND GLUTEN

Serves 6 to 8
Preparation Time: 35 minutes
Baking Time: 40 minutes
Intermediate

8 potatoes, sliced
3 cups water
3 tablespoons oil
6 onions, chopped
3 cups ground gluten
¼ cup tomato paste mixed
  with 1 cup water or
  wheat water
½ cup fresh parsley, chopped
1½ cup whole grain dry
  breadcrumbs or cracker
  crumbs

2 eggs, separated
2 cups Cheddar cheese,
  grated
4 cups milk
1 cup whole wheat pastry
  flour
½ teaspoon salt
¼ teaspoon black pepper
⅛ teaspoon nutmeg

In a covered pot, boil potatoes in water until they can be easily pierced with a fork. Remove from heat, drain and set aside.

In a heavy frying pan, heat oil over medium heat. Sauté onions until transparent. Stir in ground gluten, tomato paste and water or wheat water and parsley. Cook for 15 minutes until half the liquid has evaporated. Remove from heat. Add 2 tablespoons of breadcrumbs, egg whites and 2 tablespoons grated cheese.

In a saucepan, heat 3 cups of milk over medium heat. In a bowl, mix remaining cup of milk with flour. Gradually stir into hot milk. Continue cooking, stirring constantly, until sauce thickens. Remove from heat and add egg yolks, salt, pepper and nutmeg.

Dust a well-oiled rectangular baking dish with 3 tablespoons breadcrumbs. Arrange sliced potatoes at the bottom of the dish.

Cover with ground gluten–tomato mixture. Sprinkle with ¾ cup breadcrumbs. Pour white sauce over crumbs. Sprinkle with cheese and top with remaining breadcrumbs.

Bake, uncovered, for 40 minutes at 350 degrees and cool for 30 minutes before cutting into squares to serve.

SMALL GLUTEN BALLS WITH LEMON AND EGG SAUCE

Serves 4 to 6
Preparation Time: 20 minutes
Cooking Time: 30 minutes
Intermediate

2 cups ground gluten	1 tablespoon butter
⅔ cup soy milk powder	¼ teaspoon salt
3 onions, finely chopped	pinch pepper
1 garlic clove, minced	3 eggs
1 tablespoon dried mint, crumbled	4 tablespoons milk
	2 teaspoons arrowroot starch
⅓ cup olive oil	2 tablespoons parsley, chopped
2½ cups water or wheat water	

2 tablespoons lemon juice

In a bowl, combine ground gluten, soy milk powder, onions, garlic and mint to form a stiff mixture. If mixture is sticky, add 2 tablespoons more soy milk powder. With moistened hands, shape into balls.

In a heavy-bottomed saucepan, heat oil until water sizzles when sprinkled onto it. Fry balls until golden and crisp. Remove with a slotted spoon and drain on paper towels.

In a saucepan, heat water or wheat water, butter, salt and pepper over medium heat until butter melts. In a bowl, combine eggs, milk, starch and parsley. Pour into saucepan and reduce heat to simmer. Continue to cook for 10 minutes until sauce has thickened. Add lemon juice. Place gluten balls in sauce and simmer for a final 3 minutes.

GLUTEN BALLS IN YOGURT

Serves 4 to 6
Preparation Time: 15 minutes
Cooking Time: 25 minutes
Intermediate

2 cups ground gluten	⅓ cup olive oil
⅔ cup soy milk powder	2 cups yogurt
3 onions, finely chopped	½ cup water or wheat water
1 tablespoon dried mint, crumbled	½ teaspoon garlic powder
	pinch nutmeg

In a bowl, combine gluten, soy milk powder, onions and mint. With moistened hands, form into balls. In a heavy-bottomed saucepan, heat oil until water sizzles when sprinkled onto it. Deep-fry balls until lightly crusted. Drain on paper towels.

In a saucepan, heat yogurt, water or wheat water, garlic powder and nutmeg to a gentle boil. Reduce heat and add balls. Simmer for 10 minutes before serving.

EGGPLANT STUFFED WITH GROUND GLUTEN

Serves 4 to 6
Preparation Time: 20 minutes
Baking Time: 35 minutes
Intermediate

3 tablespoons butter	1 bay leaf
4 onions, chopped	2 eggplants
2 garlic cloves, minced	3 cups ground gluten
8 fresh tomatoes, chopped	5 onions, grated
¼ teaspoon salt	½ cup fresh mint leaves or
¼ teaspoon black pepper	3 tablespoons dried mint
1 cup water or wheat water	1 cup cooked brown rice
1 teaspoon arrowroot starch mixed with 1 tablespoon water	

In a heavy frying pan, melt butter over medium heat. Sauté onions and garlic until transparent. Stir in tomatoes, salt, pepper, water or wheat water and bay leaf. Reduce heat and simmer for 10 minutes while preparing eggplants.

Cut each eggplant in half lengthwise. Remove the seeds and pulp with a spoon, leaving a ¾-inch shell. Chop seeds and pulp fine and combine with gluten, grated onions, mint and brown rice. Spoon mixture into eggplant shells. Place stuffed eggplants in a large covered baking dish or casserole.

Stir water and starch combination into simmering tomato sauce. Continue stirring for 3 minutes until sauce thickens. Pour over eggplants. Cover and bake at 350 degrees for 35 minutes before serving.

EGGPLANT MOUSSAKA

Serves 4 to 6
Preparation Time: 40 minutes
Baking Time: 15 minutes
Intermediate

3 tablespoons butter	2 tablespoons parsley, chopped
1 onion, chopped	¼ cup oil
1 garlic clove, minced	2 eggplants, cut lengthwise in
2 cups ground gluten	½-inch slices and salted
3 tablespoons tomato paste	4 cups milk
½ cup white wine	1 cup whole wheat pastry flour
⅔ cup water or wheat water	2 tablespoons butter, melted
½ teaspoon salt	3 eggs, beaten
½ teaspoon pepper	½ cup whole grain
pinch nutmeg	breadcrumbs

1 cup Cheddar cheese, grated

In a heavy frying pan, melt butter over medium heat. Sauté onion and garlic until browned. Stir in gluten, tomato paste, wine, water or wheat water, salt, pepper, nutmeg and parsley. Reduce heat and simmer for 20 minutes while preparing eggplants.

In a heavy frying pan, heat oil until water sizzles when sprinkled onto it. Press salted eggplant slices between paper towels to remove excess moisture. Fry until dark and soft. Remove from oil and drain on paper towels.

To make cream sauce, heat 3 cups of milk over medium heat. In a bowl, mix the fourth cup of milk with flour. Stir gradually into cooking milk. Continue to cook, stirring constantly, for 10 minutes until sauce thickens. Remove from heat and stir in melted butter and beaten eggs.

In a shallow rectangular baking dish, arrange eggplant slices in a layer. Remove gluten mixture from heat and stir in ¼ cup of breadcrumbs and ½ cup of grated cheese. Pour white sauce over ground gluten mixture. Sprinkle with remaining cheese and top with breadcrumbs.

Bake at 350 degrees for 15 minutes until cheese is melted and crumbs are lightly browned. Cool for 10 minutes before cutting into squares and serving.

GREEK POULTRY RECIPES

POULTRY PIECES WITH RICE

Serves 4
Preparation Time: 10 minutes
Cooking Time: 50 minutes
Elementary

2 tablespoons butter	⅓ cup chickpea or soy flour
3 onions, chopped	pinch each of sage, marjoram,
3 tablespoons tomato paste	basil and tarragon
mixed with ½ cup water	1 egg
or wheat water	1 tablespoon milk
5 tomatoes, chopped	⅓ cup corn flour or corn meal
1½ cups brown rice	8 poultry pieces
3 cups water or wheat water	⅓ cup oil

In a heavy frying pan, melt butter over medium heat. Sauté onions until transparent. Add tomato paste and water mixture and chopped tomatoes. Reduce heat to low.

In a covered saucepan, boil 3 cups of water or wheat water. Add rice and reduce heat to low. Cook, covered, for 40 minutes until rice is tender.

To prepare poultry pieces, arrange three bowls in a row near your stove. In the first, mix flour and herbs. In the second, beat egg and milk. In the third, place corn flour. Coat each poultry piece first in seasoned flour, next in egg-milk mixture, lastly with corn meal.

In a frying pan, heat oil until water sizzles when sprinkled onto it. Fry poultry pieces on both sides until golden and crisp.

Spoon rice into the center of a serving platter. Pour sauce over rice and surround with poultry pieces.

POULTRY PIECES WITH WALNUT SAUCE

Serves 4 to 5
Preparation Time: 15 minutes
Cooking Time: 30 minutes
Elementary

pinch each of sage, marjoram, tarragon, thyme and salt	8 poultry pieces
1 teaspoon nutritional yeast	⅓ cup oil
⅓ cup chickpea or soy flour	2 tablespoons butter
1 egg	1 onion, chopped
1 tablespoon water	2 tablespoons whole wheat
⅓ cup corn flour	pastry flour
	1½ cups milk

1 cup walnuts, chopped

Arrange three bowls in a row near your stove. In the first, mix herbs, salt, nutritional yeast and chickpea or soy flour. In the second, beat egg and water. In the third, place corn flour. Coat poultry pieces first in seasoned bean flour, second in egg and lastly in corn flour.

In a heavy frying pan, heat oil until water sizzles when sprinkled onto it. Fry poultry pieces on both sides until golden and crisp. Place in a covered casserole and keep warm in a 200-degree oven while preparing sauce.

In a frying pan, melt butter over medium heat. Sauté onion until transparent. Stir in whole wheat pastry flour. Gradually add milk, stirring constantly to prevent lumps from forming. Add walnuts and cook for 10 minutes until thickened.

Remove poultry pieces from oven and pour sauce over them just before serving.

POULTRY PIECES WITH YOGURT SAUCE

Serves 4 to 5
Preparation Time: 10 minutes
Cooking Time: 30 minutes
Intermediate

2 tablespoons butter
2 onions, chopped
2 garlic cloves, minced
1 tablespoon mint leaves,
   crumbled
1½ cups yogurt
⅓ cup chickpea or soy flour
pinch each of marjoram,
   tarragon, thyme and salt

1 egg
1 tablespoon milk
⅓ cup corn flour
⅓ cup oil
2½ cups poultry pieces, cut in
   1-inch cubes

In a heavy frying pan, melt butter over medium heat. Sauté onions and garlic until transparent. Reduce heat to simmer. Stir in crumbled mint and yogurt. Continue to simmer while preparing poultry pieces.

Arrange three bowls in a row near your stove. In the first mix herbs, salt and soy or chickpea flour. In the second, beat egg and milk. In the third, place corn flour. Coat poultry pieces with contents of each bowl, in turn.

In a heavy frying pan, heat oil until water sizzles when sprinkled onto it. Fry poultry pieces on both sides until golden and crisp.

Before serving, arrange fried poultry pieces on a serving platter and pour sauce over them.

POULTRY PIE

Serves 4 to 6
Preparation Time: 45 minutes
Baking Time: 40 minutes
Intermediate

PASTRY INGREDIENTS

¼ cup water, lukewarm
1 egg, lightly beaten
⅛ teaspoon vinegar

2 tablespoons butter, melted
1½ cups whole wheat
   pastry flour
¼ teaspoon salt

FILLING INGREDIENTS

2 cups water or
  wheat water
5 onions, chopped
3 tablespoons butter
2 cups poultry pieces, cut in
  1-inch cubes
3 eggs, beaten

½ cup milk
2 tablespoons chickpea or
  soy flour
pinch each of salt, pepper and
  nutmeg
1 cup mild Cheddar cheese,
  grated

PASTRY

To make pastry, beat together water, egg, vinegar and 1 tablespoon of the melted butter. Reserve the other tablespoon for brushing the top pie crust before baking. In a large bowl, combine flour and salt. Add liquids to flour and beat for 5 minutes with a wooden spoon. Place on a well-floured board and knead for 10 minutes until smooth and elastic. Place in a bowl, cover and set aside for 20 minutes while preparing filling.

FILLING

Bring water or wheat water to a gentle boil. Add chopped onions and continue to boil for 10 minutes. Purée in an electric blender or food processor. Place in refrigerator to cool.

In a heavy frying pan, melt butter over medium heat. Fry poultry cubes until lightly browned. Remove from heat and set aside.

In a bowl, combine eggs, milk, soy or chickpea flour, salt, pepper, nutmeg, fried poultry cubes and puréed onions.

ASSEMBLING

Divide dough into 2 equal portions. On a floured board, roll pastry into 2 circles to fit a 9-inch pie plate. Line pie plate with one piece of pastry. Pour filling into pie shell. Sprinkle with grated cheese. Cover with second pastry. Trim edges, fold under excess and pinch around the rim of the plate. Prick the top crust with a fork and brush with remaining melted butter. Bake at 350 degrees for 40 minutes until top is golden.

CHAPTER THIRTEEN

African Cooking
with Wheat "Meat"

Continually more light has been shed on the once-considered "dark" continent of Africa. Along with understanding of its native peoples' customs has come exposure to their foods. Although African restaurants do not dot the avenues of American cities, some recipes have filtered west. African food uses chili but with a different style from Mexican or Latin American food. Meats are most often served in combination with fruits, vegetables and sauces, making appropriate and delectable disguises for the enjoyment of wheat "meats."

AFRICAN CUTLET RECIPES

CHOPPED CUTLETS WITH SPICED GRAVY

Serves 6
Preparation Time: 20 minutes
Cooking Time: 25 minutes
Elementary

2 tablespoons sesame oil
1 teaspoon cumin, ground
6 cutlets, cut in 1-inch cubes
2 onions, finely chopped
2 garlic cloves, minced
½ teaspoon ginger root, minced
pinch cloves
pinch allspice

pinch nutmeg
1 teaspoon paprika
pinch black pepper
pinch salt
¾ cup water or wheat water
½ teaspoon arrowroot starch
   mixed with 1 tablespoon
   water or wheat water

In a heavy frying pan, heat oil over medium heat. Stir in ground cumin. Sauté cutlet cubes until lightly browned. Add onions, garlic and ginger and sauté until onions are transparent. If mixture sticks to pan, add 1 tablespoon water. Add cloves, allspice, nutmeg, paprika, pepper, salt and water or wheat water. Reduce heat and simmer for 10 minutes. Stir in starch and water mixture and continue to stir until sauce thickens, about 5 minutes.

CURRIED CUTLETS

Serves 4
Preparation Time: 10 minutes
Cooking Time: 20 minutes
Elementary

1 tablespoon butter
2 tablespoons oil
1 teaspoon cumin, ground
¼ teaspoon salt
¼ teaspoon black pepper

4 cutlets, pounded thin
2 tablespoons scallions,
   finely chopped
1½ teaspoons curry powder
½ cup water or wheat water

½ cup sour cream

In a heavy frying pan, heat butter and oil over medium heat. Stir in cumin, salt and pepper. Brown cutlets on both sides. Place in a covered casserole and keep warm in a 200-degree oven.

To the same frying pan, add scallions and sauté for 3 minutes. Stir in curry powder, water or wheat water and sour cream. Reduce heat and continue to stir until thoroughly combined.

Remove cutlets from oven and top with sauce before serving.

CURRIED CUTLET CUBES IN JELLY

Serves 6
Preparation Time: 30 minutes
Jelling Time: 2 to 4 hours
Intermediate

3 tablespoons oil	2 onions, chopped
3 cups cutlets, cut in 1-inch cubes	1 teaspoon curry powder
	pinch nutmeg
3 cups water or wheat water	pinch cloves
1 tablespoon liquid barley malt	¼ teaspoon salt
	pinch cayenne
½ cup dried apricots, chopped	⅛ teaspoon garlic powder
1 tablespoon agar powder	

In a heavy frying pan, heat oil over medium heat. Sauté cutlets until browned and place in a gelatin mold or soufflé dish.

In a saucepan, bring water to a gentle boil. Stir in malt, apricots and onions. Sprinkle all remaining ingredients, one at a time, into the boiling water. Continue to boil gently for 10 minutes until agar is completely dissolved. Skim foam from the top. Pour over cutlets and allow to stand for 4 hours or refrigerate for 2 hours until firm.

To remove from mold, set mold in hot water for 3 minutes, then place a serving plate over the mold and turn upside down. Gently lift the mold off jelled curry.

SPICED CUTLET FRICASSEE

Serves 4
Preparation Time: 15 minutes
Cooking Time: 20 minutes
Elementary

3 tablespoons oil
1 teaspoon cumin, ground
2 cups cutlets, cut in
   1-inch cubes
2 onions, sliced
2 garlic cloves, minced

⅛ teaspoon cayenne
¼ teaspoon allspice, ground
¼ teaspoon nutmeg, ground
¼ cup orange juice
1 teaspoon liquid barley malt
4 whole cloves

2 bay leaves

In a heavy frying pan, heat oil over medium heat. Stir in cumin. Sauté cutlet cubes until lightly browned. Add onions and garlic and sauté until transparent. If mixture sticks to pan, add 1 tablespoon water. Stir in remaining ingredients. Reduce heat to low and simmer, stirring occasionally, for 10 minutes. Remove cloves and bay leaves before serving.

CUTLET AND POTATO CASSEROLE

Serves 4 to 6
Preparation Time: 20 minutes
Cooking Time: 45 minutes
Intermediate

2 tablespoons water or
   wheat water
1 tablespoon oil
4 potatoes, sliced
2 tablespoons olive oil
1 teaspoon cumin, ground
2½ cups cutlets, cut in
   1-inch cubes
3 onions, chopped
1 green pepper, chopped

4 fresh tomatoes, chopped
3 tablespoons fresh parsley,
   chopped
2 teaspoons coriander, ground
½ teaspoon cloves, ground
2 bay leaves
2 garlic cloves, minced
3 tablespoons sour cream
   mixed with ½ cup water
   or wheat water

Place 2 tablespoons water or wheat water in a covered casserole. Rub oil on sliced potatoes and place them in casserole. Bake, covered, at 400 degrees for 30 minutes until soft.

In a heavy frying pan, heat olive oil over medium heat. Stir in cumin. Sauté cutlet cubes until lightly browned. Add onions and green pepper and sauté for 5 minutes. Add tomatoes and cook for 10 minutes until moisture evaporates. Remove from heat and stir in parsley, coriander and cloves.

Remove potatoes from oven. In another casserole dish, arrange potatoes and cutlet mixture in alternating layers, ending with a layer of cutlet mixture. Tuck bay leaves into casserole. Mix garlic into sour cream and water mixture and pour over the casserole. Cover and return to oven for 15 minutes until flavors are combined.

AFRICAN STEAK RECIPES

STEAK IN GREEN CHILI SAUCE

Serves 4 to 6
Preparation Time: 15 minutes
Cooking Time: 15 minutes
Elementary

2 green peppers, chopped	½ teaspoon salt
2 fresh hot green chilies, seeded and chopped	¼ teaspoon white pepper
	½ teaspoon cardamom, ground
2 garlic cloves, minced	¼ cup water or wheat water
2 teaspoons ginger root, finely chopped	¼ cup butter
	5 steaks, thinly sliced
1 teaspoon turmeric	1 green pepper, sliced

Purée chopped green peppers, chilies, garlic, ginger, turmeric, salt, white pepper, cardamom and water in an electric blender or food processor until smooth. Set aside.

In a frying pan, melt butter over medium heat. Fry steak slices until lightly browned. Add green pepper and sauté until darkened in color and still crisp.

Reduce heat to low and pour purée into pan with steak and pepper. Cook, stirring constantly, for a final 5 minutes.

CURRIED DRIED FRUIT WITH STEAKS

Serves 4 to 6
Preparation Time: 1 hour
Cooking Time: 20 minutes
Elementary

1 cup mixed dried fruit
½ cup pitted prunes
½ cup raisins
1½ cups boiling water
3 tablespoons oil
2½ cups steak, cut in
   1-inch cubes

2 onions, chopped
2 teaspoons curry powder
2 tablespoons lemon juice
1 teaspoon arrowroot starch
   mixed with 1 tablespoon
   water
¼ cup peanuts, chopped

2 bananas, sliced

Mix dried fruit, prunes and raisins in a bowl. Pour water over them and allow to stand for 1 hour.

In a heavy frying pan, heat oil over medium heat. Sauté steaks until lightly browned. Add onions and sauté until transparent. If mixture sticks to pan, add 1 tablespoon water. Stir in curry powder, soaked fruit with its water and lemon juice. Bring to a gentle boil and stir in starch and water mixture. Continue stirring until sauce thickens. Pour onto a serving platter. Sprinkle with nuts and surround with bananas.

STEAK WITH MUSTARD GREENS

Serves 6
Preparation Time: 15 minutes
Cooking Time: 15 minutes
Elementary

2 tablespoons oil
1 tablespoon butter
3 cups steak, cut in
   1-inch cubes
2 onions, chopped

2 green peppers, chopped
1 pound mustard greens,
   stemmed and chopped
⅛ teaspoon salt
¼ cup scallions, chopped

⅛ teaspoon black pepper

In a heavy frying pan, heat oil and butter over medium heat. Sauté steak cubes until lightly browned. Add onions and sauté until transparent. If mixture sticks to pan, add 1 tablespoon water. Stir in green peppers and mustard greens and cook for 3 minutes. Add salt, scallions and pepper just before serving.

AFRICAN GROUND GLUTEN DISHES

GLUTEN PATTIES FLAVORED WITH NUTMEG AND CORIANDER

Serves 4 to 6
Preparation Time: 15 minutes
Cooking Time: 15 minutes
Elementary

2½ cups ground gluten
 1 cup soft breadcrumbs
 ⅔ cup soy milk powder
 2 onions, chopped
 2 eggs
 ¼ teaspoon nutmeg, ground

 1 teaspoon coriander, ground
 pinch black pepper
 ¼ cup oil
 1 cup vegetable broth mixed
    with 1 tablespoon whole
    wheat pastry flour

In a bowl, mix ground gluten, breadcrumbs, soy milk powder, onions, eggs, nutmeg, coriander and pepper to form a stiff mixture. Moisten hands and form into patties. Set aside.

In a frying pan, heat oil over medium heat. Brown patties on both sides. Place in a covered casserole and keep warm in a 200-degree oven.

To the same frying pan, add broth and flour. Cook over medium heat, stirring occasionally, until gravy thickens.

Remove patties from oven and smother in gravy just before serving.

GREEN PEPPERS STUFFED WITH NUTMEG AND CORIANDER–FLAVORED GROUND GLUTEN

Preparation Time: 20 minutes
Cooking Time: 30 minutes
Elementary

2½ cups ground gluten
½ cup fine whole grain breadcrumbs
2 onions, chopped
¼ teaspoon nutmeg
2 eggs

1 teaspoon coriander, ground
3 tablespoons oil
6 green peppers, whole, with stems and seeds removed
1 sweet red pepper, finely chopped

In a mixing bowl, beat together gluten, breadcrumbs, onions, nutmeg, eggs and coriander. Rub oil over the outside of the peppers and spoon ground gluten stuffing into them. Stand upright in a baking dish with opening on top and sprinkle with chopped red peppers. Bake at 400 degrees for 30 minutes before serving.

BAKED GROUND GLUTEN WITH CUSTARD

Serves 4 to 6
Preparation Time: 35 minutes
Cooking Time: 30 minutes
Intermediate

1 slice whole grain bread
1 cup milk
2 tablespoons butter
2½ cups ground gluten
4 onions, chopped
2 teaspoons curry powder
1 tablespoon liquid barley malt

¼ teaspoon black pepper
¼ cup lemon juice
3 eggs
1 apple, unpeeled and grated
½ cup raisins
¼ cup almonds, chopped
4 bay leaves
2 teaspoons soy flour

Preheat oven to 300 degrees.
Break bread into small bits and place in a bowl. Pour milk over bread and soak for 15 minutes.

In a heavy frying pan, melt butter over medium heat. Sauté ground gluten for 5 minutes until lightly browned. Pour ground gluten into a separate bowl. Return frying pan to heat and sauté onions until transparent. Stir in curry, malt, pepper and lemon juice. Reduce heat and simmer for 5 minutes. Pour over ground gluten.

Squeeze bread dry and reserve milk. Mix bread, one egg, apple, raisins and almonds into ground gluten. Pour into an oiled soufflé dish or casserole. Smooth with a rubber spatula and insert bay leaves.

With a wire whisk, beat remaining two eggs, soy flour and reserved milk until frothy. Slowly pour the egg and milk mixture over the ground gluten. Place soufflé dish or casserole in a pan of hot water 1 inch deep and place in oven. Bake for 30 minutes at 350 degrees until top of custard is firm and golden.

CHAPTER FOURTEEN

Indian Cooking with Wheat "Meat"

Indian curries are not made with the simple addition of hot pepper to a vegetable or meat. Instead, a long list of spices, precisely combined, account for the special flavor of Indian food. Most essential are fresh ginger root, garlic, cumin, coriander, turmeric, cardamom, cinnamon, cloves, black mustard seeds, black pepper and cayenne. When these flavorings are properly combined and cooked, the taste of Indian food is much more than simply hot; it is a rare taste that affects the palate from the moment it touches the lips until after it is swallowed. The strong spices bring to wheat "meat" a flavor that is unique.

INDIAN CUTLET RECIPES

CUTLET CUBES WITH WHOLE SPICES

Serves 4 to 6
Preparation Time: 10 minutes
Cooking Time: 20 minutes
Elementary

8 tablespoons oil
1 stick cinnamon
20 whole black peppercorns
15 whole cloves

5 whole cardamom pods
2½ cups cutlets, cut in
    1-inch cubes
pinch cayenne

½ teaspoon salt

In a heavy frying pan over medium heat, heat oil. Add cinnamon stick, black peppercorns, cloves and whole cardamom pods. Fry spices while stirring for 5 minutes. Brown cutlet cubes in seasoned oil. Remove with a slotted spoon and toss with cayenne and salt before serving.

CUTLETS IN SPICED YOGURT SAUCE

Serves 4 to 6
Preparation Time: 15 minutes
Cooking Time: 20 minutes
Intermediate

1 tablespoon oil
1 onion, sliced
3 tablespoons butter
2 onions, chopped
5 garlic cloves, minced
1 tablespoon ginger root,
    minced
2 bay leaves
½ teaspoon cinnamon, ground

¼ teaspoon cloves, ground
⅛ teaspoon cayenne
1 tablespoon coriander,
    ground
1 tablespoon cumin, ground
2½ cups cutlets, cut in
    1-inch cubes
2 cups yogurt
1 teaspoon turmeric

½ teaspoon salt

In a frying pan, heat oil over medium heat. Sauté sliced onion until well browned. Remove with a slotted spoon and set aside.

In the same frying pan, melt butter and sauté chopped onions, garlic and ginger until lightly browned. Stir in bay leaves, cinnamon, cloves, cayenne, coriander and cumin. Fry cutlet cubes in spices until lightly browned. Reduce heat to low. Stir in yogurt, turmeric and salt. Simmer for 10 minutes before serving.

CUTLETS WITH ONIONS AND RAISINS

Serves 6 to 8
Preparation Time: 20 minutes
Cooking Time: 35 minutes
Elementary

3 tablespoons oil
3 cups cutlets, cut in
  1-inch cubes
5 tablespoons water or
  wheat water
10 onions, chopped
4 garlic cloves, minced
1 tablespoon ginger root,
  minced
¼ cup raisins soaked in
  ½ cup water
1 tablespoon coriander,
  ground

2 teaspoons cumin, ground
1 teaspoon turmeric
4 tablespoons yogurt
2 tablespoons tomato paste
  mixed with ½ cup water or
  wheat water
1 teaspoon salt
½ teaspoon cloves, ground
½ teaspoon nutmeg, ground
½ teaspoon cinnamon, ground
pinch cayenne
pinch black pepper

In a heavy frying pan, heat oil over medium heat. Fry cutlets until lightly browned. Remove with a slotted spoon and set aside.

Add water or wheat water to pan and sauté onions, garlic and ginger root until lightly browned. Stir in raisins in water, coriander, cumin and turmeric. Bring to a gentle boil. Reduce heat to low and stir in yogurt, tomato paste and water mixture, salt, cloves, nutmeg, cinnamon, cayenne and black pepper. Simmer for 10 minutes before serving.

CURRIED CUTLETS WITH ALMONDS, PECANS AND SOUR CREAM

Serves 4 to 6
Preparation Time: 20 minutes
Cooking Time: 20 minutes
Intermediate

3 tablespoons oil
3 cups cutlets, cut in 1-inch cubes
2 tablespoons butter
4 garlic cloves, minced
1 onion, chopped
1 tablespoon ginger root, minced
1 tablespoon coriander, ground
2 teaspoons cumin, ground
2 tablespoons tomato paste mixed with ⅓ cup water
¼ teaspoon mace, ground
¼ teaspoon nutmeg, ground
¼ teaspoon cinnamon
½ teaspoon cloves, ground
½ teaspoon salt
¼ teaspoon black pepper
¼ cup almond butter mixed with ½ cup water or wheat water (Almond butter is available at all health food and natural food stores and often in the "health food" sections of grocery stores.)
¼ cup almonds, chopped
¼ cup pecans, chopped
½ cup sour cream

In a heavy frying pan, heat oil over medium heat. Fry cutlets until lightly browned. Remove and set aside.

To same pan, add butter and melt. Sauté garlic, onion and ginger until lightly browned. Reduce heat to low. Stir in coriander and cumin. Cook while stirring for 1 minute, then add tomato paste and water, mace, nutmeg, cinnamon, cloves, salt, pepper, browned cutlet cubes, almond butter and water or wheat water, almonds, pecans and sour cream. Simmer, stirring constantly, for 10 minutes until all flavors are well combined and mixture is thoroughly heated.

CUTLETS WITH COCONUT AND ALMOND SAUCE

Serves 4 to 6
Preparation Time: 20 minutes
Cooking Time: 35 minutes
Intermediate

1 tablespoon cumin, ground
1 tablespoon coriander, ground
4 tablespoons unsweetened shredded coconut
⅓ cup almonds, chopped
½ cup water or wheat water
4 garlic cloves, minced
1 tablespoon ginger root, minced
½ teaspoon turmeric
¼ teaspoon nutmeg, ground
¼ teaspoon mace, ground
2 tomatoes, chopped
½ teaspoon salt
2 tablespoons oil
2 tablespoons butter
10 whole cloves
12 peppercorns
6 whole cardamom pods
3 cups cutlets, cut in 1-inch cubes
⅓ cup yogurt

Purée cumin, coriander, coconut, almonds, water or wheat water, garlic, ginger, turmeric, nutmeg, mace, tomatoes and salt in an electric blender or food processor until smooth. Set aside.

In a frying pan, heat oil and butter over medium heat. Stir in cloves, peppercorns and cardamom pods, frying until they darken. Fry cutlet cubes until lightly browned.

Pour purée in with cutlets and whole spices. Gradually add yogurt, stirring constantly. Simmer for 10 minutes before serving.

CUTLETS WITH VINEGAR AND MINT

Serves 4 to 6
Preparation Time: 20 minutes
Cooking Time: 20 minutes
Intermediate

2 tablespoons oil
2 tablespoons butter
3 cups cutlets, cut in 1-inch cubes
4 garlic cloves, finely chopped
4 teaspoons ginger root, minced
2 onions, chopped
1 teaspoon cumin, ground
1 teaspoon cloves, ground
½ teaspoon cinnamon, ground
½ teaspoon dry mustard
⅓ cup cider vinegar
½ teaspoon salt
1 cup water or wheat water
1 tablespoon dried mint
1 teaspoon arrowroot starch mixed with 1 tablespoon water

In a heavy frying pan, heat oil and butter over medium heat. Fry cutlet cubes until brown. Remove with a slotted spoon and set aside.

In same oil, sauté garlic, ginger and onions until lightly browned. Stir in cumin, cloves, cinnamon, dry mustard, vinegar and salt. Reduce heat to simmer. Add water and mint. Return cutlet cubes. Simmer for 10 minutes. Stir in starch and water mixture. Continue stirring for 5 minutes until mint-vinegar sauce thickens slightly before serving.

CUTLETS WITH SPINACH

Serves 6 to 8
Preparation Time: 20 minutes
Cooking Time: 20 minutes
Intermediate

⅔ cup water or wheat water
3 carrots, chopped
3 pounds fresh spinach,
   stemmed and chopped
2 tablespoons butter
3 onions, chopped
4 teaspoons ginger root,
   minced

4 garlic cloves, minced
3 tablespoons oil
1 teaspoon cumin, ground
½ teaspoon cinnamon, ground
½ teaspoon cardamom, ground
3 cups cutlets, cut in
   1-inch cubes
½ teaspoon salt

In a covered pan, heat water over medium heat. In it, cook carrots, covered, for 10 minutes. Add spinach and steam until tender but still brightly colored. Remove from heat and purée in an electric blender or food processor until smooth. Set aside.

In a heavy frying pan, heat butter over medium heat. Sauté onions, ginger and garlic until lightly browned. Add spinach purée and reduce heat to low. Simmer for 10 minutes while preparing cutlets.

In a separate frying pan, heat oil over medium heat. Stir in cumin, cinnamon and cardamom. Brown cutlets in seasoned oil. Spoon cutlets into spinach purée and add salt before serving.

INDIAN GROUND GLUTEN DISHES

SAMOSAS

Serves 10 to 12
Preparation Time: 1 hour
Cooking Time: 25 minutes
Advanced

DOUGH INGREDIENTS

2 cups whole wheat pastry
 flour
½ teaspoon salt

3 tablespoons oil
¾ cup water

STUFFING INGREDIENTS

3 tablespoons oil
1 cinnamon stick
4 whole cloves
4 black peppercorns
1 bay leaf
pinch cayenne
4 garlic cloves, minced
2 onions, chopped

4 teaspoons ginger root,
 minced
1 teaspoon cumin, ground
1 tablespoon coriander, ground
4 cups ground gluten
½ teaspoon salt
4 tablespoons chickpea or
 soy flour

1½ cups oil for deep-frying

DOUGH

With fingers, rub oil, salt and flour together. Slowly stir in water to form a stiff dough. Turn onto a floured board and knead for 10 minutes until smooth and elastic. Place in an oiled bowl and cover with a damp towel. Allow to stand for 30 minutes.

STUFFING

In a heavy frying pan, heat oil over medium heat. Add cinnamon stick, cloves, peppercorns, bay leaf and cayenne. Allow to cook until bay leaf browns. Add garlic, onions and ginger. Sauté until onions are transparent. Stir in cumin, coriander, ground gluten, salt and chickpea or soy flour. Continue stirring for 5 minutes and remove from heat.

ASSEMBLING

Divide dough into 30 balls. Roll balls out on a floured surface into 4-inch circles. Cut circles in half to form 60 half-moon shapes.

Place 1 tablespoon stuffing on half the pieces of pastry. Place other half moons of dough over filling. Dip finger in water and moisten edges of dough. Seal closed with the prongs of a fork.

COOKING

Heat oil for frying in a heavy frying pan until water sizzles when sprinkled into it. Deep-fry samosas in batches of 10 until golden brown. Remove and drain on paper towels. Continue to fry samosas until all are cooked. Samosas are best served immediately but can be reheated in a 250-degree oven if necessary.

CURRIED GROUND GLUTEN WITH PEAS

Serves 4 to 6
Preparation Time: 20 minutes
Cooking Time: 25 minutes
Elementary

3 tablespoons oil	2 tablespoons yogurt
2 onions, sliced	2 tablespoons tomato paste
1 onion, chopped	2 tablespoons water or
1 tablespoon ginger root,	wheat water
minced	3 cups ground gluten
4 garlic cloves, minced	¼ teaspoon mace, ground
¼ teaspoon cinnamon, ground	¼ teaspoon nutmeg, ground
⅛ teaspoon cloves, ground	½ teaspoon salt
1 tablespoon coriander, ground	pinch cayenne
1 tablespoon cumin, ground	1 cup fresh or frozen green
1 teaspoon turmeric	peas

In a heavy frying pan, heat oil over medium heat. Sauté sliced onions until browned. Remove from pan and set aside.

To the same pan, add chopped onion, ginger and garlic. Sauté until lightly browned. Reduce heat to low and stir in cinnamon, cloves, coriander, cumin and turmeric. Cook for 1 minute before adding yogurt, tomato paste and water or wheat water. Simmer while stirring for 2 minutes. Add ground gluten, mace, nutmeg, salt and cayenne.

If using fresh peas, steam them for 3 minutes before adding to curry. If using frozen peas, thaw and add directly. Simmer for 5 final minutes.

CURRIED STUFFED TOMATOES

Serves 4 to 6
Preparation Time: 45 minutes
Baking Time: 15 minutes
Intermediate

10 tomatoes
3½ cups curried ground gluten
(previous recipe)
2 tablespoons oil
½ teaspoon whole cumin seeds
½ teaspoon black mustard
seeds
1 onion, chopped
4 garlic cloves, minced
1 cup water or wheat water
2 oranges, in sections, with
membranes removed

1 teaspoon salt
½ teaspoon garam masala
(Garam masala is a common
curry spice available at
natural foods stores and
Indian specialty shops.)
¼ teaspoon cinnamon, ground
¼ teaspoon black pepper
pinch cayenne
1 tablespoon liquid barley
malt

With a small knife cut a 1-inch cap around the stem of the tomatoes. Pull out the caps gently and discard. Using a grapefruit knife, remove the seeds and pulp and reserve to use in sauce. Fill tomato shells with curried ground gluten and arrange in a shallow baking dish.

To make sauce, heat oil in a heavy frying pan over medium heat. Add cumin and mustard seeds. Cook for a few seconds until cumin seeds begin to darken. Stir in onion and garlic. Sauté until transparent.

Purée tomato pulp, water or wheat water and oranges in an electric blender or food processor until smooth. Stir purée into onion and spices. Add all remaining ingredients and simmer for 15 minutes.

Pour ¾ cup of sauce over stuffed tomatoes. Cover baking dish and bake at 400 degrees for 15 minutes. Spoon remaining sauce over tomatoes just before serving.

INDIAN GROUND GLUTEN BALLS

Serves 6 to 8
Preparation Time: 30 minutes
Cooking Time: 35 minutes
Intermediate

GLUTEN BALL INGREDIENTS

3 cups ground gluten	pinch cayenne
¼ teaspoon black pepper	2 garlic cloves, minced
2 teaspoons garam masala	1 teaspoon ginger root, minced
1 onion, minced	¼ teaspoon cardamom, ground
2 tablespoons lemon juice	1 cup soy milk powder
¼ teaspoon cinnamon, ground	½ cup vegetable oil, for frying

SAUCE INGREDIENTS

3 tablespoons oil	1 teaspoon turmeric
4 onions, chopped	10 tomatoes, peeled and
4 garlic cloves, minced	chopped
4 teaspoons ginger root, minced	1 tablespoon paprika
2 tablespoons coriander, ground	1 teaspoon garam masala
2 teaspoons cumin, ground	½ teaspoon salt
	¼ cup water or wheat water

GLUTEN BALLS

In a mixing bowl, combine all gluten ball ingredients, except oil for frying, to form a stiff mixture. If mixture is sticky, add more soy milk powder. With moistened hands, form into balls.

In a heavy frying pan, heat oil until water sizzles when sprinkled onto it. Add gluten balls and fry until golden and crisp. Remove from oil and drain on paper towels.

SAUCE

In another frying pan, heat oil over medium heat. Sauté onions, garlic and ginger until lightly browned. Stir in coriander, cumin and turmeric. Cook spices for 5 minutes. If mixture begins to stick to pan, add 1 tablespoon water.

Stir in tomatoes, paprika, garam masala, salt and water or wheat water. Reduce heat and simmer for 20 minutes. Add gluten balls and simmer a final 5 minutes before serving.

INDIAN POULTRY RECIPES

POULTRY WITH CURRIED POTATOES

Serves 4 to 6
Preparation Time: 20 minutes
Cooking Time: 35 minutes
Intermediate

2 cups water	½ teaspoon cardamom, ground
4 potatoes, diced	½ teaspoon black pepper
2 tablespoons oil	8 poultry pieces
2 tablespoons butter	1 teaspoon cumin, ground
1 onion, chopped	2 teaspoons coriander, ground
3 garlic cloves, minced	1 teaspoon turmeric
4 teaspoons ginger root, minced	½ teaspoon garam masala
½ teaspoon cinnamon, ground	½ teaspoon salt
	2 cups yogurt

In a covered pot, boil potatoes in water for 10 minutes until they can be pierced with a fork. Drain and set aside.

In a frying pan, heat oil and butter over medium heat. Sauté onions, garlic and ginger until lightly browned. Stir in cinnamon, cardamom and black pepper. Brown poultry pieces in the same pan. Remove poultry and set aside.

Add remaining spices and potatoes to pan, stirring so potatoes are completely covered. Fry for 15 minutes until soft and crusted. If potatoes begin to burn, add 1 tablespoon water. Stir in yogurt and return poultry pieces. Bring to a gentle boil before serving.

POULTRY PIECES WITH CURRIED TOMATO SAUCE

Serves 4 to 6
Preparation Time: 20 minutes
Cooking Time: 25 minutes
Elementary

2 tablespoons butter
2 onions, chopped
4 teaspoons ginger root, minced
½ teaspoon cinnamon, ground
½ teaspoon cloves, ground
1 teaspoon cardamom, ground

¼ teaspoon black pepper
2 tablespoons oil
8 poultry pieces
1 cup water or wheat water
4 tomatoes, chopped
2 tablespoons tomato paste
½ teaspoon salt

In a frying pan, melt butter over medium heat. Sauté onions and ginger until lightly browned. Stir in cinnamon, cloves, cardamom and black pepper. Add oil and brown poultry pieces.

Reduce heat to low and add water or wheat water, tomatoes, tomato paste and salt. Simmer for 15 minutes before serving.

POULTRY PIECES IN YOGURT SAUCE

Serves 4 to 6
Preparation Time: 15 minutes
Cooking Time: 20 minutes
Intermediate

2 tablespoons butter
4 onions, sliced
2 garlic cloves, minced
4 teaspoons ginger root, minced
2 tablespoons oil

8 to 10 poultry pieces
1 cup yogurt
½ cup water or wheat water
½ teaspoon salt
pinch cayenne

In a heavy frying pan, melt butter over medium heat. Sauté onions, garlic and ginger until lightly browned. Add oil and brown poultry pieces. Stir in yogurt, water or wheat water, salt and cayenne. Simmer for 10 minutes before serving.

CHAPTER FIFTEEN

Chinese Wheat "Meat" Food

Chinese food is often an effective way to serve wheat "meats." The sauces and abundance of vegetables are a wonderful way to incorporate small amounts of leftover wheat "meats" in an otherwise protein-deficient meal. Since Chinese food enjoys great popularity in the United States, many of the ingredients basic to Chinese cooking can be found in the supermarket. Pea pods, Chinese cabbage, bean sprouts, bamboo shoots, bean curd (tofu), water chestnuts and ginger root are all easily available. However, several particularly delicious recipes in this chapter may require a trip to a specialty shop or Chinese grocer for fermented black beans and dried mushrooms.

CHINESE CUTLET DISHES

EGG ROLLS

Serves 6 to 8
Preparation Time: 2 hours
Cooking Time: 20 minutes
Advanced

DOUGH INGREDIENTS

2 cups whole wheat pastry
flour

¼ teaspoon salt
¾ cup cold water

FILLING INGREDIENTS

4 cups fresh mung bean sprouts
3 tablespoons oil
2 cups cutlets, finely diced
1 tablespoon water or
wheat water

1 tablespoon tamari soy sauce
½ cup mushrooms, finely
chopped
4 cups celery, finely chopped
½ teaspoon salt

2 tablespoons arrowroot starch mixed with
2 tablespoons water

ASSEMBLING INGREDIENTS

1 egg, beaten

3 cups oil for frying

DOUGH

In a bowl, sift flour and salt together. Gradually add water to form a stiff dough. Turn onto a floured board and knead for 10 minutes until smooth and elastic. Set aside for 30 minutes in a bowl covered with a damp towel.

FILLING

Rinse bean sprouts, removing any husks that float to the surface. Drain and pat dry between paper towels. Set aside.

Heat a wok or frying pan for 30 seconds over high heat. Reduce heat to medium and add 1 tablespoon oil and swirl it around to coat pan. Stir-fry diced cutlets for 2 minutes. Next, add water or wheat water, soy sauce and mushrooms. Stir-fry for 2 minutes. Remove from wok and set aside.

Add remaining 2 tablespoons oil to wok and heat for 30 seconds. Add celery and stir-fry for 3 minutes. Add sprouts and salt. Fry for 2 minutes, mixing well.

Return cutlets to wok. Continue cooking, stirring constantly, until liquid begins to boil. Stir in starch and water mixture until liquid thickens and coats all ingredients with a glaze. Remove from heat and cool to room temperature while rolling dough.

ASSEMBLING

Roll dough on a lightly floured surface to no thicker than $\frac{1}{16}$ inch. Cut into 16 7-inch squares.

With moistened hands, shape ¼-cup portions of filling into cylinders that are 4 inches long and 1 inch in diameter. Place diagonally across squares of dough. Fold the lower corners over the filling. Then fold over the two side corners. Three corners will be overlapping and one will be free. Brush the free corner with beaten egg, then fold over the roll. Carefully roll the wrapper to seal. Place egg rolls on a plate. Cover with a towel, then with plastic wrap and refrigerate for 30 minutes before frying.

Heat a wok or heavy frying pan over medium-high heat for 1 minute. Add 3 cups oil and heat until water sizzles when sprinkled onto it. If oil begins to smoke, immediately reduce heat to medium.

Fry 5 egg rolls at a time for 3 minutes until golden and crisp. Remove with a slotted spoon and drain on paper towels. Continue cooking egg rolls in batches until they are all ready to serve.

Although egg rolls are best eaten immediately, they can be kept warm for 30 minutes in a 200-degree oven if necessary.

STUFFED CHINESE MUSHROOMS

Serves 4
Preparation Time: 30 minutes
Cooking Time: 20 minutes
Intermediate

2 cups boiling water
20 well-formed dried Chinese mushrooms or fresh mushrooms
1 tablespoon mari soy sauce
1 tablespoon water or wheat water
1 tablespoon rice syrup

2 teaspoons arrowroot starch
1 cup cutlets, ground coarsely
8 water chestnuts, finely chopped
20 small sprigs of parsley
1 tablespoon oil
2 tablespoons vegetable broth

If using dried mushrooms, pour boiling water over them and allow to stand for 15 minutes until mushrooms have swelled and are fleshy. Reserve ¼ cup of soaking water.

In a bowl, mix soy sauce, water or wheat water, rice syrup, 1 teaspoon starch, ground cutlets and water chestnuts.

Remove stems from dried mushrooms, being careful to leave caps intact. Sprinkle remaining teaspoon of starch on the inside of mushrooms. Fill each cap with stuffing. Press a small sprig of parsley on each stuffed mushroom.

To cook, set a heavy frying pan over medium-high heat for 30 seconds. Add oil and swirl to coat pan. Place mushrooms, stuffing side up, in frying pan. Pour ¼ cup water reserved from soaking mushrooms into pan and cover. Reduce heat and simmer for 15 minutes. Remove cover and add broth. Cook for 3 minutes longer. Arrange mushrooms on a serving platter and use as an hors d'oeuvre or as a luncheon dish.

CUTLET DUMPLINGS

Serves 8 to 10
Preparation Time: 1 hour
Cooking Time: 20 minutes
Advanced

DOUGH INGREDIENTS

2 cups whole wheat pastry flour

½ teaspoon salt
¾ cup water

FILLING INGREDIENTS

2½ cups cutlet, coarsely ground
1 teaspoon ginger root, minced
1 tablespoon soy sauce

¼ teaspoon salt
1 tablespoon sesame oil
3 cups Chinese cabbage (bok choy), finely chopped

3 tablespoons oil

¼ cup soy sauce mixed with
2 tablespoons vinegar

1 cup water or wheat water

¼ teaspoon salt

DOUGH

Sift flour and salt together. Gradually mix water into flour. Turn onto a floured board and knead for 5 minutes until smooth and elastic. Place in a bowl, cover and let stand for 30 minutes.

FILLING

In a bowl mix ground cutlet, ginger root, soy sauce, salt, sesame oil and Chinese cabbage until thoroughly combined. Set aside.

ASSEMBLING

Knead dough on a floured board for 3 minutes. Divide in half and shape into two long, thin cylinders, 12 inches long and 1 inch in diameter. Cut rolls of dough into ½-inch slices. Press each slice between your palms to ¼-inch thickness. Roll on a floured board into circles ⅛-inch thick. Place on a floured board and cover with a towel to keep them from drying out while stuffing dumplings.

Place 2 teaspoonfuls of filling in the center of each circle of dough. Fold dough over the filling to form a half-moon shape. Gather edges of dough together, pleating them neatly and pressing them together firmly to form a secure case. Place each finished dumpling on a floured board and cover with a towel.

To fry dumplings, heat a heavy frying pan over medium-high heat for 30 seconds. Pour 2 tablespoons oil into pan and swirl to coat evenly. Arrange dumplings side by side in the hot, oiled frying pan. Reduce heat and fry for 3 minutes until the bottoms of the dumplings are lightly browned. Add water or wheat water and salt, cover and simmer for 10 minutes until liquid is absorbed. Add remaining tablespoon oil and gently swirl pan, being careful not to disturb dumplings. Fry for 2 minutes. Remove from pan and serve on a platter with the browned sides up. Accompany with combined vinegar and soy sauce.

SPICED BEAN CURD AND CUTLET

Serves 4 to 6
Preparation Time: 20 minutes
Cooking Time: 15 minutes
Intermediate

2 cups cutlet, ground coarsely
1 tablespoon soy sauce
1 tablespoon water or
   wheat water
1 teaspoon rice syrup
3 tablespoons safflower oil
4 cakes bean curd (tofu), sliced
1 tablespoon Chinese prepared
   black beans mixed with
   2 tablespoons water

⅛ teaspoon cayenne
1 teaspoon ginger root, minced
¼ cup vegetable broth
¼ teaspoon salt
1 teaspoon arrowroot starch
   mixed with 2 teaspoons
   water
¼ teaspoon black pepper
2 teaspoons sesame oil

In a bowl, mix ground cutlet, soy sauce, water or wheat water and rice syrup until thoroughly combined.

Place all ingredients within easy reach of your stove. Set wok or heavy frying pan on a medium-high burner for 30 seconds. Pour oil in and swirl to coat pan evenly. Fry cutlet mixture, stirring constantly, for 2 minutes. Add bean curd, black bean and water mixture, cayenne, ginger, broth and salt. Bring to a gentle boil. Stir in starch and water. Continue stirring for 2 minutes until sauce is thick and clear. Add black pepper and sesame oil. Pour into a serving dish.

CUTLET AND EGG FRIED RICE

Serves 4
Preparation Time: 45 minutes
Cooking Time: 15 minutes
Elementary

3 cups water or wheat water
1½ cups brown rice
½ cup fresh peas
4 tablespoons safflower oil

2 eggs, lightly beaten
1 teaspoon salt
1 cup cutlet, diced into
   ¼-inch cubes

1 scallion, finely chopped

Bring water to a boil, add rice, cover and reduce heat to low. Simmer for 45 minutes until rice is tender.

Steam peas for 7 minutes until color has deepened to brilliant green. Set aside.

Place all ingredients within easy reach of the stove. Heat wok or frying pan on a medium-high burner for 30 seconds. Add 2 tablespoons oil and swirl to coat pan evenly. Pour in eggs. Immediately, an egg film will form on the bottom of the pan. Gently lift this film toward the far side of the pan. The uncooked egg will flow forward and set. Repeat this procedure until all the egg has set in thin layers. Remove, mash with a fork and set aside.

Add remaining 2 tablespoons oil and swirl. Pour in cooked rice and stir until grains are coated with oil. Add salt, peas, diced cutlet, scallion and fried egg. Stir-fry for 1 minute before serving.

NOODLES WITH CUTLET SAUCE

Serves 4
Preparation Time: 20 minutes
Cooking Time: 20 minutes
Elementary

1 cucumber, seeded and sliced	4 scallions, finely chopped
4 scallions, cut in 3-inch lengths and slivered	2 tablespoons rice wine
	1 teaspoon rice syrup
1 carrot, cut in 3-inch lengths and finely slivered	2 teaspoons miso
	1 cup water or wheat water
4 tablespoons oil	1½ quarts water
½ cup cutlet, ground coarsely	

1 pound whole grain Japanese or Chinese noodles

Arrange cucumber, scallions and carrot decoratively around the edge of a large, deep platter. Set aside.

Heat wok or heavy frying pan over medium-high heat for 30 seconds. Add 2 tablespoons oil and swirl to coat pan. Reduce heat to medium. Stir-fry cutlet for 3 minutes. Stir in chopped scallion.

In a bowl, combine rice wine, rice syrup, miso and water or wheat water. Pour into wok or frying pan. Reduce heat and simmer for 10 minutes while preparing noodles.

Bring 1½ quarts water to a boil. Add noodles and boil for 7 minutes until tender. Drain and toss with remaining 2 tablespoons oil. Pour into the center of serving platter and top with sauce.

LION'S HEAD

Serves 4 to 6
Preparation Time: 25 minutes
Cooking Time: 20 minutes
Intermediate

3 cups cutlet, ground coarsely
3 tablespoons soy sauce
1 scallion, finely chopped
1 teaspoon ginger root, minced
6 water chestnuts, finely chopped
1 egg, lightly beaten
5 tablespoons arrowroot starch

4 tablespoons safflower oil
1 tablespoon arrowroot starch mixed with 1 tablespoon water
2½ cups Chinese cabbage (bok choy), thinly sliced
1 teaspoon rice syrup
½ cup vegetable broth

Mix ground cutlet, 2 tablespoons soy sauce, scallion, ginger, water chestnuts, egg and arrowroot starch. If mixture is not firm, add an additional tablespoon of starch. With moistened hands, form into 1-inch balls.

In a heavy frying pan, heat 2 tablespoons oil over medium heat. Dip balls in starch and water solution then brown on all sides. Set aside.

To the same frying pan, add the remaining 2 tablespoons oil. Stir-fry cabbage for 2 minutes until coated with oil. In a small bowl, combine rice syrup and broth. Pour into cabbage. Add cutlet balls, reduce heat and simmer for a final 10 minutes before serving.

SWEET AND SOUR CUTLET CUBES

Serves 4 to 6
Preparation Time: 20 minutes
Cooking Time: 20 minutes
Intermediate

1 egg, lightly beaten
¼ cup arrowroot starch
¼ cup soy or chickpea flour
¼ cup water or wheat water
½ teaspoon salt
2½ cups cutlets, cut in
   1-inch cubes
3 cups safflower oil
2 garlic cloves, finely chopped
1 carrot, thinly sliced at an angle

2 green bell peppers, cut in
   ½-inch squares
¼ cup vegetable broth
6 tablespoons rice syrup
3 tablespoons cider vinegar
1 teaspoon soy sauce
1 teaspoon arrowroot starch
   mixed with 2 teaspoons
   water

In a large bowl, combine egg, starch, flour, water or wheat water and salt. Add cutlet cubes and toss until well coated.

In a wok or heavy frying pan, heat oil until water sizzles when sprinkled onto it. Fry half the coated cubes at a time until crisp and golden. Remove with a slotted spoon and place in a shallow baking dish. Keep warm in a 200-degree oven while preparing sauce.

Pour frying oil out of pan, leaving only a thin coating of oil. Return to heat. Stir-fry garlic and carrot for 2 minutes. Add peppers and stir for 1 minute until darkened in color and still crisp. Pour in broth, rice syrup, vinegar and soy sauce. Bring to a gentle boil. Stir in starch and water mixture. Continue stirring for 1 minute until sauce thickens. Remove from heat and pour over fried cutlets before serving.

CUTLETS WITH ONIONS

Serves 4
Preparation Time: 15 minutes
Cooking Time: 15 minutes
Elementary

3 tablespoons soy sauce
1 tablespoon rice syrup
1 tablespoon rice wine
4 cutlets, pounded thin

2 teaspoons whole wheat
   pastry flour
2 tablespoons safflower oil
3 onions, finely chopped

2 tablespoons cold water

In a bowl, mix 2 tablespoons soy sauce, rice syrup and wine until thoroughly combined. Brush on both sides of cutlets. Sprinkle lightly with flour.

Place cutlets and all other ingredients within easy reach of your stove. Heat wok or heavy frying pan over medium-high heat for 30 seconds. Add oil and swirl to coat pan evenly. If oil begins to smoke, reduce heat to medium. Fry 2 cutlets at a time until lightly browned on both sides. Set aside.

Stir-fry onion in same pan for 2 minutes until transparent. Return cutlets to pan. Add water and remaining tablespoon soy sauce. Cook for 2 minutes until cutlets are reheated. Arrange on a serving platter before serving.

SPARES WITH BLACK BEANS

Serves 4 to 6
Preparation Time: 5 minutes
Cooking Time: 1 hour
Elementary

4 cutlets, cut in strips
  1-inch wide
1 garlic clove, crushed
4 tablespoons sesame oil
3 teaspoons rice syrup
1 tablespoon safflower oil
1 garlic clove, minced

1 cup water or wheat water
1 tablespoon soy sauce
2 tablespoons Chinese prepared
  black beans
1 teaspoon arrowroot starch
  mixed with 2 teaspoons
  water

Arrange cutlet strips on an oiled baking sheet. In a small bowl, combine crushed garlic, sesame oil and 1 teaspoon rice syrup until thoroughly mixed. Brush cutlet strips with mixture. Bake at 375 degrees for 45 minutes, basting every 15 minutes with sesame oil mixture.

To make sauce, heat safflower oil in a wok or heavy frying pan over medium heat. Add minced garlic and sauté until lightly browned. Pour in water or wheat water, soy sauce, remaining 2 teaspoons rice syrup and black beans. Bring to a gentle boil. Stir in starch and water. Continue stirring until sauce thickens.

Place gluten "spares" on a serving plate and top with sauce.

CHINESE STEAK RECIPES

NOODLES WITH STEAK AND CHINESE CABBAGE

Serves 4
Preparation Time: 30 minutes
Cooking Time: 15 minutes
Intermediate

10 dried Chinese mushrooms	1 tablespoon soy sauce
1 cup boiling water	¼ teaspoon salt
2 quarts water	4 steaks, thinly sliced
¾ pound whole grain Chinese or Japanese noodles	½ cup vegetable broth
3 tablespoons oil	1 teaspoon arrowroot starch mixed with 2 teaspoons water
1½ cups Chinese cabbage, shredded	
½ cup bamboo shoots, sliced	2 scallions, cut in 2-inch lengths and slivered

In a bowl, cover mushrooms with boiling water. Let stand for 15 minutes until swollen and fleshy. Drain and discard water. Remove tough stems and slice caps. Set aside.

In a pot, bring 2 quarts water to a boil and add noodles. Boil for 7 minutes until tender. Drain and toss noodles with 1 tablespoon oil. Spread on a baking sheet. Bake at 375 degrees for 8 minutes. Turn noodles and bake for 8 more minutes until noodles are evenly toasted.

While noodles bake, prepare sauce. Heat a wok or heavy frying pan over medium-high heat for 30 seconds. Add remaining 2 tablespoons oil and swirl to coat pan evenly. Reduce heat to medium. Stir-fry cabbage, mushrooms and bamboo shoots for 2 minutes. Stir in soy sauce, salt and steak strips. Fry for 2 minutes. Pour in broth and bring to a gentle boil. Stir in starch and water for 1 minute until sauce thickens. Remove from heat.

Pour noodles into a serving bowl, top with sauce and garnish with scallions.

STEAK WITH CELLOPHANE NOODLES

Serves 4
Preparation Time: 15 minutes
Cooking Time: 15 minutes
Intermediate

2 cups safflower oil	4 steaks, thinly sliced
2 ounces cellophane noodles	1 green bell pepper, sliced
2 tablespoons soy sauce	2 tablespoons sesame oil
1 tablespoon arrowroot starch	1 teaspoon ginger root, minced
1 teaspoon rice syrup	1/8 teaspoon cayenne

Keep all ingredients within easy reach of stove. Heat wok or heavy frying pan over medium-high heat for 30 seconds. Add oil and heat until oil sizzles when water is sprinkled into it. If oil smokes, immediately reduce heat to medium. Fry noodles, in batches, for 1 second until they puff. Remove quickly with a slotted spoon and drain on paper towels. Pour oil out of pan, leaving only a thin film, and set pan aside.

In a bowl, mix soy sauce, starch and rice syrup. Add steak strips and toss until evenly coated.

Reheat wok or frying pan over medium-high heat. Stir-fry pepper for 1 minute and remove with a slotted spoon and set aside. Add sesame oil. Stir-fry coated steak strips for 1 minute. Return green pepper and stir in ginger root and cayenne.

Pour into the center of a serving platter and surround with noodles.

STEAK WITH BROCCOLI

Serves 4 to 6
Preparation Time: 15 minutes
Cooking Time: 15 minutes
Elementary

3 tablespoons safflower oil	1 1/2 cups broccoli flowerettes
4 steaks, thinly sliced	2 teaspoons soy sauce
1 teaspoon ginger root, minced	1/2 cup water or wheat water
1 garlic clove, minced	1 teaspoon arrowroot starch mixed with 2 teaspoons water
1 1/2 cups broccoli stems, peeled and sliced	

Heat wok or frying pan over medium-high heat for 30 seconds. Add oil and swirl to coat pan evenly. Reduce heat to medium. Stir-fry steak slices for 1 minute. Remove and set aside. Stir-fry ginger root and garlic for 2 minutes. Drop in broccoli stems and fry for 1 minute. Add flowerettes and fry for 1 minute. Pour in soy sauce and water. Return steak slices and bring to a gentle boil. Stir in starch and water. Continue stirring for 1 minute until sauce thickens.

FAMILY-STYLE BEAN CURD

Serves 4 to 6
Preparation Time: 30 minutes
Cooking Time: 30 minutes
Intermediate

20 dried Chinese mushrooms	3 teaspoons ginger root,
2 cups boiling water or	minced
wheat water	2 garlic cloves, finely chopped
3 cakes bean curd (tofu),	2 onions, each cut in
sliced	16 wedges
1 cup safflower oil	½ cup bamboo shoots
4 steaks, thinly sliced	15 water chestnuts, sliced

2 teaspoons arrowroot starch mixed with
4 teaspoons soy sauce

Cover dried mushrooms with boiling water or wheat water. Soak for 15 minutes until swollen and fleshy. Remove stems, slice and set aside. Reserve water.

Place bean curd slices between paper towels to remove excess moisture.

Heat a wok or heavy frying pan over medium-high heat for 30 seconds. Add oil and heat until water sizzles when sprinkled onto it. If oil begins to smoke, immediately reduce heat to medium. Fry bean curd, several slices at a time, until golden and crisp on both sides. Remove with a slotted spoon and drain on paper towels.

Pour oil out of pan, leaving a thin film. Return pan to heat. Stir-fry steak slices for 3 minutes. Add ginger and garlic and fry for 1 minute. Stir in onions and fry until transparent. Add bamboo shoots, water chestnuts and mushrooms and fry for 2 minutes. Pour in reserved mushroom water and bring to a gentle boil. Stir in starch and soy sauce mixture and fried bean curd and stir gently and continually for 3 minutes until sauce thickens.

TOMATO STEAK CHOW MEIN

Serves 4 to 6
Preparation Time: 15 minutes
Cooking Time: 20 minutes
Intermediate

2 tablespoons safflower oil
1 teaspoon ginger root, minced
1 garlic clove, minced
3 onions, each cut in 16 wedges
4 steaks, thinly sliced
8 tomatoes, each cut in
  8 wedges

1 cup water or wheat water
2 teaspoons arrowroot starch
  mixed with 2 teaspoons water
2 quarts water
1 pound Chinese or Japanese
  whole grain noodles

Heat wok or heavy frying pan over medium-high heat for 30 seconds. Add oil and swirl to coat pan evenly. If oil begins to smoke, reduce heat to medium. Stir-fry ginger root and garlic for 1 minute. Add onions and fry until transparent. Stir-fry steak slices for 1 minute. Add tomatoes and fry for 2 minutes. Add water or wheat water and bring to a gentle boil. Stir in starch and water. Continue stirring for 2 minutes until sauce thickens, then reduce heat to low. Simmer while preparing noodles.

In a pot, bring 2 quarts water to a boil. Add noodles and boil for 7 minutes until tender. Drain noodles and pour into a serving platter. Pour sauce over noodles just before serving.

CHAPTER SIXTEEN

Japanese Wheat "Meat" Cooking

A delicate sense of art and beauty permeates the Japanese style of cooking and serving a meal. Food is prepared with attention to shape, design and taste. The meal is served with simplicity and grace. Foods are presented in bowls, beautifully garnished, with sauces for dipping served alongside. There is a sense of calm in a well-prepared and -presented Japanese meal. We have tried to convey this unique appreciation for beauty characteristic of Japanese cuisine in the wheat "meat" recipes in this final chapter.

Preparing Japanese dishes requires some specialty foods that, although not available at a supermarket, can readily be found in most health food stores. Tofu (soybean curd), miso (fermented soybean paste), tamari soy sauce, fresh ginger root, rice vinegar, sesame seeds, rice syrup and sesame oil are the traditional Japanese foods required in these wheat "meat" recipes. In addition, rice wine (sake) is occasionally used in Japanese cooking. However, if unavailable, a dry white wine may be substituted. For those who do not wish to use wine, water is the next best alternative. Finally, to appreciate the full effect of Japanese eating, chopsticks are highly recommended.

JAPANESE CUTLET RECIPES

CUTLETS WITH GRATED RADISH

Serves 4
Preparation Time: 15 minutes
Cooking Time: 15 minutes
Elementary

2 tablespoons sesame oil
1 teaspoon cumin, ground
4 cutlets, cut in 1-inch cubes
¼ cup rice wine

⅓ cup tamari soy sauce
⅓ cup water or wheat water
½ teaspoon ginger root,
    finely grated
2 cups white radish (daikon), grated

In a heavy frying pan, heat oil over medium heat. Stir in cumin. Sauté cutlet cubes until browned. Add rice wine, soy sauce, water or wheat water and ginger. Reduce heat and simmer for 5 minutes.

Place ½ cup grated radish on individual plates. Remove cutlet cubes from broth with a slotted spoon and arrange on beds of radish. Serve broth in small dishes as a dipping sauce for cutlet cubes.

CUSTARD, CLEAR SAUCE AND CUTLET BITS

Serves 4
Preparation Time: 15 minutes
Cooking Time: 30 minutes
Intermediate

4 eggs
½ cup vegetable broth
1 tablespoon soy flour
½ cup water or wheat water
1 teaspoon tamari soy sauce
1 teaspoon rice syrup

½ teaspoon arrowroot starch
    mixed with 1 teaspoon water
½ cup fresh peas
1 tablespoon oil
1 cutlet, cut in ⅛-inch cubes
¼ cup chives, finely chopped

In a bowl, beat together eggs, broth and soy flour. Pour into 4 oiled custard cups. Place cups in a pan of water 1 inch deep and bake for 30 minutes at 350 degrees until firm.

In a saucepan, bring water or wheat water, soy sauce and rice syrup to a gentle boil. Stir in starch and water mixture. Continue stirring until sauce thickens slightly.

In a frying pan, heat oil over medium heat. Add cutlet cubes and fry until lightly browned.

Steam peas for 5 minutes until darkened in color.

To serve, top custard with cutlet and green peas, fill each cup with clear sauce and garnish with chives. This dish can be served hot or can be chilled and served cold.

CUTLETS AND WHITE RADISH WITH ORANGE SAUCE

Serves 4 to 6
Preparation Time: 15 minutes
Cooking Time: 15 minutes
Elementary

⅔ cup tamari soy sauce	2 tablespoons oil
⅓ cup rice wine or water	4 cutlets, cut in 1-inch cubes
1 cup fresh orange juice	1½ cups white radish (daikon),
2 teaspoons ginger root, finely grated	sliced

In a saucepan, mix soy sauce, rice wine or water, orange juice and ginger. Simmer for 5 minutes and set aside.

In a heavy frying pan, heat oil over medium heat. Fry cutlet cubes until lightly browned. Add radish and sauté for 1 minute.

Place sautéed cutlet cubes and radish in individual bowls and top with orange sauce.

MIXED CURRIED VEGETABLES WITH CUTLETS

Serves 4 to 6
Preparation Time: 20 minutes
Cooking Time: 25 minutes
Elementary

1 tablespoon oil
3 cutlets, 1 inch thick and thinly sliced
3 onions, sliced
1 garlic clove, minced
1 teaspoon ginger root, minced
2 teaspoons curry powder
3 teaspoons butter
1 cup water or wheat water

1 eggplant, diced
2 carrots, thinly sliced at an angle
1 tomato, chopped
1 green pepper, chopped
2 teaspoons tamari soy sauce
1 teaspoon arrowroot starch mixed with 2 teaspoons water

In a heavy frying pan, heat oil over medium high heat. Sauté sliced cutlets until lightly browned. Add onions, garlic and ginger and sauté for 1 minute. Sprinkle with curry powder. Add butter, melt, then stir in water or wheat water, eggplant and carrot. Reduce heat and simmer for 10 minutes. Stir in tomato, pepper and soy sauce. Simmer for 2 minutes. Stir in starch and water mixture. Continue stirring until sauce thickens before serving.

POTATO SHREDS SAUTÉED WITH CUTLETS AND GREEN PEPPER

Serves 4 to 6
Preparation Time: 15 minutes
Cooking Time: 20 minutes
Elementary

¼ cup sesame oil
4 potatoes, cut in fine shoestrings
4 green peppers, sliced

4 cutlets, 1 inch thick, finely sliced
½ teaspoon salt
¼ teaspoon black pepper

In a heavy frying pan, heat oil until water sizzles when sprinkled onto it. Fry potatoes, stirring constantly, for 5 minutes. Add cutlet strips and sauté until lightly browned. Sauté green peppers for 1 minute until color deepens. Season with salt and pepper before serving.

CUTLET AND CUCUMBER SALAD WITH MUSTARD DRESSING

Serves 4 to 6
Preparation Time: 10 minutes
Cooking Time: 10 minutes
Elementary

3 tablespoons oil
4 cutlets, 1 inch thick
2 cucumbers, sliced
2 raw egg yolks

¼ cup rice vinegar
1 teaspoon powdered mustard
2 tablespoons rice syrup
2 tablespoons carrot, grated

In a heavy frying pan, heat oil over medium heat. Fry cutlets on both sides until browned. Remove from heat and cut into thin slices. Place in a salad bowl, cool and toss with cucumbers.

In a small bowl, mix egg yolks, rice vinegar, mustard and rice syrup until thoroughly combined. Pour dressing over cutlets and cucumbers and toss well. Garnish with carrot before serving.

CUTLETS WITH BELL PEPPERS AND MUSHROOMS

Serves 4 to 6
Preparation Time: 20 minutes
Cooking Time: 20 minutes
Elementary

2 tablespoons scallions, minced
1 garlic clove, minced
1 teaspoon ginger root, minced
¼ cup tamari soy sauce
1 tablespoon lemon peel, grated
2 tablespoons rice syrup

¼ cup rice wine or water
1 tablespoon lemon juice
⅛ teaspoon cayenne
3 tablespoons oil
4 cutlets, cut in 1-inch strips
1 cup mushrooms, sliced
5 bell peppers, sliced

In a bowl, mix scallions, garlic, ginger, soy sauce, lemon peel, rice syrup, rice wine or water, lemon juice and cayenne until thoroughly combined.

In a heavy frying pan, heat oil over medium heat. Brown cutlet strips. Add mushrooms and fry for 5 minutes until darkened. Stir in peppers and fry for 2 minutes. Add prepared sauce and toss until vegetables and cutlets are well coated.

JAPANESE POULTRY DISHES

STEAMED PUMPKIN WITH GROUND POULTRY

Serves 4
Preparation Time: 15 minutes
Cooking Time: 30 minutes
Elementary

4 cups water or wheat water
½ cup rice syrup
4 tablespoons tamari soy sauce
3 cups pumpkin, peeled and
   cut into 1-inch cubes

1 tablespoon rice wine
1 cup poultry pieces, ground
1 teaspoon arrowroot starch
   mixed with 2 teaspoons
   water

In a large pot, bring 3 cups water or wheat water, ¼ cup rice syrup and 2 tablespoons soy sauce to a gentle boil. Add pumpkin, cover, reduce heat and simmer for 30 minutes until soft.

In a saucepan, combine remaining cup water or wheat water, 2 tablespoons soy sauce, ¼ cup rice syrup, wine and ground poultry. Simmer for 5 minutes. Stir in starch and water mixture. Continue stirring for 3 minutes until sauce thickens.

Drain pumpkin and spoon into individual bowls. Top with sauce before serving.

STEAMED POULTRY BALLS

Serves 4 to 6
Preparation Time: 15 minutes
Cooking Time: 90 minutes
Intermediate

1¼ cups water or wheat water
½ cup brown rice
2 cups poultry pieces, ground
2 onions, minced

1 cup mushrooms, finely
   chopped
3 tablespoons arrowroot starch
1 garlic clove, crushed

⅓ cup tamari soy sauce mixed with
3 tablespoons water

In a pot, boil water or wheat water. Add rice, cover, reduce heat and simmer for 1 hour until rice is mushy.

Combine cooked rice, ground poultry, onions, mushrooms and arrowroot starch. With moistened hands, shape into balls. Steam for 20 minutes in a steamer until firm.

Mix garlic with soy sauce and water mixture. Place balls on individual dishes and spoon sauce over them.

BUCKWHEAT NOODLES WITH POULTRY AND WALNUTS

Serves 4 to 6
Preparation Time: 15 minutes
Cooking Time: 25 minutes
Intermediate

2 quarts water	8 poultry pieces, thinly sliced
1 pound Japanese buckwheat noodles (soba)	2 cups water or wheat water
	6 tablespoons tamari soy sauce
8 teaspoons fresh ginger root, grated	3 tablespoons rice syrup
	3 tablespoons sesame oil
4 tablespoons rice wine or water	pinch salt
	1 cup scallions, chopped
1 tablespoon arrowroot starch	⅔ cup walnuts, chopped

¼ cup carrot, slivered

In a pot, boil water. Add noodles and boil for 7 minutes until tender. Drain and rinse. Set aside.

Squeeze ginger with a garlic press to extract ginger juice. Continue until 2 teaspoons juice is obtained. If ginger root is dry, more than 8 teaspoons may be needed to yield 2 teaspoons juice.

In a bowl, combine ginger juice, rice wine or water, and arrowroot starch. Add poultry and toss until well coated. Set aside.

In a saucepan, combine water or wheat water, soy sauce, rice syrup, 2 tablespoons oil and salt. Bring to a gentle boil. Reduce heat and add noodles. Simmer for 5 minutes.

In a heavy frying pan, heat remaining tablespoon oil over medium heat. Sauté coated poultry slices and scallions for 3 minutes.

To serve, place noodles with broth in individual bowls, sprinkle with chopped walnuts, top with fried poultry, scallions and raw slivered carrots.

POULTRY PIECES WITH BAMBOO SHOOTS

Serves 4 to 6
Preparation Time: 15 minutes
Cooking Time: 25 minutes
Intermediate

4 teaspoons ginger root, grated
8 poultry pieces
3 egg whites, beaten until frothy
2 tablespoons arrowroot starch

½ cup oil
1½ cups mushrooms, sliced
1½ cups bamboo shoots, slivered
1 cup water or wheat water

1 teaspoon tamari soy sauce mixed with
1 teaspoon arrowroot starch

Press grated ginger with a garlic press to extract juice. Extract 1 teaspoon ginger juice. If root is dry, it may require more than 4 teaspoons grated ginger to yield 1 teaspoon juice.

Place poultry pieces in a bowl. Pour juice over them and toss to coat evenly. Dip pieces in frothy egg whites and sprinkle lightly with arrowroot starch.

In a heavy frying pan, heat oil until water sizzles when sprinkled onto it. Fry poultry until golden. Drain on paper towels.

Pour off oil, leaving only a thin film in pan, and return pan to heat. Sauté mushrooms for 5 minutes until darkened and decreased in size. Stir in bamboo shoots and water. Bring to a gentle boil. Stir in soy sauce and starch. Continue stirring until sauce thickens. Stir in fried poultry just before serving.

POULTRY WITH ORANGE-FLAVORED SOY SAUCE

Serves 4 to 6
Preparation Time: 15 minutes
Cooking Time: 20 minutes
Elementary

¼ cup white radish, grated
¾ cup fresh orange juice
¾ cup tamari soy sauce
 3 cups water or wheat water
 1 tablespoon nutritional yeast
½ teaspoon salt
¼ teaspoon sage
¼ teaspoon thyme
¼ teaspoon tarragon
¼ teaspoon rosemary

½ teaspoon turmeric
 2 tablespoons oil
 3 cups poultry pieces, cut in
    1-inch cubes
 1 cup white radish (daikon),
    sliced
 2 cups Chinese cabbage (bok
    choy), sliced
 1 cup mushrooms, sliced
¼ cup scallions, finely chopped

In a bowl, mix grated radish, orange juice and soy sauce until thoroughly combined. Set sauce aside.

In a saucepan, combine water or wheat water, nutritional yeast, salt and herbs. Bring to a gentle boil. Reduce heat and simmer.

In a heavy frying pan, heat oil over medium heat. Brown poultry. Stir in sliced radish, Chinese cabbage and mushrooms. Add hot water and herb stock and simmer for 5 minutes.

Pour into a large serving bowl and sprinkle with scallions. Serve orange-flavored soy sauce in small individual plates. Poultry and vegetables are dipped in sauce just before eating.

JAPANESE SEAWHEAT RECIPES

SEAWHEAT IN SOY AND GINGER SAUCE

Serves 2 to 4
Preparation Time: 5 minutes
Marinating Time: 6 to 8 hours
Elementary

1½ cups water or wheat water
 3 tablespoons tamari soy
    sauce

2 teaspoons ginger root, finely
   grated
1½ cups seawheat

In a bowl, mix water, soy sauce and ginger. Add seawheat and toss. Marinate for 6 to 8 hours or overnight. Serve cold or heat for 5 minutes before serving.

SEAWHEAT, CUCUMBER, ASPARAGUS AND RADISH IN ICE WATER

Serves 4
Preparation Time: 20 minutes
Elementary

2 cups asparagus tips
2 cups seawheat
1 cucumber, sliced
1 white radish (daikon), sliced
2 cups ice water

10 ice cubes
1 cup rice vinegar
⅓ cup tamari soy sauce
1 tablespoon ginger root, finely grated

Steam asparagus tips for 5 minutes until they have darkened in color and are still crisp. Place asparagus tips, seawheat, cucumber, radish, ice water and ice cubes in a large bowl.

In a small bowl, mix vinegar, soy sauce and ginger. Pour sauce into small individual bowls. Traditionally, seawheat and vegetables are removed from large bowl with chopsticks and dipped in sauce before eating.

SEAWHEAT WITH BEAN CURD AND VEGETABLES IN CASSEROLES

Serves 4
Preparation Time: 20 minutes
Baking Time: 15 minutes
Intermediate

1 cake bean curd (tofu), cut in 1-inch cubes
1 cup yellow miso
1 teaspoon ginger root, finely grated
16 pieces seawheat

1 cup mushrooms, sliced
2 cups Chinese cabbage, thinly sliced
4 cups water or wheat water
4 tablespoons scallions, finely chopped

Broil tofu cubes until tops are browned. With fingers, coat the inside of small individual casserole dishes with miso. Sprinkle with ginger. Arrange broiled tofu, seawheat, mushrooms and Chinese cabbage in each dish. Pour a cup of water or wheat water in each dish. Bake at 325 degrees for 15 minutes until cabbage is cooked but still crisp. Sprinkle with chopped scallions before serving.

SEAWHEAT WITH VINEGARED MISO

Serves 4 to 6
Preparation Time: 15 minutes
Cooking Time: 10 minutes
Elementary

3 teaspoons dry mustard
¼ cup water or wheat water
3 tablespoons miso
⅓ cup rice vinegar

¼ cup tahini
2 cups seawheat
4 tablespoons scallions, finely chopped

In a bowl, mix mustard, water, miso, vinegar and tahini until smooth. If a thinner sauce is desired, add 2 additional tablespoons water.

Place seawheat in individual bowls, top with sauce and garnish with scallions.

DRIED MUSHROOM, SESAME AND SEAWHEAT SALAD

Serves 4 to 6
Preparation Time: 30 minutes
Intermediate

10 dried mushrooms
1½ cups boiling water
2½ tablespoons tamari soy sauce
3 tablespoons rice syrup

¼ cup sesame seeds, toasted and chopped
3 tablespoons water
3 tablespoons rice vinegar
1½ cups seawheat, diced

¼ cup white radish (daikon), grated

Soak dried mushrooms in boiling water until swollen and fleshy. Drain, slice and place in a saucepan with 1 tablespoon soy sauce and 1½ tablespoons rice syrup. Cover and cook over medium heat for 10 minutes until liquid evaporates. Set aside to cool.

In a large bowl, mix remaining 1½ tablespoons soy sauce and 1½ tablespoons rice syrup, sesame seeds, water and vinegar until thoroughly combined. Add mushrooms and seawheat and toss well. Place on individual serving plates and top with grated radish before serving.

BIBLIOGRAPHY

Airola, Paavo. *Are You Confused?* Phoenix: Health Plus Publications, 1972.

Airola, Paavo. *How to Get Well*. Phoenix: Health Plus Publications, 1975.

Ballentine, Rudolph. *Diet and Nutrition*. Honesdale, Pa.: Himalayan International Institute, 1978.

Hur, Robin. "Vegetarianism for a World of Plenty." *Moneysworth*, March, 1979, pp. 18–19.

Lappe, Frances Moore. *Diet for a Small Planet*. New York: Ballantine Books, 1975.

Null, Gary. *Protein for Vegetarians*. New York: Jove, 1974.

Null, Gary and Steve Null. *The New Vegetarian*. New York: William Morrow and Company, Inc., 1978.

Nutrition Research, Inc. *Nutrition Almanac*. New York: McGraw-Hill, 1979.

Reuben, David. *Everything You Always Wanted to Know About Nutrition*. New York: Simon and Schuster, 1978.

Sussman, Vic. *A Vegetarian Alternative*. Emmaus, Pa.: Rodale Press, 1978.

INDEX

African recipes, 186–194
Aging, premature, 8–9
All-American recipes, 29–78
Amines, 8
Amino acids, 12
Ammonia, 7
Amyloid, 8
Antibiotics, 9
Apple and cutlet pie, 109
Arteriosclerosis, 7, 10, 13
Austrian recipes, 159–172
Avola, Paovo, 8

Bamboo shoots and poultry pieces, 228
Barbecue recipes:
  cutlet, 71–73
  ground gluten, 77–78
Barley malt, liquid, 16
Bean curd:
  family-style, 219
  spiced, and cutlet, 212
Bean flour, 13
Beans:
  black, cutlet spares with, 216
  black, steak in tomato sauce with, 96
  kidney, with cutlets, 177
  lysine content, 13
  white, casserole with cutlets and spiced links, 130

Beef:
  calorie content, 3, 14
  cost of, 14
  fat content, 7
  protein content, 12
  saturated fat content, 13
Bircher, Ralph, 8
Blood pressure, high, 7, 13
Bread, whole wheat submarine, 51
Breast milk, DDT in, 10
British recipes, 108–119
Broccoli, with steak, 218
Buckwheat:
  cakes with spiced bits, cholesterol-free, 69
  pancakes with spiced bits, 67
Buns, whole wheat burger, 50
Burgers, 52
  casalinga, 149
  grilled, 77
  Italian outdoor, 78

Cabbage:
  cutlets with, 125
  stuffed with ground gluten, 48
Cakes:
  buckwheat, with spiced links, cholesterol-free, 69
  corn, with spiced bits, cholesterol-free, 70
  poppy seed, with spiced links, 69

Calories, 3, 13, 14
Cancer, 7, 8, 10
Cardiovascular disease, 7, 13
Casseroles:
  cutlet and potato, 189
  seawheat, with bean curd and vegetables, 230
  seawheat, scalloped, 63
  white bean, with cutlets and spiced links, 130
Cattle raising, 4–5, 6, 9–10
Cereal, 26
Cheese, stuffed, 85
Chemical residues in meat, 9–10
Chickpea:
  flour, 29
  stew, 136
Chili, hot, 92
Chili peppers stuffed with whipped cream and nut sauce, 103
Chinese recipes, 207–220
Cholesterol, 3, 13
Chow mein, tomato steak, 220
Chowder:
  Manhattan, 36
  New England, 37
  rice and spiced link, 35
Clams. See Seawheat
Coconut, steaks in, 97
Coloring agents, 8
Corn:
  cakes, with spiced bits, cholesterol-free, 70
  pie with ground gluten, raisins and olives, 101
Corn meal stew, 145
Cornell University, 7
Crackers, gluten-free, 24–26
Creole fried poultry, 61
Cucumber and cutlet salad, with mustard dressing, 225
Cutlets:
  African recipes, 187–190
  American recipes, 38–40
  and apple pie, 109
  Austrian recipes, 160–166, 168
  barbecued, with orange dip, 72
  with bell peppers and mushrooms, 225
  braised, with carrot-currant sauce and parsley, 126
  braised, with paprika and caraway, 165
  British recipes, 109–111
  with cabbage, 125
  casserole with white beans and spiced links, 130
  Castilian-style barbecue, 71
  with cheese, 38
  Chinese mushrooms stuffed with, 209
  Chinese recipes, 208–216
  chopped, with spiced gravy, 187
  chops with herbs, 39
  with coconut and almond sauce, 198
  with cream and mustard sauce, 124
  cream of tomato soup with, 30
  cubes with whole spices, 196
  and cucumber salad, with mustard dressing, 225
  curried, 187
  curried, in jelly, 188
  curried vegetables with, 224
  curried with almonds, pecans, and sour cream, 198
  custard, clear sauce and, 222
  in dill and paprika sauce, 160
  dumplings, 210
  and egg fried rice, 212
  in egg rolls, 208
  eggplant purée with, 176
  French recipes, 121–127
  Greek recipes, 174–177
  with green peppers, 176
  Indian recipes, 196–200
  Italian recipes, 143–144
  Japanese recipes, 222–225
  in kettle goulash, 161
  with kidney beans, 177
  Lancashire hot pot, 110
  in layered sauerkraut, 170
  lemon loaf, 40
  Lion's Head, 214
  marinated, 160
  in marjoram sauce, 162
  Mexican recipes, 81–82
  with mint sauce, 109
  with mushrooms, 164

with onions, 215
with onions and raisins, 197
in orange sauce, 132
with paprika, 163
parmigiana, 143
with peanut sauce, 80
in pecan sauce, 80
pie, with feta cheese, 174
pilaf, 175
and potato casserole, 189
preparation of, from raw gluten, 18–19
with prunes and cream sauce, 125
with radish, 222
sauce, noodles with, 213
sautéed with potato shreds and green pepper, 224
scaloppine gypsy style, 140
scaloppine with Italian spices, 144
scaloppine with zucchini, 132
in sherry sauce, 133
skewered, with curry-lemon sauce, 72
soup, cream of, 31
in sour cream, 165
Spanish grilled, 71
Spanish recipes, 132–134, 140
spares with black beans, 216
and spiced bean curd, 212
spiced fricassee, 189
with spiced links and pickles, 168
in spiced yogurt sauce, 196
with spinach, 200
and steak pie, 118
stew with cream sauce, old-fashioned, 122
stew with fruit, 81
stew with spring vegetables, 121
stew with tomatoes and mushrooms, 123
stuffed, 38
sweet and sour cubes, 214
tacos, 82
with vinegar and mint, 199
and white radish, with orange sauce, 223
Wiener Schnitzel, 163

Dairy products, 13
DDT, insecticide, 10

Defoliation, 4
DES, hormone, 10
Diabetes, 10
Diet for a Small Planet (Lappe), 5
Dumplings:
    cutlet, 210
    steak, filled, with tomato sauce, 98

Ecology, 4
Egg rolls, 208
Eggplant:
    and ground gluten sauce for spaghetti, 147
    Moussaka, 181
    purée with cutlets, 176
    with spiced links, 152
    stuffed with ground gluten, 180
Eggs:
    cholesterol content, 13
    lysine in, 12, 13
    poached, with spiced link hash, 64
Empanaditas, 88
Enchiladas:
    fried, 89
    red, 94

Fats, saturated, 7, 13
Fertilizers, 9
Food and Drug Administration (FDA), 8, 9
Food poisoning, 9
Food processor, 16
French recipes, 120–130
Fruit, dried, curried with steaks, 191
Fuel conservation, 5–6

Ginger root, 221
Gluten, 3, 14, 16
    preparation of, 17–18
    wheat "meats" made from, 17–18
Gluten flour, 12
Ground gluten:
    African recipes, 192–194
    American recipes, 46–53
    with apples, olives and almonds, 102
    Austrian recipes, 169–172
    baked, with custard, 193
    balls, Indian, 204
    balls in yogurt, 180

Ground gluten (*Cont.*)
  balls with lemon and egg sauce, 179
  brown loaf, 47
  brown loaf with cream, 47
  burger casalinga, 149
  burgers, 52
  burgers, grilled, 77
  burgers, Italian outdoors, 78
  cabbage stuffed with, 48
  cheese stuffed with, 85
  chili, hot, 92
  corn pie, with raisins and olives, 101
  in curried, stuffed tomatoes, 203
  curried, with peas, 202
  eggplant Moussaka, 181
  and eggplant sauce, for spaghetti, 147
  eggplant stuffed with, 180
  Empanaditas, 88
  Enchiladas, fried, 89
  Greek recipes, 178–182
  green peppers stuffed with, with nutmeg and coriander, 193
  Indian recipes, 201–205
  Italian recipes, 146–150
  lasagne, baked, 154
  Latin American recipes, 101–104
  lysine content, 13
  manicotti, 157
  meat ball submarines, 51
  meat balls and sauce, Italian, 150
  Mexican hash, 85
  Mexican recipes, 85–93
  patties with nutmeg and coriander, 192
  pie, mashed potatoes 'n' hash, 49
  potato Moussaka, 178
  preparation of, from raw gluten, 20–21
  ravioli, 155
  Samosas, 201
  sauce on pasta shells, 146
  Sloppy Joes on whole wheat buns, 50
  in steak roulades, 169
  stuffed chilis, with whipped cream and nut sauce, 103
  tacos, 90
  tamales, 87
  tartare, 148
  tostadas, 91
  in wheat "meat" strudel, 171
Gluten, raw:
  preparation of, 16–18
  rinsing solution uses, 18, 24–26
  storage of, 18
Gluten-free crackers, 24–26
Goulash, kettle, 161
Gravy, 42, 46
Greek recipes, 173–185

Hamburger, 14. *See also* Ground gluten
Harvard University, 7
Hash:
  browns with spiced links, 64
  Mexican, 85
  old-fashioned, 55
  pie, with mashed potatoes, 49
  Spanish, 136
  spiced link, with poached eggs, 64
Heart attack, 7
Heart disease, 7, 13
Hominy grits, and spiced links, 65
Hormones, given to cattle, 9–10
How to Get Well (Avola), 8

Indian recipes, 195–206
Italian recipes, 142–158

Japanese recipes, 221–231

Lancashire hot pot, 110
Land resources, 4
Lappe, Frances, 5
Lasagne, baked, 154
Latin American recipes, 94–107
Leek pie with poultry pieces, 114
Lentil soup with spiced links, 32
Life expectancy, 9
Lion's Head, 214
Longevity, 9
Lysine, 12

Manicotti, 157
Masai (African tribe), 9
Mayer, Jean, 5–6

Meat:
  and aging, 8–9
  calorie content, 3
  and cancer, 7–8
  chemical residues in, 9–10
  cost of, 3
  U.S. comsumption of, 10
Meat balls (wheat):
  Italian, and sauce, 150
  with lemon and egg sauce, 179
  submarines, 51
  in yogurt, 180
Meat grinder, 16
Medical costs, 10
Mexican recipes, 79–94
Milk products, lysine in, 12, 13
Minestrone, 34
Miso, 16, 221
Moussaka:
  eggplant, 181
  potato, with ground gluten, 178
Mushrooms:
  Chinese, stuffed, 209
  cutlets with, 164
  and seawheat bisque, 36
Mustard greens, with steak, 191

New England chowder, 37
Nitrosamines, 8
Noodles:
  buckwheat, with poultry and walnuts, 227
  cellophane, with steak, 218
  with cutlet sauce, 213
  soup, with poultry pieces, 35
  with steak and Chinese cabbage, 217

OPEC (Organization of Petroleum Exporting Countries), 5, 6

Pancakes:
  buckwheat, with spiced bits, 67
  buttermilk, with spiced bits, 68
  cholesterol-free, with spiced links, 69
Pasta, sauces for, 146–149
Peas:
  black-eyed, soup, with spiced links, 33

split, cream soup, with spiced links, 32
split, soup, with spiced links, 31
Peppers, green, stuffed with nutmeg and coriander-flavored ground gluten, 193
Pesticides, 9
Pie:
  corn, with ground gluten, raisins and olives, 101
  cutlet, with feta cheese, 174
  mashed potatoes 'n' hash, 49
  pot, 44
  poultry, 184
  poultry pieces and leek, 114
  Shepherd's, 112
  steak and cutlet, 118
Pilaf, cutlet, 175
Pizza, spiced link, 152
Poppy seed cakes with spiced links, 68
Pork, 13
Pot pies, 44
Pot roast, 56
Potato(es):
  curried, with poultry, 205
  and cutlet casserole, 189
  mashed, 46
  mashed, and hash pie, 49
  Moussaka, with ground gluten, 178
Poultry pieces:
  in almond sauce, 139
  American recipes, 59–62
  with artichoke hearts and olives, 138
  balls, steamed, 226
  and bamboo shoots, 228
  British recipes, 114–116
  buckwheat noodles and walnuts with, 227
  in chili-nut sauce, 106
  cold, pickled, 105
  creamed, on toast, 59
  with curried potatoes, 205
  with curried tomato sauce, 206
  fried, Creole, 61
  fried, spicy, 60
  with fruit juice, 107
  Greek recipes, 182–185
  Indian recipes, 205–206

Poultry pieces (*Cont.*)
   Japanese recipes, 226–229
   jellied, with tomatoes, 104
   jellied, with vegetables, 105
   Latin American recipes, 104–107
   and leek pie, 114
   with lemon and cream sauce, 115
   in noodle soup, 35
   with orange-flavored soy sauce, 228
   with oranges, 139
   pie, 184
   preparation of, from raw gluten,
      23
   pumpkin with, 226
   with rice, 182
   salad, 59
   southern fried, 61
   Spanish recipes, 138–140
   in tomato sauce, 107
   with walnut sauce, 183
   in yogurt sauce, 206
   with yogurt sauce, 184
Preservatives, 8
Protein:
   complete, 12–13
   metabolism of, 8
   in wheat "meat," 3
Pudding, Yorkshire, 113
Pumpkin:
   baked. stuffed with steak, 97
   steamed, with poultry pieces, 226

Ravioli, 155
Rawitscher, Mary, 6
Rice:
   egg fried, and cutlet, 212
   and spiced link chowder, 35
Rice syrup, 221
Rice vinegar, 221
Rice wine, 221
Roast:
   American recipes, 55–58
   boiled, 58
   British recipes, 111–113
   hash, old-fashioned, 55
   in a pot, 58
   pot roast, 56
   preparation of, from raw gluten, 22
   in red wine, 137
   sandwiches, hot, 57

Shepherd's pie, 112
Spanish recipes, 137–138, 141
   with Spanish spices, 138
   spiced, 111
   stuffed slices, 141
   with Yorkshire pudding, 113
Roulades, steak, 169

Sahara Desert, 4
Sake, 221
Salad:
   poultry, 59
   seawheat, dried mushroom and
      sesame, 231
Salmonellosis, 9
Samosas, 201
Sandwiches, hot, 57
Saturated fats, 7, 13
Sauces, for pasta, 146–149
Sauerkraut:
   layered, 170
   spiced links with, 54
Sausages (meat):
   calorie content, 14
   saturated fat content, 13
Sausages (wheat). *See* Spiced links
Scaloppine:
   gypsy style, 140
   with Italian spices, 144
Schwartz, P. H., 8
Seawheat:
   American recipes, 62–63
   with bean curd and vegetables in
      casseroles, 230
   and cucumber, asparagus and
      radish in ice water, 230
   deep-fried, 62
   Japanese recipes, 229–231
   Manhattan chowder, 36
   and mushroom bisque, 36
   New England chowder, 37
   preparation of, from raw gluten, 23
   salad, with dried mushroom and
      sesame, 231
   scalloped, casserole, 63
   in soy and ginger sauce, 229
   with vinegared miso, 231
Sesame oil, 221
Sesame seeds, 221

Seventh-Day Adventists, 7–8
Shepherd's Pie, 112
Shish Kebab, 76
Sloppy Joes, 50
Sodium nitrate, 8
Soups, 30–37
 black-eyed pea, with spiced links, 33
 cream of tomato, with cutlet chunks, 30
 cutlet, cream of, 31
 lentil, with spiced bits, 32
 Manhattan chowder, 36
 minestrone, 34
 New England chowder, 37
 poultry noodle, 35
 rice and spiced link, 35
 seawheat and mushroom bisque, 36
 split pea, cream of, with spiced links, 32
 split pea, with spiced links, 31
 tomato and steak, 30
Soy flour, 16
Soy sauce 16, 221
Soybean curd, 221
Soybean paste. *See* Miso
Spaghetti:
 with ground gluten and eggplant sauce, 147
 with spiced link sauce, 151
Spanish recipes, 130–141
Spiced links:
 American breakfast recipes, 63–70
 American recipes, 53–55
 and apples, 66
 Austrian recipes, 168–170
 black-eyed pea soup with, 33
 with braised sauerkraut, 129
 British recipes, 116–119
 and buckwheat cakes, cholesterol-free, 69
 buckwheat pancakes with, 67
 buttermilk pancakes with, 68
 casserole with white beans and cutlets, 130
 corn cakes with, cholesterol-free, 70
 in cream of split pea soup, 32
 in crust, 54
 with cutlets and pickles, 168

 with dried fruit, 66
 with eggplant, 152
 enchiladas, 94
 French recipes, 129–130
 fried, 63
 with green peppers, 53
 hash browns, 64
 hash with poached eggs, 64
 and hominy grits, 65
 Italian recipes, 151–158
 jellied wheat "meat" loaf, 117
 in lasagne, 154
 in layered sauerkraut, 170
 in lentil soup, 32
 lysine content, 13
 in manicotti, 157
 Mexican recipes, 93–94
 pancakes with, cholesterol-free, 69
 with pineapple, 65
 pizza, 152
 poppy seed cakes with, 68
 preparation of, from raw gluten, 21–22
 in ravioli, 155
 and rice chowder, 35
 roast slices stuffed with, 141
 sauce with spaghetti, 151
 with sauerkraut, 54
 scaloppine gypsy style, 140
 Spanish recipes, 140–141
 in split pea soup, 31
 in steak roulades, 169
 tarts, 93
 Toad-in-the-Hole, 116
Steak (beef). *See* Beef
Steak (wheat "meat"):
 American recipes, 40–46, 73–77
 Austrian recipes, 167–168
 in bean curd, family-style, 219
 breaded, fried, 42
 with broccoli, 218
 Bullfighter's, 135
 with caraway seeds, 167
 with cellophane noodles, 218
 chickpea stew, 136
 Chinese recipes, 217–220
 in coconut, 97
 corn meal stew, 145
 cubes, smothered in juice, 136
 curried, dried fruit with, 191

Steak (wheat "meat") (*Cont.*)
  and cutlet pie, 118
  dumplings, filled, and tomato sauce, 98
  and gravy, 42
  in green chili sauce, 190
  grilled, with Italian sauce, 73
  hash, Spanish, 136
  Italian recipes, 145–146
  Latin American recipes, 96–101
  Mexican recipes, 83–84
  with mushrooms, 41
  with mustard greens, 191
  noodles and Chinese cabbage with, 217
  olives and, 146
  pie with peaches and meringue, 99
  pot pies, 44
  preparation of, from raw gluten, 19–20
  in pumpkin, baked, 97
  ranch-style, 75
  rolls, stuffed, 76
  roulades, 169
  sautéed in wine sauce, 128
  sautéed, with mustard sauce, 127
  Shish Kebab, 76
  on skewers, 74
  Spanish recipes, 134–137
  stew, chunky, 40
  stew, cinnamon tomato, 134
  stew, with peas and lima beans, 134
  stew in a pot, 84
  strips with onions and peppers, 168
  stroganoff, 45
  Swiss, 43
  Teriyaki-style barbecue, 74
  tidbits, 83
  tomato, chow mein, 220
  in tomato sauce with black beans, 96
  and tomato soup, 30
  tortillas filled with, 83
Stew:
  chickpea, 136
  chunky, 40
  corn meal, 145

cutlet, with cream sauce, old fashioned, 122
cutlet, with fruit, 81
cutlet, with spring vegetables, 121
cutlet, with tomatoes and mushrooms, 123
steak, cinnamon tomato, 134
steak, with peas and lima beans, 134
steak in a pot, 84
Stroganoff, steak, 45
Strudel, wheat "meat," 171
Submarine sandwich, 51
Sweet and sour cutlet cubes, 214
Swiss steak, 43

Tacos:
  green, white and red, 82
  ground gluten, 90
Tamales, 87
Tamari soy sauce, 16, 221
Tartare, ground gluten, 148
Tarts, spiced link, 93
Toad-in-the-Hole, 116
Tofu, 221
Tomato:
  curried, stuffed, 203
  soup, cream of, with cutlet chunks, 30
  soup, steak, 30
Tortillas, 83
Tostadas, 91
Tranquillizers, 10
Turnovers, Mexican empanaditas, 88

Veal, 14, 159
Vegetarian diet, 7
Visek, Willard, 7

Water reserves and pollution, 6
Wheat flour, whole, 3, 14, 16, 17, 18
Wheat germ, 13
Wheat "meat:"
  about, 11–15
  calorie content, 3, 13, 14
  chemical residues in, 9
  and cholesterol, 3, 13
  cost of, 3, 14
  freezing, 16
  lysine content, 13